To

All my bosses and mentors who made a difference in my professional career.

"Human nature has a propensity to eventually become exactly what we imagine or see ourselves as becoming, so picturing is just positive thinking taken a step further. The world's happiest and most successful individuals do this. We are the products of our thoughts, thus adopting a positive outlook might actually alter our life, while adopting a pessimistic outlook can ultimately lead to our demise. Being mindful urges you to enter the present. It teaches you how to feel at peace in your own skin, at ease among other people, and how to let tension and worry go. You may reconnect with yourself, your heart, and the present moment by using these techniques."

- Dr. Amit Das, Motivational Speaker, Leadership Coach , Counsellor, and Mentor.

90 MINUTES MINDFULNESS

MASTERING A MOMENT-BY-MOMENT AWARENESS OF YOUR THOUGHTS, FEELINGS, AND SURROUNDING ENVIRONMENT WITHOUT ANY INTERPRETATION OR JUDGEMENT.

DR. AMIT DAS

Made with ❤ on the Notion Press Platform
www.notionpress.com

Contents

Foreword

"My success, part of it certainly, is that I have focused in on a few things." -Bill Gates

Dear Reader,

Thank you for taking the time to learn more about "**90 Minutes Mindfulness**" and the rewarding outcome of increasing your personal productivity. This is a book with a stunning design that is packed with motivational sayings and tried-and-true advice on utilising optimism to build a life you love.

Do you frequently find yourself at a location—such as at work or home—but not there? This book teaches you how to lay a solid foundation for your pursuit of mindfulness. The author of this book will demonstrate to you, for instance, how merely pausing for a moment or regulating your breathing can assist you in learning to bring yourself more fully into the present moment, increase awareness of your thoughts, and practise receiving the wisdom of your body in a spirit of open, friendly inquiry. Each chapter includes step-by-step guidelines for immediately incorporating mindfulness into your workday.

The author is on a mission to find a solution to the symptoms of distraction. He's spent over two decades researching productivity and has discovered that you're now living in a new world of information overload. In a world where there is always more work, steaming, or networking you can do to spend your time, that's why you'll need modern answers to current problems, as well as a major paradigm shift in your thinking.

He discusses the relationship between the brain and the body and how habits may alter this relationship. In order to help you perform better in your active life, he also presents healthy exercises for creativity and cognition and offers ideas to improve memory. He explains his easy-to-learn yet incredibly powerful meditation methods in this book. The advantages of mindfulness and meditation are widely known, and this author modernises this age-old practise for those of you who value time the least.

The author hopes that by following a simple guideline, many young people will be able to create a fortune by staying focused. Many individuals are unaware that they are being distracted since the world is filled with pop-ups. In today's society, mindless scanning of news feeds, checking of WhatsApp messages every few seconds, and turning on Instagram reels, YouTube and Netflix has become the new normal. This is influencing a lot of individuals in a subtle way. It diverts attention away from more important aspects of life and produces uneven outcomes.

This book covers a variety of disciplines, including new-age spirituality and methods for emotional emancipation. In order to let readers pick the approach they might like to try out to solve their current difficulties, the author gives sufficient information.

This book will help you to understand how to preserve harmony among leaders and employees even in times of turbulence and quick change. Avoid the hidden costs of workplace conflict and antagonism by protecting your career and workplace. You may learn how to deal with the daily barrage of irritation with the help of how to reduce workplace conflict and stress without letting your confidence, mood, or momentum suffer.

This book will guide attaining financial and emotional accomplishments that energise and maintain workforces. These uniform guidelines have helped organisations save millions of dollars for more than ten years. It's time to take charge if you or someone you care about experiences the sometimes crippling effects of stress or anxiety. We all understand that persistent stress and worry are bad for us, and this book will discuss ways to deal with them.

You will learn how to detect stressful ideas, disassociate from them, and de-stress. You will also understand how stress affects the body and how we manage it. How does mindfulness meditation alter brain chemistry? How and why meditate? How to alter your way of life to reduce stress. This book will assist you in lowering the stress in your life, regardless of how much you are currently under pressure. You can do this if you take the time to put what you learn into practise. As you experience improvements in your own life, you will improve the lives of those around you. People frequently wait until stress becomes unbearable before dealing with it; this is the incorrect course of action.

Have you reached a dead end and lack the resources to get out? It's easier than you might imagine. This book will assist you in quitting scrolling through other people's tales so that you can start concentrating on your own by pushing you to make tiny, personal decisions. Every decision we make in life is our own. To an invitation, a job, or a companion, we have the option of saying "yes" or "no." We simply need to practise making that choice.

The author has been able to clearly demonstrate how our self-critical ideas and attitudes can result in a variety of physical and psychological problems that can have a disastrous impact on our lives. If you modify your way of thinking, everything may be healed. Your body will then be healthy and fit. The book is entirely focused on the intricate connection between the body and mind. Let's offer ourselves and others we love this present so they can always be fit and healthy. Avoid negative ideas and beliefs, and you will observe changes in your life. Your desires may be realised and a life with a happily ever after can be created just by using basic healing practises.

The author of this book will just go right to the point and concentrate on outlining what you must do to address the stress issue in your life. There is nothing in this book that you haven't already heard about. The majority of the concepts are ones you are already familiar with. The issue is that while you may have a lot of knowledge, you are probably not using it. You'll discover how to provide the body with the right nutrition, how to implement these changes into your everyday routine, and how to live a happier, healthier life with less stress. Body health is significantly influenced by your thinking.

After reading this mindfulness book, your job-related stress and anxieties that come from connecting with loved ones, strangers, coworkers, or other people's fears that have prevented you from taking action; added tension from ineffective time management; your mental habits can help you face your anxieties and feel less stressed; your physical well-being will help you feel less anxious about marital tension or financial anxiety. While following his techniques, you'll be happy that you did. methods to reduce stress, coping mechanisms, and stress. It is a book that offers practical tips for lowering anxiety and stress. Straightforward medical and psychological ideas on how to use proven stress management methods?

For its substance, the book is praised by a wide range of people. The author offers direction for choosing the best way to mend your life. Significant topics will be covered in this book:

- How to permanently stop having negative thoughts?
- How to find the most important formula for success?
- How to use the power of your subconscious mind to make your dreams come true?
- What phrases and words you use most frequently and how they affect your life?

He is one of today's most inspirational author demonstrates how to see a bright future for yourself and explains how the technique of "imaging" might assist you in: resolving your financial issues; overcoming concern; getting rid of isolation and stress; boosting your health; strengthening your faith and self-belief; and better interacting with others.

This book will help you to discover how the power of your physical presence may serve as a catalyst to enable you to access your own unique magic and advance in life. There must be a deep-seated need for some sort of understanding or mode of being that, while it may seem unattainable, is yet very desired. If not, you wouldn't even bother picking up a book like this.

If you're seeking a means to protect yourself against these unpleasant features of modern life, look no further. You can now choose. Clicking the order button now can either transform your life for the better or worse for the foreseeable future compared to doing nothing.

Once again, thank you for taking the time to learn more about how you would reframe your mental attitude towards everyday situations to find a positive perspective in your life? Thank you for taking the time to read this book.

Carpe diem.

Dr. Amit Das

Leadership Coach , Counsellor, and Mentor.

Preface

"I don't care how much power, brilliance or energy you have, if you don't harness it and focus it on a specific target, and hold it there you're never going to accomplish as much as your ability warrants."-Zig Ziglar

Always be mindful of the beauty that is there in every moment, no matter how tiny. Give it some serious thought and take some time to properly look.

Each of us has attempted to reason our way out of harmful thinking patterns and poor behaviours, only to give up with an unbalanced mind and chaotic daily routines. See how praising and praying will alter your thinking. What if practising mindfulness might help you make significant changes in your life? What if deliberate attention might enhance your health?

Together, we will explore the topic of mindfulness as if you had never heard of it, had no clue what it was, or had no understanding of what meditation was or why it could be beneficial to practice.

There are several materials available if you want to dive further. The topic of mindfulness encompasses a vast world. It has a huge number of features and galaxies. It's infinitely deep and wonderful, and thankfully, there are a plethora of excellent teachers—past and present—whose books, writings, and living retreats can be extremely beneficial for you to connect with throughout this lifetime, your lifetime.

You can create habits that will enable ideas to permeate your mind. I claim that in order to achieve the fantastic, one must imagine the impossible, and that it's critical to understand that issues are small in comparison to dreams and don't really matter. Additionally, I contend that success is a decision, not an accident.

In this first chapter, which I call mindful fundamentals, I will help you learn the fundamental skills you will need as a foundation for workplace mindfulness. I begin by talking about the first step in mindfulness practice: pausing to become present. With the expectations and frantic speed of our culture, we live in a difficult period when it's easy to lose sight of who we are and what really counts. In the moment where your lives are genuinely happening, you're not there. You've been drawn to mindfulness learning, whether you're a service professional or executive, team member, consultant, healthcare worker, or new to the workforce, because it will improve your job and life. Maybe you wish to improve your ability to think clearly and perform well. You may be trying to find a method to feel more balanced and at ease, or you may feel stuck in behaviours that are hurting your relationships at home and at work.

Increasing awareness is the first step in changing where you are.

Although we spend most of our waking hours on computers and smartphones, humans are builders and creators by nature, and utilising our hands is an integral part of that. This book exhorts you to reestablish contact with your surroundings. Nothing is limiting about this book. As much as it is about concentrating on yoga and meditation, it is also about embracing delicious food, wine, and love.

Are you prepared to make life changes?

Sometimes it seems like we are being pushed in a million different directions since life can be so unexpected. But it is possible to lead a contented, purposeful life! Realising that change is both essential and inevitable is the first step. Knowing this reality will make it easier for you to overcome any reluctance or fear and concentrate on what's most important.

Determine your advantages and disadvantages so you can focus your time and efforts on areas where you can improve your skills. Choose your main objectives and then divide them into manageable stages. Finally, create a method that will keep you accountable to yourself by tracking your progress toward your objectives and constantly reviewing your strategy. People find themselves enjoying work more, feeling less stressed, and eventually prospering in their personal and professional lives by taking tiny actions every day.

We are not supposed to be static but to constantly sharpen the saw is exactly what this book seeks to achieve. This book serves as a reminder that our goal is to constantly sharpen the saw rather than to stand still. My goal in writing this book is to uplift you and give you advice on how to apply the suggestions made in order to be more productive in life. This book strives to inspire readers, touch their hearts, and alter their outlook on life. This book succeeds in instilling a sense of positivity and well-being while also being inspiring and motivational. I will draw knowledge from the scriptures, mythology, and ordinary occurrences and offer tried-and-true strategies for altering your life so that you are a contented soul.

Your mental programming, or paradigm, will attempt to prevent you from doing anything unusual. Continue moving forward if you want to succeed. Your paradigms may be covered with complacency, concern, anxiety, insecurities, self-doubt, mental haste, and self-loathing, which keep you trapped, confined, and deprived of your goals and aspirations. You must alter your paradigm in order to transform your life. Although the adjustment is difficult, it is worthwhile, and the outcomes are long-lasting. I will demonstrate the tried-and-true techniques to you.

I document the true benefit of self-renewal comes from within. Observing our own development gives us delight. Knowing that we are acting correctly brings us peace. We get stronger as we overcome challenges. When we're committed to realising our dreams, we feel alive. This book's main objective is to motivate you to take control of your life, starting right now. There is no easy way out; perseverance and hard work are the only paths to success. However, because it demonstrates how to develop beneficial habits (like sharpening the saw) that produce greater results, my counsel makes achievement appear possible (self-renewal). You'll become more driven than ever once you understand why these habits are crucial; you'll start enjoying successes rather than focusing on setbacks, and you'll start looking ahead rather than back. I'd like to conclude by emphasising the importance of self-renewal to the readers. We are not intended to remain still.

Our natural cycles are disrupted by bad habits like skipping meals, working out when it's convenient, working late into the night to enhance productivity, and then attempting to "catch up" on sleep during the weekend. The human body is extremely sensitive to these rhythms, down to the genetic level, as evidenced by a growing amount of chronobiology research. Small adjustments can be the difference between fighting with our bodies and smoothly controlling weight, sleep, stress, inflammation, and other factors.

You may begin by forming new habits and persistently pursuing your objectives by doing actions that advance those goals each and every day. This book demonstrates how to accomplish that. You are capable of doing it. You merit it. You can actually design a better, healthier, and richer existence thanks to this book. Simply put, you need to quit waiting and get moving!

Success and happiness don't just happen to certain individuals and not others by coincidence. They are the result of certain worldly thought and behaviour. I have conducted research on extremely successful and productive individuals and has condensed the key tactics and approaches that will enable the reader to start thinking like a super-achiever. Learn how to control your thoughts and emotions, have unwavering self-confidence, and transform into the person you truly want to be.

Is it possible to learn to pay attention to details?

Organisations lose a lot of money because they don't pay attention to the details. You either have it or you don't have it when it comes to paying attention to details. With today's market's emphasis on soft skills, more businesses are preferring to teach staff to be more detail-oriented. Not only in human hours to rectify the problem, re-build connections, and so on, but also in attempting to find out where and why something happened, industries lose a lot of money due to a lack of attention to the details. Mistakes, misunderstandings, dropped balls, and missed KPIs result from a lack of attention to detail. Employees who aren't detail-oriented may find it difficult to stay focused, meet deadlines, and produce high-quality output. Workers may be at risk of underemployment and professional stagnation if they don't have the skills to develop detail-oriented.

There is no one-size-fits-all approach to being inspired and taking action.

Most executives today travel with technology that keeps them connected to a constant stream of communications and data, 24 hours a day, seven days a week. As a result, there are now expectations of rapid and continuous availability, reinforcing your need to be connected and, as a result, your ongoing distraction. And, if distraction is your issue, time management isn't the answer. Attention is the cure for distraction. Your capacity to regulate your attention is your most significant protection against a world that is always trying to take it away from you. The battle for the public's attention has never been more fierce. All that implies is that your most important resource is now your attention. At first glance, this may appear abstract and difficult, but it isn't. Even with your hectic schedule, here's how you can accomplish it.

I will finish this book with my final thoughts for a useful practise you may do to strengthen your awareness and progress with it throughout your workday. With mindfulness, you may pause after writing an email before pressing the "send" button, pause before having a challenging discussion, or even halt before getting into your car to drive to work. You can take a little break in the middle of your typical workday activity to focus on being present. Take note of how doing something makes you feel. I've used my many years of teaching expertise to write a book that will assist you in working more humanely, stress-free, and clearly. You'll learn how to create a transforming meditation practise from this book, and more significantly, you'll discover how to apply that insight and equilibrium to the difficult circumstances that crop up at work and in your personal life. You began the process of what I refer to as "coming into presence" during your daily practise sessions. You experimented with pausing, sensing your bodily feelings, and being conscious of your mental moods.

I'll discuss what it is, how to practise it, and the potential health, sickness, and stress advantages it may have. Of course, I can only cover those portions that are intended to increase your motivation, which instructs you on how to actually practise mindfulness, as well as provide you with a conceptual framework for understanding why it makes sense to engage in something that seems so strange as to be meaningless on a regular, systematic, and disciplined basis in order to cultivate your own mind and what I would refer to as your deep inner resilience.

When you learn how to practise mindfulness, you may pause, breathe, and reach a space of greater clarity and empathy rather than responding. Then, you may react in a more intelligent, considerate, and reasonable manner. Athletes, musicians, healers, martial artists, and leaders have all learned how to employ the power of mindful breathing throughout time. I will concentrate on this crucial core ability for the following chapters of this book, "90 Minutes Mindfulness," backed by the presence and compassion I discovered in my life. Later, I'll help you understand how to use your laser-like attention to become aware of your thoughts, feelings, and bodily sensations, as well as your relationships with others. You'll also learn that you don't have to leave the house or limit your practise of mindfulness to a dimly lit space or a certain meditation position. Whatever the moment, including during the course of your workday, in any circumstance you may find yourself, you can practise attentive awareness.

The key to maintaining constant concentration and attention involves being aware of your breathing. As you carry out the remainder of your workday, try to be attentive to your breathing. Wouldn't it be wonderful to be able to reply to a stressed-out coworker, demanding employer, unhappy kid, or angry spouse in a cool-headed manner? It's feasible, but having developed this skill makes it easier to react quickly. Try to set aside a few minutes each day to practise mindfulness breathing.

I will provide advice throughout the book to assist you on your path to serenity from a personal viewpoint. This book cuts success down into achievable, tiny stages that won't overwhelm you. In this book, I will show you how to recognise your distraction patterns, which begins with recognising that distractions may come from a variety of sources. Internal distractions, such as your own thoughts or anxieties, are also possible.

So let's start reading by taking a moment to be present. To help you stay attentive while still remaining relaxed, find a sitting position that allows you to feel at ease when at rest. Either a chair or the floor are options for seating. Sitting a bit farther forward on a chair is preferable to leaning against the back. Ensure that your hands can comfortably rest on your knees or your lap. Gently shut your eyes. Or, if you'd rather, keep them open while gazing softly and receptively. Feel how the Earth is sustaining you and the force of gravity. Take a moment to be aware of the current condition of your body in this basic, judgment-free presence. Take a moment to relax with whatever is now available and pay attention to it. Recognise the advantages of simply being in the moment, and realise that you can do this repeatedly.

Finally, I'm thrilled to have this connection with you, and I do so in the hope that whatever it was that pulled you to the appeal of mindfulness, that exact urge may be investigated and fostered in order for it to grow and develop. Also, even if most of it was traumatic and maybe still is, we always build on what has come before in our lives, and each of us contributes our own brilliance to such journeys. When it comes down to it, our entire past—whatever it may have been—becomes the fundamental foundation for carrying out the tasks of being in the present. And it becomes both the challenge and the adventure of a lifetime to free ourselves from being bound by our history or our beliefs in favour of reclaiming the one moment we are ever actually guaranteed to have, which is always this one. Additionally, taking care of this one can have a notable impact on the present, the one after that, and so forth.

Mindfulness gives a reliable and trustworthy road home. As you become more aware of your body, you will understand how your ideas and the corresponding emotions affect your physiology. Your body will then send signals to your brain about how well you are thinking.

Acknowledgements

*At the outset, I will thank my family for supporting me throughout the journey of writing my book and encouraging me to live my dreams; my son has always been instrumental in giving his inspiration to complete the writing of this book. Despite the fact that I am listed as the author of this book,"***90 Minutes Mindfulness***" would not have been published if I had depended entirely on my own talents. Creating this book required more than anything—it took a family of dedicated and caring people who were always prepared to lend a hand.*

Writing a book while working full-time is no simple task, so I'd want to express my gratitude to my amazing coworkers who act as cheerleaders in equal measure. Thank you, too, to my students and clients for your patience and unflinching support while I worked on this book!

Thank you to everyone who has listened to me argue for doing everything you can to make your life, including your work life, more progressive. I appreciate everyone's assistance throughout the process. This book would not have been possible without each of you having had an impact on my life in some manner.

Lastly, I would like to thank all the people with whom I have been associated. You gave me power. I would like to thank Notion Press for publishing my book. Finally, thank you all for gifting your time to read this book.

I'd want to convey my heartfelt appreciation to the almighty God for bestowing his blessings and being so gracious.

CHAPTER ONE

The Science Of Mindfulness And Art Of Mindful Living

"A clear vision, backed by definite plans, gives you a tremendous feeling of confidence and personal power."- Brian Tracy

With so many distractions in today's society, it's more vital than ever to know what matters most, what you should pay attention to, and what you should disregard.

Today's attention is under threat. The very devices we use to increase our productivity also divert our attention while marketing to us. Unfortunately, the majority of us have led lives that have been constantly distracted. A constant barrage of information leads to a lack of focus, as neuroscience is increasingly proving. And the continual barrage of information only adds to the tension. Hence, distractions have become a common feature of the modern workplace, whether you're working from home, your favourite coffee shop, or in a crowded office. Distractions can be beneficial in some situations, particularly for creative endeavours. Distractions can help you break out of a rut known as cognitive fixation, which may seem contradictory. You have an inherent desire to be distracted as well.

In today's environment, there is no shortage of things that demand our attention. People now have more options to connect to the outside world because of technological advancements. However, these conveniences can make it difficult to concentrate on your task. As a result, reclaiming control over what captures your attention on a daily basis is critical. According to new research from the Technical University of Denmark, our collective global attention span is shrinking as the amount of information we are exposed to grows. We now have more things to concentrate on, so we are able to concentrate for shorter periods of time. Because there is so much other stuff vying for our attention, there is less time for depth of focus.

"People think focus means saying yes to the thing you've got to focus on. But that's not what it means at all. It means saying no to the hundred other good ideas that there are. You have to pick carefully. I'm actually as proud of the things we haven't done as the things I have done. Innovation is saying no to 1,000 things." -Steve Jobs

There are several materials available on mindfulness if you want to dive in further My current working definition of mindfulness is paying intentional, non-judgmental attention in the present moment as if your life depended on it. Actually, mindfulness is nothing more than paying nonjudgmental attention to the present moment as if your life depended on it. Now, awareness is something we are all very familiar with but also very unfamiliar with. Therefore, the "mindfulness" that we'll be learning together is actually just the development of a resource that you already have. It doesn't involve travelling or purchasing anything, but it does involve some degree of learning how to live in a mental space with which we are often unfamiliar, even though, of course, without it, we would already be dead. Although mindfulness is frequently described as the core of Buddhist meditation, it is actually universal because, as I just mentioned, it is about attention and awareness, two abilities that are present in all of us.

Mindfulness is truly universal and has nothing to do with Buddhism in the sense that you don't have to be a Buddhist to practise it, or even that you need to meditate in order to acquire it. But if you truly understand meditation, you can't possibly cultivate awareness without engaging in meditation since they are essentially the same thing. We already possess this profound degree of consciousness, but because we are so unfamiliar with it, we are unable to use it when we most need it.

One of the most common regrets I heard people -- hundreds of people -- express as they died was that they had not lived authentically. I may spend my entire life trying to live up to other people's norms and expectations while never truly living my own life. Using a phone app, Harvard researchers monitored the thoughts and satisfaction levels of thousands of participants and discovered that, 50% of the time, their thoughts were unrelated to the task they were performing. However, they also discovered that people are happiest when they are present and concentrated on what they are doing, whether it's talking to someone at work, strolling down the street, or doing anything else.

Being mindful means focusing on the present moment and what is going on both within and outside of you. This starts with a pause, which is really easy to do. Imagine seeing a thriller in a theatre while completely engrossed. The display abruptly freezes. You stop getting lost in the activity and start to pay attention to your surroundings, the people in them, the noises and colours, the pulsating tension in your body, and your thoughts and feelings. You get access to this while there is a pause.

Developing the ability to pause in the middle of your life forces you to focus on the present moment. The movie hasn't captivated you. Additionally, you may more clearly and firmly observe what you are thinking and feeling as well as what is happening around you during this period of reflection. Imagine one of the following happening to you: getting stopped in traffic on the way to work; your laptop breaking down and costing you hours of work; receiving an unexpected criticism from your boss; or seeing a temper outburst from a stressed-out coworker.

You as a leader are inundated with everyday interruptions these days: urgent email, appointments every fifteen minutes, and choices ranging from recruiting to overall vision. This constant barrage of distractions diverts attention away from the task at hand; those ostensibly urgent calls and alerts may not be that important. Working to maintain clear concentration on a task despite distractions engages the brain's attention circuitry on a regular basis. Unfortunately, a laser-like concentration on objectives isn't the only sort of attention that you require. For example, creativity and invention need a more open and easygoing mindset. This is where self-awareness comes in handy: monitoring attention allows us to see if our form of focus is appropriate for the scenario. Details may appear small, but if they are ignored, they can quickly grow in importance. If you're aware that you lack attention to detail, make a commitment to train yourself to appreciate the various aspects that can help you regularly excel at the activities you set out to complete. You'll know you've mastered the principles of becoming detail-oriented when you start catching your blunders ahead of time or using the nuggets of knowledge you gleaned by paying careful attention.

It is fair to argue that the Buddhist tradition has produced the most sophisticated and evolved explanations of mindfulness throughout history and how to practise it. Actually, the mind and states of mind are what those statues of Buddha and other works of Buddhist art are all about. And the Buddha stands for a mental condition that can be categorically described as awake, and he did speak about it in his own way. As a result, all human minds—not just Buddhists or Buddhist meditation practitioners—gained profound insights into the nature of the human mind. Additionally, the Buddha devised a method of meditation that included regulating and calibrating the mind so that it could perform the difficult job of penetration. Obviously, if you were attempting to look at the moon and you set your telescope on something like a lake bed and then tried to find the moon, you'd lose the moon in the telescope every time you changed your stance, even the slightest bit. The mind operates in a similar manner. If the mind wants to explore itself, it must first master at least the basics of mind stabilisation so that it can undertake the task of paying attention and being aware of what is truly occurring underneath the surface of our own mind's activities, which frequently include what?

I prefer to think of the Buddha as a scientist—a genius of a scientist, really—who utilised his own body and intellect—his own tools—to great effect in order to investigate the complex issues that fascinated him, such as what is the nature of the mind and what causes suffering? Naturally, you must calibrate any instrument before stabilising the platform on which it stands in order to acquire accurate results, whether it's a radio telescope, spectrophotometer, or scale.

How do you feel when you are under a lot of pressure?

Instead of a clear and focused mind, you're usually caught up in feeling hurried, nervous, and distracted. You could be prone to interrupting others, have trouble setting priorities, or experience problems finishing tasks on schedule. In essence, you're reacting rather than intelligently reacting to what's going on around you. In no way would cultivating a sense of comfort and tranquilly make you sluggish, weak, or inactive. You're creating a state of mind and feeling that is ideal, similar to a flow state in athletics. So that you may respond to whatever comes with your full potential and abilities, being both calm and awake is necessary. This enables you to react in a quick, effective, and advantageous manner for all parties.

Cognitive management is critical for your leadership skills, along with your self-management, which requires the capacity to focus on an intention and the discipline to stick to it despite distractions and setbacks. You don't have to pay attention to anything if you have the ability to focus. There isn't anything like it. They have informed you that you can pay attention to this or that, which is a fallacy of modern psychology. You seem uninterested in anything. You are simply paying attention. Everything that is in the vicinity automatically attracts your attention. Because the pace of modern life is quickening and the number of electronic distractions is increasing, it is up to you to take control of your surroundings, which includes setting limits on your gadgets. As I shared my thoughts earlier, you have more power than you think, and taking measures to become indestructible enhances everything, from your performance to your capacity to connect with others and to the bigger purpose of your lives.

Do you check to see if the sun has risen or not when you get up in the morning? Not at all. You've awoken, and the sun has entered your body. Because you are awake, all that is there enters into you. I hope you'll commit to developing your own unbreakable habits now that you've seen how much power you have against the forces of destruction. There's no better time than now to make little adjustments that will make a significant difference in your career and life. Finally, the top two guidelines, which I would like to refers to as mindfulness, are to focus only on your present activity for at least a few minutes and to keep distractions to a minimum during that time.

Never try to execute two major cognitive activities at the same time, switching milliseconds by milliseconds, otherwise your attention will be fractured, and both will suffer. When you need to give a task your whole concentration, you should invest in noise-canceling headphones or go to a quieter environment. You may schedule a time when you're available for drop-ins on your calendar. This way, if someone approaches you with a query, it won't throw your entire timetable off. Learning how to focus and using effective attention-span-improvement techniques will help you become a better employee. Though distractions are unavoidable, understanding how to cope with them and discovering what works best for you are excellent places to start.

What would you do if your worried employee had previously called numerous times during the day and made yet another call just before the day was about to end? Or when your overbearing employer assigns you a significant project right before the weekend? What is your reaction? Erupt in rage? Withdraw inside and flare up? Pretend that none of this matters and disengage? Your freedom of choice is made possible by this understanding.

Let's first take a minute to just breathe. Inhale deeply, slowly, and consciously. This calms the pulse and helps to level out the ragged breath of frustration. Taking a breath allows you to consider your options and, ideally, answer more lucidly, assuredly, thoughtfully, and kindheartedly.

I'll concentrate on the mindfulness technique that is widely practised worldwide: awareness of breath. Fundamentally, breathing connects you to everything around you, including the exhalations and inhalations of trees, the wild and chilly winds that sweep over the landscape, and all of the other individuals you interact with on a daily basis. I breathe in the same air as everything alive. Even in the sometimes chaotic environment of my workplace, being aware of my breathing may help to quiet and stabilise my attention and increase my capacity to focus on whatever I'm doing.

Breath control is not actually breathing awareness. Increasing awareness of what the breath is truly doing is the goal. This should be kept in mind. Your objective is to just observe the breath with interest, attentiveness, and non-judgement. You want to allow it to breathe naturally and in accordance with its own constantly changing rhythms. Remember to use patience when you start this activity. It requires consistent practise, much like acquiring any art or ability, whether it's playing the piano, shooting baskets, or making a speech. Recall the puppy I mentioned. You want to maintain a calm, present state of mind while being nice and considerate of yourself. You want to maintain a calm, present state of mind while being nice and considerate of yourself. This is acceptable if, initially, you can only focus on two or three breaths. Simply bring your focus back to your breath whenever it wanders. Even though breathing awareness is so straightforward, it is revolutionary. This is due to the fact that you can train your mind and master the skill of paying attention to where you are right now, as opposed to developing lifetime habits of being distracted or dozing off. So let's start the exercise of breathing with mindfulness. Allowing oneself to sit down with grace and dignity. Create the basic sensation of being present, and do your best to let your body and mind relax.

Do not make great gestures or attempt to save the entire planet. Instead, carve yourself a space in the thick forest of your life and patiently wait there until the song of your life lands in your clasped hands. You can feel greater aliveness, clarity, and heart with even a little stop that creates a clearing.

While I will refer to sitting in the following practises, if for whatever reason you are unable to sit, it is okay to stand with your arms at your sides or to lie down with your legs crossed as long as you are awake. As you become motionless, it's as if you're coming to a halt and entering presence. Pay mindful attention to how your body is feeling right now. Breathe in deeply and fully, then slowly exhale so that you can feel the sensations of the breath moving through your chest, throat, and nose. Allow your breath to begin to flow naturally once more, and acknowledge that you may now unwind. It would may be warm, chilly, relaxed, or tense. Also take note of how your heart and thoughts are right now—whether they are pounding or peaceful, happy or unhappy. Hold everything in a considerate manner. Simply be conscious of your presence and the at-ease feelings that come with being here at this time. It's important to realise that no matter how good or unpleasant your current situation may be, you can still be present in it. With an open and compassionate presence, mindfulness observes and unwinds around everything.

Again, consider your physical condition and pay it careful attention. Maybe you sense it in that kind-hearted half-smile. Take two slow, deep breaths, paying attention to how your breath fills and then releases your body. Allow the breath to return to its normal rate. Take note of where in your body you can feel or detect the breath the easiest. It could be a warm sensation on the upper lip, a chill, or tingling in the back of the neck or the nostrils. It might be the ups and downs of the chest or stomach, or it could be the feeling of breathing throughout the entire body. Rest your compassionate attention there, or wherever you can experience the natural breath rhythm most readily. Put your palm on your tummy and watch how it rises and falls with each breath if any of these methods make it impossible for you to feel the breath. The following three inhalations and exhalations should be felt, and while you do so, let your body and mind unwind. Please take three more breaths. For some time, maintain this peaceful, at-ease focus on your breathing. When you sense your attention straying, simply softly bring it back. No criticism or annoyance—just a pleasant reply. Currently, this breath keep feeling the breath. Feel each breath as you naturally inhale and exhale, and notice how it might help you calm down and relax. Try to notice five or six breaths in succession while unwinding and practising peaceful awareness. You may just start over if you become lost even after only one or two breaths.

It can be both long and short. Feel the rhythm in each moment just as it is. Being mindful of this breath allows you to feel its calming and easing effects. Now pay attention to whether the phrases "calm" and "ease" are helping you calm your body and mind and focus on your breathing more effortlessly. If so, keep using them. If not, let them go and carry on with quiet awareness if they feel artificial or get in the way of your ability to directly experience your breath. Make an effort to stay present as much as you can. I'll wait a little longer to allow your focus to grow. As you go through the remainder of this day, keep practising attentive breathing. If it helps you to relax, say, "Calm with the intake and ease with the outflow." Be steady, kind, and patient. Be steady, kind, and patient. Learning any skill, such as learning a new language, takes time. Because it can be applied to every scenario in your life, mindfulness is a great art. The next time you find yourself starting to feel nervous or agitated, I ask you to try this quiet, easy breathing technique and see how it changes your experience.

I practise it because I want to be able to use the talent when I need it. Just keep repeating the attentive breathing techniques. The more often you do this, the simpler it is to put into practise when it matters. Slowly, with peaceful attention, check if you can perceive five or six breaths in a row. If you get lost, don't worry; you can easily start over.

Continue to breathe or softly come back to it. "To win, you must be present." That neatly encapsulates a lot of what

I've been learning. You might already be noticing through your daily mindfulness practise that when you arrive in a calm and clear presence, it becomes easier to live, study, and work with more vitality and flow. I'll keep working on a skill that is essential to staying present in any activity in this session. According to research, mindfulness training helps your mind become less disorganised and distracted. This indicates that mindfulness has a good impact on all of the essential mental processes that are necessary for success and making a difference, including remembering, thinking, planning, and problem-solving. Your capacity to remain stable and present for each moment will steadily deepen with consistent practise of mindful breathing. While I begin this course with the breath, this deeper presence will naturally affect how you engage in meetings, the quality of your problem-solving, and your ability to collaborate and influence more effectively over time. The contrary of this, as you know, won't work.

You've probably realised that we're not normally this aware. Why is that, then? If you ask yourself right now, "What's stopping me from feeling at ease?" you'll be sick. Simply follow your intuition. This question reveals the stress and strain I'm carrying for a lot of people. You know, we have a lot going on throughout the course of our days—meetings, emails, projects, phone calls, producing reports, and more—and these constant demands cause stress and physical strain. I can see that throughout the course of our working hours, I spend a significant amount of time fretting, thinking, planning, regretting, attempting to satisfy everyone, and being someplace other than where I am. The present moment is often lost on us. I'm so preoccupied with the tasks, the next meeting, and the upcoming project. A cartoon depicts a family travelling through the Sahara desert on camels, with the parents riding one camel and the three children on the next three smaller camels. "Stop asking whether I'm almost there yet," the father responds to the last young child. "I'm a nomad, for goodness' sake." A large portion of my existence is spent waiting to get somewhere else. I sometimes discover that I've been gone for minutes or even hours, much like waking up from a dream. When we have a tendency to travel to another location, I miss out on whatever is in front of us. "Well, I despise my work," or "Driving on the same stretch of highway every day is dull, so why not zone out?" are some possible responses. However, the propensity to become sidetracked can also cause you to miss out on the aspects of your work that really matter. The intricacy of interpersonal communication, the delight of seeing coworkers use their imagination, the chance to approach an issue in a new manner, or the fleeting expression of thanks.

"Discovering what you really want saves you endless confusion and wasted energy." -Stuart Wilde

Everybody who is alive can use these universally applicable methods. Although we don't have a good track record with the dead, as long as you're still alive and breathing, regardless of what's wrong with you, there's more right with you than bad from our perspective. Thus, the present moment turns into a truly amazing starting point for this trip of a lifetime.

Why is it so important in our life?

Every day, humans have between 50,000 and 70,000 ideas (mental chatter, images, or movies playing in their heads). 95% of these ideas are repeats from the previous day, and 80% of habitual thoughts are unfavourable.

"Focus is a matter of deciding what things you're not going to do."-John Carmack

You've all been in circumstances where you just can't seem to pay attention. You try our hardest, but it's impossible to prevent the mind from straying. Some of you begin to have vivid daydreams, while others methodically consider all of the tasks that need to be completed. You have a lot of interesting thoughts, but you don't pay attention to what you're meant to be doing. You can't help but lose track of time, and you frequently don't even realise it. It keeps you from paying attention, making it extremely difficult to concentrate on the work at hand. No one wants to admit it, yet you all lose concentration more frequently than you'd like.

You'll never have enough time in the day to do all you should or want to do. Individuals become happier, healthier, and more productive as a result of flawless attention, which I have observed or acknowledged. By mastering attention management, I want to help you convert your career and life into the vision you create for yourself. Your capacity to focus has become a rare commodity in today's environment, when distractions abound. You're continuously aroused, and you're restless for no apparent reason. When it comes to focusing on the main chores that will allow you to advance toward your objectives, there are frequently a slew of other things to do. You may go for a stroll, grab a cup of coffee, check your emails, or reorganise your files instead of working toward your objectives.

Everything appears to be a good idea, with the exception of the thing you should be doing. You can do most of your difficult activities after you learn to remove distractions and move away from this continual state of excitement and restlessness. You will become more productive and happier as a result of doing so on a regular basis. You must learn how to eliminate overstimulation and feel focused and peaceful at work, feel naturally motivated to work on the key tasks that will help you achieve your biggest goals instead of procrastinating, eliminate unproductive activities and distractions, and skyrocket your ability to focus, among other things.

"You don't get results by focusing on results. You get results by focusing on the actions that produce results."- Mike Hawkins

Do any religious theories, practises, prayers, pilgrimages, or other religious rituals actually advance our cause? Do they aid us in developing our spiritual selves and beginning a journey? If we don't strive to alter who we are within, can we truly affect anything in the environment around us? Genuine spirituality is more concerned with truth and eternal realities than with serenity and enjoyment. Finding the truth about oneself, flaws and all, is the most important aspect of any serious journey. But how many of us are willing to look ourselves in the eye and accept who we really are?

Through practice, concentrate on thinking positive thoughts. It will become simpler as you continue to practise and these ideas become second nature. Every day, try to think at least three positive things about yourself. This will help you overcome negative ideas and make you feel better and more confident throughout the day.

No matter how you're feeling or why your viewpoint is more pessimistic, being happier and more upbeat can improve your wellness and increase your sense of fulfilment in life and your role within it. Work on striving for optimism as much as you can, keeping in mind that viewpoints may alter based on personal control.

How can you change your view to have a positive outlook?

If you alter your perspective, the difficulties of life might become more bearable. You may adopt a more upbeat view by using these suggestions for perspective switching.

- Sing aloud an uplifting inner monologue.
- Make a conscious effort to employ the power of positivity to actively alter your inner dialogue because it's common for self-talk to be negative in nature.
- Set a daily reminder to think happy thoughts to boost your confidence and make you feel better. Even better, each morning, compose and repeat a longer affirmation.

Physical and mental health are inextricably linked. When you exercise frequently, drink enough water, and get adequate sleep, it's a lot simpler to have a happy outlook. Finding that fresh perspective and maintaining a happy mindset may require making little adjustments like obtaining eight hours of sleep each night or taking daily walks.

You may weave this into talks, for instance, if your viewpoint on women serving as heads of state or CEOs has evolved. You may immediately put into practise your decision to have a positive outlook on life by maintaining pleasant interactions with others and even with yourself. The ability of nervous-system-level rewiring. But it goes beyond that. Your controlled nervous system aids in the control of the nervous systems of your family, employees, and other people you come into contact with in the grocery store. Their neurological systems are always looking around them for danger. The others around you will subconsciously sense when your neurological system is balanced, and they will gain from it too, whether they can express it or not. This means that the more of us who understand how to control our neural systems, the safer, more just, and less stressful the world will be.

I genuinely believe this. Research shows that cultures and organisations that prioritise nervous system health and activation of the social engagement system increase creativity and productivity as well as foster a sense of our shared humanity and foster altruism, compassion, and love. That is my motivation for offering you this education. For you, the company you work for, and our entire globe, I wish for more of that. I urge you to persist with your nervous system plan and welcome any questions or comments you may have. I appreciate your time and consideration. I'm hoping the best for you.

You may be familiar with the breath and gratitude techniques from your mindfulness and meditation classes. Some of these practises that are intended more particularly for regulating your nervous system may be more accessible and helpful for you if you find it challenging to sit still with your eyes closed and concentrate on your breathing. This is because they are less introspective. If you're immobile, you could definitely stay there for a very long time with your eyes closed, but that's more because you're numb and shut down than because you're actually present. And it's really challenging to expect oneself to remain cool and collected while you're mobilised, isn't it? So, what are you going to do? Balancing a ball on a book is an excellent exercise for controlling your nervous system. It requires concentration and makes it challenging to become lost in your thoughts.

The goal is to try to maintain breathing while engaging in the act of trying to balance it; the goal is not to keep the ball on the book perfectly; it may slide off. You could rest your pen on your finger if you don't have a ball. Try this with me right away if you're sitting at your desk. You'll observe that it requires a lot of concentration and is an active method of keeping your mind on the present. Think basic while engaging in these sorts of regulatory techniques, since they are all about being present in your body in low-risk, safe ways. Giving yourself a massage might help you regulate, and applying lotion to your hands, particularly one with a nice scent, could help you bring your attention back to the present moment and your body.

A client of mine recently sent me a handwritten note in the mail to thank me for the job we had accomplished together. Her words were sincere, and as I read them, a pleasant feeling spread through my chest. At that point, the entire world seemed a little bit brighter. The vagus nerve region involved with social involvement was probably stimulated by the warm expansion I felt in my chest. Amazing, huh? What's also interesting is that research demonstrates that the gratitude exchange would have benefited both my client who sent the note and me who received it because, whether given or received, gratitude stimulates your social engagement system, which in turn helps you feel more positive emotions, boost your immunity and general health, and help you cope with stress and adversity. Try it then. Think of a person from your past who helped you achieve your goals. This person may have been a mentor, a family member, a former boss, or a teacher. If it's comfortable for you, close your eyes and think of this individual. If you're having trouble thinking of someone, try picturing your dog greeting you at the door when you get home. How does it feel inside of you? You could experience warmth, a burst of energy, or a relaxing of your shoulders. Allow yourself to linger there for a while. Think about anything else that makes you thankful if you start to feel your feelings of gratitude waning. For example, you can be grateful for a recent act of kindness from a coworker or for having enough food to feed your family. Take note of your breathing. Take note of your breathing. Consider taking a few deeper breaths to see if you can expand or breathe into your feeling of thankfulness. When you're ready, open your eyes and spend a short while observing the results of choosing thankfulness.

How can you tell when someone is feeling grateful?

This is significant because the advantages of gratitude do not result from merely forming a mental list because appreciation is more than just a notion. Feeling it brings about the benefits. So, here is your homework. Create a routine to encourage a genuine sense of thankfulness. You could make a list of your blessings at the end of the week and then take some time to reflect on them, or you could express your gratitude when you sit down to eat with loved ones. You could also make it a habit to express gratitude by writing thank-you notes to clients or telling coworkers when you value something they've contributed. Look for things you could be taking for granted on days when you feel stuck, and when things seem to be going nowhere, go back to a period in the past when you had a really great experience that you can draw on. Life can be so tragic, frightening, irrational, and unjust. And although I often think it's cruel to advise being thankful, even in the darkest periods, you may find little instances that inspire reverence or compassion. The neighbour who brings you food when a loved one passes away or the stranger who holds a door open for you on a day when you're feeling lonely It's not weak or overused to decide to be grateful for those times. It serves as a powerful resource for health and resilience and is hardwired into your neurological system.

As I mentioned earlier in this chapter, an excellent technique to reset your nervous system is to actively monitor your breathing. Because when you're anxious, you undoubtedly notice that your breath is quick and that you intake more air than you exhale. Additionally, when you're shut down, your breathing is more likely to be shallow or almost motionless, with an increased focus on exhales. Additionally, your breath tends to be fuller and more well balanced between inhalations and exhalations when you're feeling focused and secure. However, the five-breath technique is my preferred breathing technique. It requires touch and movement to track your breath, which appeals to me. The movement and tactile aspect can allow you to break out of a numb or immobile condition, and because it slows your breathing, it can also help you relax if you're feeling nervous or agitated. Now let's test it. Use your other hand's index finger to position it at the base of your thumb while holding out one hand with your fingers spread wide. Consider your own finger for a moment and notice its weight and warmth. Trace your finger up to the top of your thumb as you start to inhale. The opposite side of the exhalation is returned. Exhale, and swoop back down after taking a breath up your index finger. Therefore, keep breathing at your own rate, inhaling more and exhaling less, and try to notice any pauses at the top and bottom of each breath. Go the other way when you discover that you have reached the bottom of your pinkie side. Inhale deeply, exhale downward, and then inhale fully.

Become conscious of feeling your finger trace the other fingers in addition to syncing your breath with the action. Did counting to five allow you to regain control of your neurological system? If not, it's okay. When you're completely immobile and your breath is quite calm, or when you're anxious and your breath is quick and shallow, it might be challenging to work with your breath. If it applies to you, there are other techniques that could be more effective. Although it did help, I still advise you to take five whenever you need to demobilise or remobilise yourself. However, I also urge you to use this tool and others even when you don't feel like you need them, since it will be simpler to enter or remain in your social engagement system the more safety and connection signals you send to your neurological system.

How to stop appeasing others?

A people-pleaser is someone who, on the whole, constantly says "yes," always offers to assist, never moans, takes care of everyone, completes the task, frequently arranges and organises things, and is kind. And you have to admit, that individual sounds really wonderful. They could be, for those who are on the outside and cannot see what is actually happening. But people-pleasers frequently fall short in one area.

We realise that if we want the best outcomes in anything, it is the most crucial factor in the world. They primarily fall short when it comes to caring for themselves. They don't give themselves enough time. When they are exhausted, they don't say no. They don't make an effort to maintain constant physical and mental relaxation. Everything goes apart if you don't manage your daily tasks. How can you prioritise your needs without causing a commotion? Do you believe you can maintain a high level of activity before becoming exhausted? Don't you think it would be necessary to take care of yourself before you burn out and are unable to look after your father, children, career, or home? Which is worse: being a bit selfish and scheduling some downtime each day, even if it means upsetting the people you care about, or being drowsy and unable to concentrate while you're with your dad, your kids, or at work? Be mindful of your kinship. They are the ones who truly count. Ignore what people think about the way you spend your life. By lowering your expectations, you may simplify your life and take full advantage of it.

I will continue by advising you to make even more lifestyle changes, start saying "no" when you are weary or don't feel like doing things, and come up with more clever solutions for your daily responsibilities so that you could prioritise yourself. Because people who like to please frequently go in one of two directions, the reality is either they collapse and burn out, or they begin to despise those around them.

A person's mental and physical health begin to deteriorate after they have neglected themselves for an extended period of time. They eventually reach a point where they can no longer be of much use to anybody, or they begin to hate people, and they find it difficult to engage in once-enjoyable activities such as socialising. They could experience tension or even depression, and they are vulnerable to being used by others. This frequently happens to people who only try to please others in specific situations, such as when they are with strangers or higher-ups. Resentment toward that particular group of individuals might develop over time, and if that happens, the people-pleaser may feel as though they must entirely shun that group. There will come a moment when everything comes apart if we don't prioritise taking care of our own needs before attempting to take care of others. Start with this easy practise if you suspect that you could be a people-pleaser. To take care of your own physical and emotional welfare, take a look at your calendar and block out time as often as you need.

How to manage your feelings to combat negativity?

93% most individuals can think of a moment when their feelings gained control in a bad circumstance and heightened anxiety instead of calming it. How therefore, in the face of negativity, can you effectively manage your emotions? Try the effective frame method. As in, keep in mind to adopt this mindset when confronted with this circumstance. This is where it starts. Observe your ideas. Many ideas and emotions are triggered by negative experiences. How do you keep from responding in a way that makes the situation worse? Your reaction might become erratic and impulsive due to emotions. Instead, pay attention to your thoughts rather than your feelings. Imagine that you are taking part in a job interview. That isn't going well at all. You experience fear and embarrassment.

Having been there You can choose to concentrate on these counterproductive feelings, which will lead you astray even more. Alternately, you may concentrate on the idea "This isn't going well, how can I adjust?" by taking a moment to reflect and answer, for instance. Much more effective, yes? Then give the emotion a name. I'm feeling ashamed and anxious. After that, ignore the emotion and concentrate on the fundamental idea. Since things aren't working out, I need to change. Advancing the methodology keep in mind that it is just temporary. According to recent studies, feelings connected to bad events are greater than those connected to good ones. These unpleasant feelings then leave a more profound, enduring impression, making bad circumstances seem more permanent.

Define bad circumstances as a moment in time, something fleeting, and not something that lasts forever. Then, start the transformation. Consider unpleasant emotions as a signal light blinking, signalling that a change may be necessary. Say, for instance, that whenever you interact with a certain coworker, your emotions are volatile. Take your emotions as a hint that you need to improve your fundamental connection with that individual rather than letting your responses get the best of you. Or you may explain that you have demotivation whenever you perform specific tasks for your job. as like you are wasting your time. Take such sensations as a hint that you need to alter some of your obligations or even change instead of concentrating on them and sinking into despair. The good news is that we think more critically when we are negative than when we are positive. That could help you realise exactly what needs to be changed. You should now lessen the mood as well. Bad moods are accompanied by a barrage of unfavourable feelings that can ruin your entire day. Observe your emotions in context. The way things are doesn't always reflect your mood or how you're feeling. Just your counterproductive emotions are in charge. It's not true that you are unappreciated just because you feel that way. Describe your current state of mind: "I feel underappreciated today." Then inquire as to your motivation.

It's possible that no one praised you for your efforts on a challenging job, or your child whined that his favourite shirt wasn't clean when it seems like you're always doing laundry. When you label your mood, you are compelled to pinpoint the event that set it off. Additionally, details are something tangible that you can process. Additionally, be aware that research demonstrates a connection between your emotions and bodily experiences. Simply put, a bad mood may be the result of not getting enough sleep, not eating breakfast, or being dehydrated. This will conclude the technique: engage to comprehend. When you engage in unfavourable situations, such as finger-pointing, placing blame, or expressing annoyance, you only serve to make matters worse. Instead, take the time to comprehend, think, and listen. And remember to ask questions rather than make demands. Come from a place of curiosity and want to assist rather than asking questions and expecting reasons or answers. Apply this perspective and visualise yourself successfully managing your emotions.

"The difference between successful people and really successful people is that really successful people say *no* to almost everything." — Warren Buffett

Our profession determines how we live and why we are here. We may have many interests and be many things to many people, but we only devote our entire, daily attention to the skill to which we are devoted. Our resolve to pursue progress every day eventually determines the difference between a life of fulfilment and one of discontentment. We surpass the constraints imposed by our body or psyche.

How will you set goals in a situation where everything feels like a priority?

Being overburdened just makes it worse when you feel like you have a million things to do but not enough time to do them. Here are three strategies for regaining control. Make a list of all the things you need to accomplish and write them down first. Your subconscious is continuously on the lookout to make sure you don't forget something when it's circling in your thoughts. That implies that it will continue to reappear at inconvenient times, such as in the middle of the night. Instead, write it down so that your brain can unwind. Next, plot the items on your to-do list onto your calendar. Find a precise time and date for each assignment. I'm going to write the report on Tuesday from 3 to 5 p.m. I'm also conducting the project debrief with the team on Friday at 10:00 a.m. When you have a certain time in mind for completion, your anxiety decreases. Finally, score a minor victory for yourself. We frequently work on complicated projects that take a while to complete. It can feel incredibly depressing in the middle, which could last for months or even years, like you're not moving forward. Make sure to record any little accomplishments you may celebrate in their place. Creating the prototype, writing the marketing copy, and running the project are all victories, even though the new project may not debut for two years. And it's crucial to be aware of it so you can track your development as you go. Although everyone of us has a lot to accomplish, these three tactics may make it seem a lot more doable.

What should you do if your objectives keep getting put off?

What a wonderful world it would be if we could consistently focus on our most important objectives, but of course, that is not how it is. It's certain that there will be emails to reply to or tedious paperwork to finish. However, if your objectives keep being put off over time and you never appear to be able to achieve them, that's a problem. Here are three approaches to handling it:

- First, set higher stakes first. Perhaps you aren't pursuing your objectives because you don't feel they are urgent or significant enough. The urgency can be increased by concentrating on the long-term effects of inaction. What would it look like, for instance, if you didn't do X in six months, a year, five years, or 10 years? When you begin to consider your objectives in that way, it frequently inspires you to take action.
- Second, search for patterns. Do certain aspects of your life consistently take precedence over others? For instance, there will undoubtedly be hectic times at work when you'll have to put in extra hours and prioritise your profession over everything else. But if you consistently behave in that manner, ultimately you'll realise that you have no personal life, and your health will begin to deteriorate. To avoid jeopardising your overall health, you must maintain equilibrium over time.
- Third, it could be time to completely rethink things. If a given aim isn't being accomplished, you probably need to adjust your strategy. For instance, can you outsource it, or do you have to do it yourself? Is there anything you're doing right now that you could cease doing

entirely to give yourself more time to concentrate on your goal? Give yourself permission to have other thoughts. What if the objective had to be attained at all costs? What could you possibly do to make it happen? That could open up new innovative avenues for solving the problem. We are unable to consistently concentrate on our top priorities. Sometimes life's little details get in the way. But we must make certain that we finally reach them. and using these tactics ensures that you will.

"Your destiny is to fulfill those things upon which you focus most intently. So choose to keep your focus on that which is truly magnificent, beautiful, uplifting and joyful. Your life is always moving toward something."-Ralph Marston

Destructive thoughts fade away as you shift your focus to more constructive ideas. You will become a living embodiment of serenity if you do this regularly. Under the garb of a spiritual guru, finding peace is a choice rather than something that calls for intense study.

How can you deal with persistent complainers?

Few things tyre you more than someone who constantly complains. Negativity is when someone corners you with their misery. Once someone starts the complaining train, it's difficult to stop it, but this is how. The next time you're around someone who constantly complains, consider why they're moaning in order to help you react more positively rather than whining about it, which simply makes matters worse. I'll help you decide how to reply and prompt you to consider what could be motivating this individual to complain. Let's examine to comprehend the psychology of why we complain. It starts with complains, but I can't figure out the issue. Your complainant could simply be really irate at their inability to remedy the problem. If you suspect this is the case, politely inquire whether they would like your suggestions for resolving the problem. Talk them gently out of irritation and into a solution-seeking mentality. The next step is grab attention, as if the complainant is looking for some. They may feel abandoned or alone in coping with their issue. Pay attention to them, and pay close attention if you think that their whining is a cry for attention. The primary motivation for complaining is frequently a simple desire to be heard and understood. However, if it starts to become a habit and you find yourself continuously accommodating their whining and need for attention, speak up and let them know that, while you are always willing to listen to them and offer assistance, your willingness to do so is being drained by their incessant whining. Underlying insecurity and understanding situation is your third step in going forward with complainers. Using complaints as a cover for our unhappiness with our shortcomings I frequently moan to coworkers about a significant change at work, but the truth is that I was just anxious about how well I would adapt to the change. If you see someone else moaning out of insecurity, you may find encouraging things to say to them to make them feel better.

One of my employees responded to my complaint by saying, "The change might be difficult, but you usually manage to adjust so well to new things." And guess what? It was beneficial. Your next option for stress alleviation. It's only natural that we have all expressed our displeasure in the past by letting our guard down. You are aware that taking action will help you feel better. If you notice that this is the case, provide the person with a reasonable outlet to prevent them from storing up their anger, and then highlight any positive aspects of the circumstance to make them feel better. Understand your environment is your final step, as in "consider your surroundings." At work, are they surrounded by whiners, and at home, are they surrounded by whiners? In this situation, politely follow up to let them know their complaints are having an impact on other people. They're probably used to it. I understand the irritation you're expressing, but you might not be aware of the effect it's having on others. Now, if it's you who complains frequently, use this method to investigate why. Now that you have the mothod you want, you can use this effective method to deal with persistent complainers.

"We each focus on what we're going to buy, but that's an incorrect focus. Focus instead on why you want to spend the money on this or that. What feeling in you does it satisfy?"

We all know that having objectives and achieving them is essential to our success, yet life may sometimes feel out of control because virtually every professional has a long list of tasks to complete. Everything being a top priority might cause paralysis and prevent you from moving forward with anything. In order to accomplish progress in a fast-paced environment with many conflicting objectives, we must seize control of the situation. You now know how to successfully prioritise tasks so you can complete the most crucial ones and gain the respect you deserve at work by using the methods I covered in this chapter.

How your priorities are influenced by your values?

Your values may not seem to have much of an impact on your priorities on a daily basis. And they might not when it comes to something as simple as returning emails. But over time, the decisions you make are shaped by your principles, and those decisions add up. It's helpful to consider three distinct periods when deciding what to prioritise in order to obtain a clear picture. What's most crucial right now is the first and simplest question. You're probably using your time well if your employer is pressing you to complete a task or if you're working on a project that is essential to the success of your business. The majority of the time, though, it is a little less clear where we should focus more of our attention. Does that networking event truly pay off? What course do you need to take for professional development?

Zooming out to other periods is useful because nothing is urgent right now. What will have made me proud of myself in a year? Make a list while keeping in mind both your personal and professional goals. Volunteering to head a committee at work can seem like a burden, but if you want to advance to a leadership role in a year, that team-leading experience might be quite beneficial and help you do so.

What decisions can you make now to improve your current situation and your quality of life in the future? Starting language classes now is an excellent option, for instance, if you want to go into a position that requires you to work internationally. Making decisions today can be improved by taking the long view and considering your priorities in the long run.It might not seem like your values and priorities are closely related on a daily basis. And they might not when it comes to something as simple as returning emails. But over time, the decisions you make are shaped by your principles, and those decisions add up. It's helpful to consider three distinct periods when deciding what to prioritise in order to obtain a clear picture. What's most crucial right now is the first and simplest question. You're probably using your time well if your employer is pressing you to complete a task or if you're working on a project that is essential to the success of your business. The majority of the time, though, it is a little less clear where we should focus more of our attention.

"Once you have mastered time, you will understand how true it is that most people overestimate what they can accomplish in a year--and underestimate what they can achieve in a decade!" --Tony Robbins

You're overworked, and the CEO's project delivery deadline is putting a lot of pressure on your team. Your thoughts are primarily clouded by fears and uncertainties. Can we actually accomplish this? Is this the best course of action to pursue? What if I'm unable to keep my promises? Now, tell me which emotion you believe is now controlling your actions. It's anxiety. Overthinking and fear frequently coexist. This is so that your nervous system can be alerted to produce stress hormones like cortisol and adrenaline when fear sets off your body's fight-or-flight reaction. Your frontal cortex, which is in charge of self-control, attention, and concentration, almost shuts down. Your brain's amygdala, a primitive region, takes control. No matter how strong the emotion, you have the power to control it before it controls you.

Let's look at a couple approaches to managing it with assurance and making quick decisions. Grounding is a mindfulness practise that might help you regain control. Your frontal brain comes back online, allowing you to think properly, and your parasympathetic nervous system, the opposite of your stress reaction, is activated. You can try a variety of excellent grounding activities, such as regulated breathing, a rapid body scan, or a little meditation.

Fear often leads us to catastrophise when we anticipate the worst-case scenario. Instead, face the worst-case scenario. Push your fear to the limit. You'll discover that no matter what life throws at you, you can come up with a strategy for it. Consider both the positive and negative outcomes in equal measure. Flip your hypotheticals. What if my suggestion is embraced by the senior leadership team? What if it isn't foolishness but rather the innovation the team needs to advance? After facing the worst-case scenario, come up with a strategy on how to handle it. If-then logic may be used to provide solutions for problems. For instance, I may resolve to write 100 words, no matter what they are, if I find myself putting it off. This is referred to as "implementation intentions" in psychology, and studies have shown that they can lower anxiety and improve emotional regulation. Scheduling time to worry is a second, slightly peculiar recommendation. Yes, I do. Give yourself 15 to 20 minutes to reflect on your anxieties and come up with solutions. Make a list of your anxieties and mark those that you can influence or control by taking action or by altering your perspective. It may seem contradictory, but the more you expose yourself to fear, the more your amygdala gets trained to stop responding to unpleasant events. You'll become increasingly adept at addressing these circumstances with confidence as you practise.

"Excellence is an art won by training and habituation. We do not act rightly because we have virtue or excellence, but we rather have those because we have acted rightly. We are what we repeatedly do. Excellence, then, is not an act but a habit." -Will Durant

There are a few priorities that are "do this or you'll be fired," but the majority of what we spend our days doing is less obvious. What is the best way to use our time when there are so many things we might be doing? Here are three evaluation and decision-making frameworks you may utilise: The first instructs you to weigh the importance of the urgent versus the importance of the significant. It is a traditional method known as the Eisenhower matrix since the former president popularised it. Act immediately if something is both significant and urgent. Don't do anything if it isn't urgent or vital. After finishing what is both urgent and important, you should take care of the middle-of-the-road tasks that are either important but not urgent or urgent but not important. The Pareto principle, named for the Italian economist who developed it, is the second framework. It is sometimes referred to as the "80/20 rule," which states that only 20% of your efforts will produce 80% of your outcomes. Therefore, it is vital to consider what actually generates revenues, customer pleasure, or whatever metric you are measured on when deciding how to spend your time. Concentrate on those as there are probably only a few important items. Third, consider your own and the business's potential for growth. Which tasks or efforts will teach you the most and help you develop the most? Ideally, you should focus your efforts on initiatives with the potential to revolutionise things. It's challenging to prioritise your lengthy to-do list, but these three frameworks can assist you.

The first step is sometimes the most difficult when it comes to taking action toward your goals. You could have felt helpless. But now that you know what has to be done at a high level, here are four methods to start with. Look over your list of priorities first, and then estimate how long it will take you to do each activity. The fact that so few individuals care to do something despite its importance. We frequently fall short in our implementation because we vastly underestimate the time required. But if we can develop precise estimation skills, we'll be much more productive. Track the evolution of your estimations. Track the evolution of your estimations. You'll eventually discover that it takes two hours, not one, to complete the memo for your boss. This allows you to realistically choose where to schedule it in your calendar and complete it.

The second step is to arrange your tasks together. If you need to make a phone call, do it all at once while you're in the zone rather than spreading it out over the course of the day. You'll be able to move considerably more quickly.

The third step is always ask yourself what tasks you can complete to make everything else simpler. If your desk is really disorganised and you need to find documents for every other project you're working on, clearing it up first might ultimately save you time.

Finally, sometimes the best course of action is to simply take action. Utilise the "Pomodoro Technique," in which you set the timer for 15 or 20 minutes, dive in, and start working. Whatever you decide to do, you'll go forward, which frequently motivates you to keep moving. It's challenging to break the cycle of inertia on your objectives, but these four strategies can help you take that crucial first step.

According to a new book, "One Second Ahead," by Rasmus Hougaard, an acknowledged authority on mind training, there are certain fundamental guidelines that may actually help you manage your concentration and awareness in all job tasks. A little gaffe may go unnoticed at times, and the only penalty for those responsible is embarrassment. An ignored error, on the other hand, can occasionally result in serious issues, causing a range of things to go wrong for a team, a project, or an organisation. That's why having a keen eye for detail is so important. Some workplaces place a premium on getting things done fast. Rushing through a task or project, on the other hand, allows plenty of leeway for mistakes to creep in.

Aside from catastrophic and costly mistakes, even a minor blunder at work may undermine the organisation's and an employee's credibility. Employees that are unable to create high-quality work due to a lack of attention to detail cost much more to hire, whether it is for internal or external communication or a project. It might be a waste of corporate resources to hire extra people only to check the work of other employees. Inattention to detail leads to mistakes and misunderstandings. "Missing execution due to a lack of attention to detail has a greater impact on the worker's reputation.

In a society where perception is everything, no one wants to be known as the one who constantly drops the ball or makes mistakes." Continued missed execution owing to a lack of attention to detail has a higher impact on the worker's personal reputation. No one wants to be seen as the one who constantly drops the ball or makes mistakes in a society where perception is everything." Assignments that were not completed and goals that were not met.

Importance of being mindfulness at work

- It instils a sense of urgency. When you keep concentrating on a single task, you're more likely to do it quickly. Knowing that you're capable of completing tasks can help you stay positive and motivated to achieve your next objective.

- It increases efficiency. You'll be able to finish more things overall if you're able to stay on target. Distracting yourself as little as possible is a terrific way to stay in the zone and allow your brain to digest what requires your attention. When you focus your attention as a working professional, you're more likely to get more work done.
- It helps relieve tension. You'll reduce any strain and pressure that has built up by keeping on track and enhancing your productivity. When you concentrate only on one task, you may cross more items off your to-do list and free up more time in your calendar.
- Your ability to direct your energy will ensure that you don't fall behind on work or hurry through it. Building a friendly and collaborative corporate culture requires communication with your employees, colleagues, and business partners. Spending too much time chatting about "Game of Thrones" or gossiping, on the other hand, is not just a significant distraction. Hearsay can also contribute to a poisonous work environment.
- Your ability to channel your energy will ensure that you don't get behind on work or hustle to meet deadlines at the last minute.
- It produces higher-quality results. Your capacity to concentrate is critical to your professional success. The higher the quality of work you do, the more time and focus you can commit to it. You'll not only do things faster, but you'll also ensure that they're error-free.
- A little blunder might sometimes go unnoticed, and the only punishment for those involved is humiliation. However, an overlooked error can occasionally cause major problems, causing a variety of things to go wrong

for a team, a project, or a firm. That's why it's crucial to have a great eye for detail. Staying on target requires overcoming temporary, unpleasant, and unavoidable setbacks. That is why the ability to concentrate is so important.

"Do not pay attention to anything. There is a way of heightening the level of attention that you are in right now. If you become far more attentive, everything is in your attention. If you try to pay attention to this and that, you will just lose your mind."

When it comes to accessing concentration, it's like a kid learning to walk. The toddler can take a few steps, but falls down frequently. Absorption focus, on the other hand, is comparable to an adult who can stand and walk for a full day without falling down. A current analogy would be a spinning top. The top necessitates constant attention in access focus, wobbles frequently, and collapses. In absorption, the top spins on its axis in a centred manner.

How will you increase your ability to focus on the current task?

Everyone has known since the dawn of time that if you drop anything, it will fall to the earth. Why was the question? By focusing intensely, Isaac Newton was able to make great discoveries. Everyone has known since the dawn of time that if you drop anything, it will fall to the earth. Why was the question? Isaac Newton did not have an apple fall on his head and immediately comprehend gravity, as folklore has it. Instead, beginning in 1666, he began to see various items fall and questioned whether these occurrences were related to why the moon circled the earth. He was able to explain the law of universal gravitation after two decades of investigation.

Pure focus is a two-edged sword with the edge of single-pointedness or steadiness on one side and clarity and intensity on the other.

To achieve single-pointedness, we must first exert tremendous effort; however, if we exert too much effort, we will lose our single-pointedness and our minds will begin to drift toward other things. We must modify our effort to ensure that it is neither too tight nor too loose, similar to how a musician must tune the strings of an instrument. Researchers once found out that mental acuity and focus are so pronounced in martial arts when they conducted a study on karate experts and discovered that their stronger punching forces occurred as a result of better muscle control in the brain rather than an actual increase in muscular strength.

Assume you're holding a little rubbery party balloon. It clearly inflates as you blow air into it. The balloon is about to explode after 4 or 5 more puffs. Balloons, although being simple to inflate, don't actually serve much of a function-you let go, and it deflates practically instantly. You might use them as a decoration or as a present for someone's special day. Perhaps you simply enjoy blowing them up and watching them fly about. Nonetheless, they serve no practical use. The air mattress is time-consuming, but it is also beneficial. Consider an air mattress that you can inflate.

You put in the same amount of work as the balloon, yet there is no discernible difference. You don't feel like you're making much of a difference when it comes to inflating this monster. If you continue to blow air into the mattress, you'll see that it gradually expands as a consequence of your constant efforts. You don't notice the consequences of your activities until you've been doing them for a long time. You continue to inflate the object until it is completely inflated.

Finally, you realise you have something worthwhile – you can sleep, sit, or simply lie peacefully on it. What are you saying? It's a good thing you have what you have. It won't be exactly where you want it if you stop halfway through, but it will still serve a function.

You typically spend a lot of time trying to figure out how to get ahead faster. You want to save money. You want and hope for a fast track to greatness. The unfortunate fact is that taking shortcuts yields nothing worthwhile. What makes anything precious to us is the difficulty and work that we put into it. You're searching for the work we put into something that will eventually provide the most return.

You may find yourself treading a route with numerous distractions on your way to your highest dreams, losing focus on what you want to achieve. You can find yourself traversing a route with numerous diversions on your way to your biggest aspirations, losing concentration on what counts by trying to pick up something simpler and easier. By blowing air into something that doesn't matter, you're diverting your focus away from what really matters. The balloon represents all of the roadblocks that we encounter.

You put a fraction of effort into something in the hopes that it will make a significant difference—it almost never does. You'll have to blow air into the air mattress and distract attention away from all of the balloons of quick satisfaction if you want to make a meaningful difference in your life. True transformation takes time. The work we put into anything isn't immediately recognized. It takes time for the proof to emerge. Multiple self-help and business publications, such as James Clear's Atomic Habits and Darren Hardy's The Compound Effect, express this principle. The compound interest of everyday practises and habits has a long-term influence.

Always ask yourself:

- Is this bringing me closer to my objectives?
- Is this the most important thing for me to concentrate on?
- Is this a source of distraction?
- Is this going to be of any use to me in the long run?
- Is this a hydrogen balloon or an air mattress?

So, keep this metaphor in mind the next time you feel yourself losing concentration. Use it as a reminder to remind you of what really important to you and whether or not what you're doing right now is worth the work you're putting in.

"That's been one of my mantras - focus and simplicity."-Steve Jobs

That focus, though, must not be myopic. It must look beyond this quarter and the next, to the medium-to long-term prerequisites for success. It might be difficult to stay focused on the most important growth initiatives. The urgent – that is, the day-to-day necessities of getting the task done – may readily divert management focus away from what is vital. The management team's devotion, discipline, and perseverance are put to the test when it comes to staying focused on essential tasks.

One day, the Zen master wanted to demonstrate a new arrow-shooting skill to his disciples. He advised his trainees to put a towel over his eyes before shooting his arrow. When he opened his eyes, he found a target without an arrow, and when he glanced at his students, they were humiliated that their instructor had missed.

"What lesson do you suppose I aim to give you all today?" the Zen master inquired. "We expected you'd show us how to fire at the target without seeing," They said. "No, I taught you that if you want to be successful in life, you must remember the aim," the Zen teacher said. You must keep your eyes on the objective at all times, or you may miss out on a fantastic chance in life. They exchanged glances, impressed by the lesson. The conclusion of the narrative is that we must maintain a steady focus on what we desire and recognise that, because we feel what we think about, our thoughts have a direct impact on our emotions. We attract into our lives what we focus on and feel. Our ideas have a continuous influence on our fate. Tips on how to regulate your thoughts. Focus when confronted with a problem or difficulty, spend 5% of your time addressing the issue and 95% of your time coming up with inventive and creative solutions.

"Life isn't measured by the number of breaths we take, but by the number of moments that make us gasp for air."

Most of you recognise the necessity of focusing on your goals in life. At the same time, it's critical to understand exactly what you're not going to do. You must have a thorough grasp of the actions that do not support your objectives. It is quite important to know what keeps you from achieving your objectives. Simultaneously, it is beneficial to recognise the acts that do not advance you. While it's critical to understand why you're dealing with a certain issue, it's also critical to discover answers to it. The majority of individuals overlook the second step. They notice a problem and whine about it, but they do nothing to address it.

"The successful warrior is the average man, with laser-like focus."-Bruce Lee

According to Bruce Lee, mental focus may be the difference between being ordinary and amazing. He emphasises the numerous advantages of being able to achieve the maximum degree of attention and focus. However, he also points out that if we can improve our focus abilities, we can be far more than average.

"You don't get results by focusing on results. You get results by focusing on the actions that produce results." - Mike Hawkins

"The Importance of Concentration" It may seem counterintuitive to say that concentrating on fewer things may help one grow more quickly, yet it is true. And you realise you've been wasting a lot of time chasing after things that have no or little bearing on your driving ability. To grow faster, concentrate on fewer things. In business as well as in life, less is more. More is actually less in this case. It may seem counterintuitive to imply that concentrating on fewer things can help you improve more quickly, yet it is true. Management time is the most valuable resource in a business. What gets done and what doesn't depends on how this time is used. That is the strength of managerial attention and focus. It's a no-brainer: if we devote more management time and attention to a certain area, that area will begin to improve.

Concentration is similar to a dilithium-crystal in that it is a concentrated centre of energy, intellect, and sensitivity. Concentration is like the moonlight, which shines so clearly that the stars of stray lies fade away. So much clearer if you can hold aloft the flame of knowledge. It eliminates emotional bonds by irrigating the buds of insight. Concentration improves with practise, and it is the most effective technique to increase willpower and clarity.

Meditation, on the other hand, is not something that can be truly practised. It's the state in which you're left afterward. Meditation is like complete eyesight, including peripheral vision, whereas concentration is like tunnel vision. That makes sense, right? It is not meditation if there is any effort involved. Concentration requires effort; meditation is just revelling in your own brightness. However, it appears counterintuitive, because meditation is far from a mind that is lethargic. On its own, concentration is like being on one leg; walking in harmony with the stream of being on one leg is really tough. On its own, meditation is like standing on one leg; walking in harmony with the current of being with only one leg is extremely difficult.

"Energy is the essence of life. Every day you decide how you're going to use it by knowing what you want and what it takes to reach that goal, and by maintaining focus."- Oprah Winfrey

When you put in the effort to ensure that your task is completed fully and efficiently, you provide value to your firm. This is why "attention to detail" is frequently included as a needed ability in job listings. It increases your value and saves lost time when you offer your supervisor or customer well-completed, high-quality work the first time. Detail-oriented people are also better at spotting errors that might cost them money.

Furthermore, paying attention to detail is a sign of having other desirable employee attributes like organisation, thoroughness, and focus. Some occupations, such as accounting, engineering, medical research, and others, require you to teach yourself to pay attention to details in order to succeed. In other professions, having a high level of attention to detail is the characteristic that will get you promoted to a position where you will be expected to think about the broader picture. Finally, if you are the team's "go-to" details guy, everyone else may unwind a little. They'll probably toss you other tasks as a reward because they know the project is in good hands. This will eventually result in your growth.

How will you maintain momentum toward your goals?

The Journal of Environment and Behavior estimates that the average human makes more than 35,000 decisions each day, including more than 200 decisions about eating alone. You decide what to wear and which tasks to prioritise. Should I go to this gathering? How should I respond to my boss's email? "Decision fatigue" is the idea that each of these options depletes the meagre mental and emotional energy you have available each day. Stress and decision fatigue both directly lead to overthinking. The more exhausted you are, the more prone you are to analytical paralysis, future tripping, or ruminating. This is precisely why managing your energy is the key to producing better work. Finding what works for you in terms of managing your energy is a personal journey. But to help you get going, here are a few suggestions. Think about placing priorities first.

Consider what, if any, significant choices you'll have to make the next day, such as approving a budget or choosing a vendor. Then, make every effort to plan your day so that you can make these choices first thing in the morning, when your energy is at its maximum. If a crucial request or query arises in the late afternoon or evening when you're already exhausted, put it on your to-do list for first thing the following morning when you're rested. Additionally, try to remove any unnecessary choices.

Find strategies to automate decisions to save mental energy, such as making a weekly food plan or assembling a capsule wardrobe, which consists of a small number of items, so that you don't have to spend as much time and effort deciding what to wear each morning. You'll have more energy for the important things if you do it that way.

Another excellent tactic is to schedule buffer time throughout the day. This is something I prefer to accomplish by giving myself at least 15 to 20 minutes in between visits. This enables me to find my centre and comprehend the information that is being presented to me. Take a whole lunch break away from your desk, while we're on the subject of breaks. Naturally, staying energised is important, but it also enables you to return to your work with new eyes.

Finally, turn off your device when the day is through. If your workday doesn't have a clear conclusion, you're more likely to keep worrying about job-related issues after work. Set an alarm 30 minutes before you want to close up business to remind yourself to do it. Create a closing ritual, such as listing your top goals for the next day or your three biggest victories from the day. Don't forget the fundamentals when it comes to controlling your energy wisely. Get enough sleep. I realise that the thought of extra downtime may seem lazy because I am a high achiever. One more suggestion to change this perspective. Consider recovering instead of telling yourself you need to rest. Recovery is a more active, intentional process that will serve as a reminder to you that controlling your energy is important and required to beat overthinking.

The murky middle is so-called for a reason. There is sometimes a lot of excitement when you initially begin working toward a goal, but soon, reality settles in. There can be obstacles along the road because this is taking longer than you anticipated. It's simple to become dejected. So, here are three things you can do to keep moving forward.

First, each person has a favourite method for achieving goals. Some people prefer to start each day by tackling the most difficult task because it feels good to complete it, and everything else becomes easier. Others favour accumulating minor victories so you can see tangible results and feel accomplished, even if that specific activity isn't the most important one. Change your approach if you sense that you are stuck. Go for a modest gain if you've been doing the toughest thing first, and vice versa. You might feel better after changing your routine.

Second, if you're battling nature, you won't produce your finest work. Match your energy levels to your tasks. If you're a morning person, do creative or important work then, when you're most awake. Instead of trying to push yourself to be productive later in the day when you're distracted and worn out, you'll make a lot more progress this way.

Third, too many of us treat ourselves like cruel masters. We frequently push ourselves to work at our desks for excruciatingly long periods of time without a break because we believe it to be the sign of productivity. Take little pauses instead to help you regain your concentration. To avoid feeling exhausted, even a 15-minute walk outside or five minutes of stretching might be beneficial. The most difficult part of a project is frequently the middle. You may maintain your progress even when things become difficult or uninteresting by using these three strategies.

Sustaining the drive to achieve your objectives.

We always project our inner selves outward. When we connect and speak with people, our actual nature is always shown. If we are sincere, kind, and compassionate toward others, that is, let's say, if we comprehend others and accept them for who they are, then all of these positive traits of ours show themselves in our personalities.

A person's personality is a mirror of his or her inner self. The process of thinking itself is what shapes and frames both character and personality.

The personality also exhibits negative traits, including brutality, dishonesty, and unkindness. Outstanding people usually motivate others around them. The statements made by these individuals do not serve as inspiration or stimulus. Actually, it is these people's entire aura and vibrations that function and perform the magic. If the speaker is skilled, even the bare words of someone who does not follow his or her own advice may be praised. These statements will, however, not sway others. They won't significantly alter anyone's life. On the other side, someone who speaks their mind has the power to alter the world by influencing millions of others. The true definition of the word "personality" has been lost through time. It now has a more outward appearance.

A person's personality can be described in terms of his appearance, his communication abilities, his gait, etc. An attractive individual is always assumed to have a positive demeanor. Numerous personality development courses are offered nowadays in numerous locations. These seminars are taught by eminent speakers from many disciplines who help students who lack confidence develop their personalities. These seminars teach students how to handle themselves, smile, walk, speak, and use other mannerisms. But personality is much more than just what is often thought of as it. Instead, the development of confidence and positive traits within is what manifests outside.

Candidates are only granted jobs at reputable firms following a successful interview. In reality, the candidate's personality is taken into consideration during these job interviews in addition to his credentials and talents. It's crucial to see how he conducts himself and handles the entire interview process. Every employer seeks candidates with strong personalities who can manage the demands of the job and inspire others to foster a sense of teamwork. No matter how skilled a person is, if they cannot maintain their composure under pressure during the whole crisis, they will never be of any help. A positive personality is necessary for success in all spheres of life.

Any person can begin a project. However, not everyone completes them. Because it's so uncommon, having a reputation as someone who gets things done has a significant positive impact on your career. You can achieve your aim by using one of the following three methods. Make deadlines work in your favour first. Everyone is unique. A deadline can inspire some people to labour tirelessly until the very last second. As long as you reach the deadline, that is not at all an issue. It might be a terrific technique to motivate oneself to complete tasks. Like me, other people prefer to take their time and finish things early.

Consider your prior experiences to gain understanding. Consider your prior experiences to better understand how you relate to deadlines and how you might use them to your advantage. Second, even when you don't feel like doing anything, you may frequently find motivation by considering other people. Who is in need of your services? Are you delaying them by not responding to them or by failing to finish your portion of the project? Even if they don't behave in their own best interests, many people will do anything to avoid upsetting or hurting their loved ones' coworkers. Consider your relationships and the other people working on the project.

Finally, a lot of us waste a lot of time doing the things we enjoy and avoiding the ones we find unpleasant.Try to outsmart yourself if there's a chore you avoid performing on a regular basis by adding it to your schedule and perhaps setting up a coworking session with a coworker through video or in person where you're both working hard so you know it will get done. Otherwise, it's far too simple to stick with what you know how to do well and avoid critical activities or initiatives where you need to hone your abilities. The genuine mark of a professional is project completion, and that attracts attention. You can accomplish that with the aid of these three strategies.

Personality development programmes can only influence external change. This modification is only cosmetic. It can simply go since it is only surface-level and not deeply rooted. For instance, they preach that you should always smile, no matter what circumstances arise in your life. It is not at all simple to achieve this.

A person who is insecure on the inside cannot smile through times of crisis and difficulty.

If a person continues to supply phoney information when internally agitated, it is useless. His personality is readily affected by all of these internal turbulences and disturbances. His entire aura conveys the message that he is unable to handle challenging situations any more and that his grin will no longer be able to save him. On the other hand, a person who is calm and relaxed doesn't even need to grin; instead, his calm demeanour comes across extremely easily. Only modifications that must be made on an external level are covered in personality courses. If efforts are made to bring about changes on a surface level, they are useless. True internal adjustments must be made at deeper levels.

Individuals aren't what they seem to be. Therefore, there is one behaviour that the majority of individuals exhibit that keeps them from genuinely comprehending other people. As soon as we identify it and learn how to deal with it, our ability to comprehend why other people behave in a particular way improves. That phenomenon is known as the actor-observer bias in psychology. This is the propensity we have to believe that when we do something poorly, it is due to outside forces, but other individuals act the way they do because of who they are as people. In other words, we frequently form opinions about others based on their actions. But when it comes to ourselves, we frequently justify our choices in light of what other people say or how our lives were at the time. Imagine you are driving and you come to a stop at a red light. The automobile in front of you doesn't move even if the signal turns green. In fact, they stand there for so long that you have to blow your horn at them to encourage them to move; otherwise, you risk missing the light. It's evident that the driver of the vehicle is inattentive and should be removed from the road.

Have you ever acted like that idiot? The likelihood is that if you drive a car, you have experienced this, and you may even have become irritated with the impolite driver who honked their horn in front of you. After all, it's not a huge thing, and failing to see the light at the time doesn't make you stupid or inattentive, does it? You were only sidetracked by your situation. The point is this, even if this is an oversimplified example that only applies to those who drive automobiles and experience mild road rage.

Nobody ever attempts to play the villain. Based on the knowledge and resources they are aware they have available to them, everyone always performs the best they can at the time. In order to avoid the actor-observer bias, we must keep this in mind if we wish to understand other people and why they act the way they do. This will enable us to cease making snap judgments about others based on our cursory observations of their conduct. It becomes much simpler for us to feel confident among people when we realise that everyone normally strives to make the most of what they have since we will understand that we are all there trying to live our lives as best we can.

At the very least, we'll be better able to comprehend and overlook our own mistakes as well as those of others. It will be simpler to connect with others around us when we realise that everyone, regardless of how outgoing or timid they appear to be, is simply trying to do the best they can in any given circumstance. Therefore, this activity is for you to practise. When you observe someone do something that makes you respond adversely, ask yourself, "What good were they attempting to achieve with what they did?" This will train you to understand people's reasons rather than just their actions, and it will also greatly increase your empathy. Doing this will train you to see people's motivations rather than just their behaviours.

People frequently mistakenly assume that those around them are more at ease, self-assured, or in charge than they actually are. Although that may be true occasionally, it is not always the case. And if we don't correct this thinking mistake, we'll pass up a lot of chances. Let me relate the first time I witnessed this occur to someone in real life, in front of my very eyes. It occurred many years ago while I was out with some friends at a pub, and ever since then, I have tested and seen it several times in a variety of circumstances and locations. At the pub, I saw one of my friends—they frequently mistakenly assume that those around them are more at ease, self-assured, or in charge than they actually are.

Although that may be true occasionally, it is not always the case. And if we don't correct this thinking mistake, we'll pass up a lot of chances. Let me relate the first time I witnessed this occur to someone in real life, in front of my very eyes. It occurred many years ago while I was out with some friends at a pub, and ever since then, I have tested and seen it several times in a variety of circumstances and locations. At the pub, I saw one of my friends—let's call her Lima—talking to a man who was standing near the bar. I was familiar with Lima, and this guy seemed to be just her kind. I could tell she liked him because of the expression in her eyes as she turned to face me.

However, a few minutes later, she returned to our table by herself. She was informed by my question. She said that the man had lost interest and just departed because she had become overly anxious and was at a loss for words. I felt that this wasn't quite right. Lima is a stunning, wise, and hilarious girl, so I firmly doubted that the man would have gone after a short while if all she had been worried about was chatting with him. So, to Lima's great humiliation, I made the decision to investigate. I approached the man and started up a discussion before saying, "Look, I really have no business asking you this, but I'm simply curious." Why did you leave that vent when I spotted you chatting with her over by the bar? She had not shown any interest in speaking with him, and he shrugged. After waiting for a while to possibly ascertain what business that was of mine, I asked him how. Lima is a stunning, educated, and humorous young lady, so I had serious reservations about the person he claimed was quite obvious. She responded quickly, looked away toward her friends rather than at me, and crossed her arms—all of which are common signals. I had an unexpected thought.

When we're anxious and stressed out, we behave and present our bodies in a way that is strikingly similar to how we behave and present ourselves when we're attempting to subtly reject someone. However, neither Lima nor this guy realised that the reason they weren't connecting was because they were both feeling a bit apprehensive and uneasy since they each thought the other was assured and in charge of the situation. The narrative would have ended quite differently for them if one of them had realised that the other might be just as frightened and not truly confidently rejecting them. Since that evening, I have often seen this in a variety of circumstances and have tried to raise awareness of it.

Humans frequently believe that those around us are more informed than we are.

We assume that others can see that they are anxious or uneasy, since it is so evident to us when we are that we imagine it would be obvious to them. However, the reality is that if we attempt it, it's really simple to mask our emotions. Therefore, when other individuals aren't entirely honest about their feelings, we frequently have a very hard time understanding those feelings. It gets much tougher if we're already feeling nervous or stressed in that circumstance. As a result, when we try to infer someone's thoughts or feelings from their actions, the halo effect we discussed earlier joins forces, and we frequently conclude that their emotional condition is better than our own.

We overlook the reality that various emotions can be represented through behaviours that are strikingly similar, not to mention the fact that people frequently act in ways that completely contradict their feelings. Fortunately, the answer to all of this is pretty straightforward. Just though it seems clear to us, we simply have to quit assuming that we know what other people are thinking or feeling. We should stick to one straightforward guideline instead.

We have to presume that people are interested in whatever conversation we're having with them right now, as long as they are paying attention to us. If we act on that premise, we'll stay in the conversation longer and frequently get through any impeding feelings we or the other person may be experiencing. And once that occurs, we'll start seeing more of the desired outcomes. not to mention how much your confidence grows as you learn that some people are truly hesitant to speak with you.

How should you handle others' expectations on you?

Rahul, a colleague and occasionally coworker, was born too late and has a history of being late. He's just not interested in the idea of keeping a schedule or predicting time. Rahul frequently arrives hours late for events, and he is completely content with that. I, on the other hand, am usually right on time. This makes for an unusual connection because anytime Rahul and I are going to do something together, whether it be going to the movies or conducting a combined class, we both have to bear in mind these distinctions between us. I am not late, I am not early, I am right on time. In order to avoid driving each other crazy, we must be sure that we have realistic expectations of one another. It's likely that if I count on Rahul to arrive on time, I'll be dissatisfied and perhaps even irritated when he doesn't. And if I am, it is entirely my fault. Because reality rarely lives up to our expectations, we frequently become disappointed, irritated, and other negative emotions. And it would be foolish of me to anticipate anything different given that I am aware that Rahul is perpetually late.

However, if I prepare for Rahul to be late, I'll be able to entirely avoid irritation and get the desired outcomes. If I ask Rahul to the movies, I'll make sure he believes the film has already begun when it hasn't. In order to avoid having to wait for Rahul to get ready when Rahul and I are giving a workshop together, I always make sure that I'm the first speaker in the morning. In other words, we need to make sure that our expectations of others are accurate if we wish to prevent, or at least decrease, sentiments like irritation and disappointment. So how do we go about doing that? Actually, it's rather simple. In order to control your expectations of people, you must focus on what they really do rather than just what they say they'll do or what you believe they ought to do.

By doing this, we may lessen our disappointment and annoyance with others while also planning our interactions with them in a way that is more likely to produce the outcomes we desire. Not to add, we won't be as frequently taken aback or perplexed by their actions, which will make us feel much more comfortable with them. Having said that, if you discover that someone in your life is unacceptable to you in terms of what they do or who they are, end the connection and look for one with a better match for you. This is not a justification for you to put up with individuals in your life who shouldn't be there.

By using this easy strategy, you'll start developing real connections with individuals that complement you and your life based on who they actually are rather than what you expect, wish, or imagine them to be. And it will do wonders for our confidence to know that we are surrounded by real connections with individuals we see for who they really are. It will merely put an end to many of our social anxieties and uncertainties.

As a result, you have learned some fundamental truths about the human brain and how it has evolved to undermine your happiness in the previous chapters. You've also uncovered a very stunning new piece of brain science research that reveals why your brain is primarily a social organ motivated by a feeling of identity, community, and belonging to a group. An unsettling number from the State of the American Workplace study was revealed. The first fact is that just around one-third of US workers say they are engaged at work. This suggests that disengagement is present among more than two-thirds of American workers, which equates to a loss of over $500 billion in income. What else might serve as a wake-up call to the business world if not that?

Look at ways to apply these four pillars of comfort, contribution, connection, and compassion to help you invest in your happiness while also achieving your business goals, rather than looking at ways for you personally to find more engagement, a sense of purpose, a sense of meaning, and happiness at work.

Making decisions today can be improved by taking the long view and considering your priorities in the long run.

It's critical to be able to keep your attention, especially in times of information overload. If you focus all of your attention on your goals, unnecessary distractions will no longer significantly reduce your productivity. Distractions usually hinder us from focusing our entire attention on a single part of our life. However, once we are able to overcome these obstacles, we will be able to do a lot. Even the most ambitious among us understand how difficult it is to maintain a high level of focus, particularly when fatigued or bored. Lack of concentration may be a major issue, which is why we've compiled a list of the most motivating focus quotes to help you get back on track. All we have to do is concentrate intensely on mastering a particular area without allowing distractions to distract us.

When faced with an issue, we may either compulsively analyse it and moan about it, or we can focus our efforts on finding a solution. Many of life's most difficult problems were addressed by those who refused to complain about the issue, which aided them in finding a solution. You'll need a fire glass to focus the sun's rays if you wish to burn something with them. However, you must also aim the beams at a specified target. If you don't do so, nothing will ever catch fire. The same may be said about achieving life's objectives. It's improbable that your activities will yield the desired results if your approach is unfocused and undirected.

"Whenever you want to achieve something, keep your eyes open, concentrate and make sure you know exactly what it is you want. No one can hit their target with their eyes closed."- Paulo Coelho

The notion of an eight-second attention span has its origins. Because of a study performed by Microsoft in Canada in 2015, most individuals will tell you that their attention span is shorter than that of a goldfish. They're all incorrect, but don't hold it against them. From The Daily Telegraph to TIME, a slew of respected publications and magazines announced that Microsoft had discovered that our attention span has shrunk to that of a fish. All of them were mistaken as well.The Microsoft study is undeniably true. It includes impressive-sounding quantitative surveys and neurological research, as well as an infographic showing human attention spans "dwindling" from 12 seconds in 2000 to eight seconds in 2013, The only problem is that the infographic wasn't based on Microsoft's own research findings. It comes from a website called Statistics Brain. The Statistics Brain website has a number of different sources for this and other statistics. Human or goldfish attention spans do not appear to be mentioned in any of them. The statistic that has dominated a large number of marketing conversations since May 2015, when looked at in any degree of depth.

As an example, consider a business meeting. In a very short period of time, a lot may happen. There can be a lot of fascinating connections made. There is a lot of information that may be shared. It might be difficult to concentrate on a topic when there are so many distractions. When people are striving to address an urgent creative challenge, focus is especially vital. While it may appear straightforward in principle, it is not always a natural talent for employees to master. If you're still not convinced, consider the data from Udemy's 2018 Workplace Distraction Report:

- 70% of workers are distracted at work
- 54% are not performing as well as they should
- 75% believe they could get more done if distractions were reduced.

Do you know about your internal vs. external locus of control?

What's the difference and why does it matter? The perplexing aspect is that, despite warnings about the dangers of information overload, you continue to multitask, check email constantly, text while driving, and multitask some more. It's the equivalent of a statistician who likes playing slots. Location of internal control people who have an internal locus of control feel they are in charge of or can affect their own fortunes and lives. They may or may not consider themselves leaders, but they believe they are in command of their lives. Those with an external locus of control think that other people, environmental elements, the weather, malevolent gods, the alignment of celestial bodies, basically any and all external events, have the most effect on their lives. Individuals with an external focus of control will either applaud or blame the outside environment, respectively. The locus-of-control construct may be measured using conventional psychological tests and has been shown to predict work success.

It also has an impact on a successful management style. This means that you should be aware of the variations in motivational styles and take care to assign autonomous work to those with an internal locus of control and more limited occupations to those with an external locus of control. Managers underestimate the true depth of their employees‘ thoughts by assigning shallow incentives to them and then failing to provide them with the things that genuinely inspire them.

It's difficult to be innovative on the spur of the moment. The majority of us require time for thought, which necessitates thinking alone and without interruptions. To solve an issue, it's also necessary to be able to breathe, think, and take in a large amount of data. You can uncover some amazing chances to be incredible leaders if we adjust our mindset from being conscious of our emotions to using them as tools. These tools aren't external, but because of our limited internal locus of control, they're frequently hidden from view. You all have the potential to manage our reactions to certain events.

You may become a better leader by looking at leadership through the lens of regulating your own psychology. This will help you become not just self-aware but also take control of your thoughts and emotions. You can uncover some amazing chances to be incredible leaders if we adjust our mindset from being conscious of our emotions to using them as tools. These tools aren't external, but because of our limited internal locus of control, they're frequently hidden from view. Taking charge of your own psyche indicates that you are in command. Each of you have your own reality, which is a blend of what is actually happening to yourselves and around you and your objective and our brain's subjective perception of these occurrences. You believe you have no power over reality, when in fact, you do. Taking charge of your own psychology suggests that you are in command of your ideas, feelings, and actions. It's a purpose-driven perspective that reminds people that they have the capacity to create meaning in their lives and don't have to accept their current situation.

What is the major obstacles to your Attention?

The first reason is that I wanted to reveal the hidden psychology behind how companies like Facebook, Twitter, Slack, instagram reels and WhatsApp keep us coming back to their products. I've worked with many top performers in my corporate job, from the most junior employees to business leaders and business promoters. These are professionals at the pinnacle of their professions. They're well-organised, motivated, and self-disciplined.

However, many people fall short when it comes to monitoring how they use their mobile devices, such as iPhones and iPads. You're probably in the same boat. Tristan Harris, a former Google design ethicist, spends his time raising awareness about technology's ability to influence your attention and build an addiction to the stimulus that comes from your mobile devices all the time. Status updates, alarms, noises, and sensations all obstruct your ability to pay attention and concentrate. I've seen how strong habit-forming technologies can be firsthand. One major risk is that mobile gadgets provide "intermittent changeable incentives," as Harris describes them. Your devices constantly bombard you with fresh information, likes, news stories, messages, and so on. The random but continuous nature of these stimuli is precisely what makes them so appealing and addicting. The release of dopamine is triggered by each new piece of information, providing the conditions for gadget addiction. You wind up checking your phone and email hundreds of times each day as these habits build.

I aim to help you increase your attention and avoid the main dangers of daily device use. I'd like to suggest three ideas for you to consider. First and foremost, consider how much time you're wasting. Consider how interruptions impede your flow. Assume you're sitting at your home computer, doing some armchair research on a beloved subject or completing a major deliverable for a critical project.

"The key is not to prioritise what's on your schedule, but to schedule your priorities." -Stephen Covey

While the relationship between attention and greatness is sometimes overlooked, it pervades practically everything we strive to do. Attention: The Hidden Driver of Excellence, by Daniel Goleman, dives into the power of focus. Attention acts like a muscle, he adds. If you use it poorly, it will wither; if you use it effectively, it will develop. Goleman contends that attention is more important than knowledge in achieving success in life. It is something I adhere to! Productivity is all the rage these days. We all want to complete tasks as quickly as possible. But, have we considered anything as simple as how to concentrate? How, for example, do you stay focused when completing an assignment or exercise?

What effect does social media have on our memory?

Along with a shorter attention span, we are also observing a shorter memory, which is partially due to the Internet and social media. Because of information overload, our brain is unable to remember all the details it absorbs, which is often unnecessary. Your smartphone can act as a calendar, a reminder, and a notebook for all of the things you need to remember. And if you have a question, all you have to do is look it up on Wikipedia or Google. Another problem we've already explored is what Google does to our brains.

Furthermore, you no longer need to remember your friends' birthdays since Facebook will remind you. All you have to do is go through your calendar events for birthdays and make appropriate wishes. However, when our brains learn to work in new ways, it's not always simple to tell what's beneficial from what's not, causing us to forget essential knowledge accidentally. Accidents may result from a loss of concentration due to a shorter attention span, which is a concern that should not be overlooked.

How can you overcome the attention span of social media users?

Gone are the days when you could sit in peace for hours and read a book. It's difficult to lose sight of time these days without succumbing to the Internet's allure. This isn't to say that technology should be shunned. Yes, avoiding distractions is growing harder by the day, but it is up to us to have the power to manage our time and focus appropriately. Learn to say no and set aside time to concentrate on vital activities. Leave your phone at home, if feasible, switch off the Wi-Fi, and try to concentrate on one activity as much as possible. It's only a question of self-control!

Students must focus once they have determined where they want their thoughts to go, begun their job or problem solving, and persevered in getting the work started. It's tough to focus one's attention and concentrate on one's thoughts. Because higher level thinking requires a lot of energy, as I said in the persistence post, the brain will try to save energy in any way it can. The brain may conserve energy in a variety of ways, one of which is the polar opposite of perseverance. The brain will enter a state of neutrality. Relaxing and allowing your mind to wander, doing neutral chores, and daydreaming all have advantages, but they do not represent higher-order thinking.

Researchers from the University of Texas at Austin, the University of California at San Diego, and Disney Research recently conducted a study to see how simply having your smartphone near you, even if you aren't looking at it or using it, might alter your cognitive function. "Merely having their cellphones phones out on the desk led to a minor but statistically significant decrease in participants' cognitive function," the researchers concluded in a Harvard Business Review summary of their findings, "on par with the consequences of lack of sleep." Participants who uses mobile phones close by showed a reduction in their capacity to learn, reason, and generate innovative ideas.

Humans learn to reflexively pay attention to items that are regularly relevant to them, even when they are concentrating on other activities, the researchers add. This is why, even if you're in the middle of a discussion with someone else, your ears perk up when you hear your name spoken across the room. When you try to resist the draw of your smartphone, you're putting up an effort to do so, which is a distraction that impairs your ability to think clearly.

How often do you find yourself tempted to conduct a little more research or to take a break from your job to check your email, read the news, or just scroll through your friend's social media posts? It'll take a second, but if you're like most people, seconds will turn into minutes before you realise it, and you'll have wasted significant time looking at useless or slightly relevant content and lost your concentration. It takes a lot of effort to reclaim it. It takes almost 20 minutes on average to refocus on what you were doing before the interruption. I'd want you to consider the impact of distractions on your flow. Make a list of your observations and the level of attention required for the job. You may employ the best form of concentration for the circumstance by identifying the scenario's needs.

Have you ever felt remorseful for being preoccupied?

You have a tendency to believe that our inability to focus is our fault, and we might berate ourselves for it. You wonder why it's so difficult for you to concentrate. Distractibility is, first and foremost, a physiological and psychological trait. While a racing mind may not assist you prepare for an important presentation when you're ready to go on stage, it is a critical aspect of a stress reaction that has developed to defend you in life-threatening situations.

Distractibility and the capacity to think quickly can really assist you in making vital judgments. Then there's the fact that your mind is built to generate ideas. Your mind is continuously working in addition to maintaining your body's operating system. According to studies, the human mind creates between 50000 and 70,000 thoughts every day. This is fantastic for creativity, but not so much for getting hard, boring work done. While you're attempting to concentrate, your mind wants to hop all over the place, making new connections. Your behaviour has an influence on your capacity to focus. If you're like most people, you spend the majority of your waking hours in front of a computer or on a mobile device.

The amount of knowledge you've been exposed to appears to be growing at an exponential rate. Simply put, you're inundated with a massive amount of data that you can't handle. The pace of change in the information world has outpaced your ability to keep up. Consider that for a moment. It took thousands of years to get from clay tablets to illuminated manuscripts, which were only accessible to and read by a select few. After that, it took nearly 400 years for the Gutenberg Press to become global, making books available to the general public. However, in a little over 25 years, the current waves of information distribution, the internet, and portable wireless gadgets have become ubiquitous. As a result, your concentration suffers.

Now that you have a better understanding of why focusing is difficult, I'd want to assist you in figuring out why your attention patterns are so difficult to break. Above all, whether you recognize it or not, your mind and body are designed to keep things as they are. Consider that for a moment. Your body temperature must retain constancy from a physiological standpoint. Your heart must maintain a constant pace of blood pumping and so on. The same may be said about our emotions and ideas. Whether useful or not, the patterns of behaviour, thinking, and emotions you've developed throughout your life have shaped who you are. As you continue on your focus journey, recognise that it takes time and dedicated effort. Be patient with yourself as you work to reclaim your focus.

Have you ever noticed how your thinking alters when you're stressed?

If you're like the majority of individuals, you've undoubtedly noticed that your mind is racing, filled with anxiety, bad ideas, and sentiments. We can't all be Sherlock Holmes, the calm in the midst of a storm who solves complex mental puzzles while under duress. You may, however, learn to reclaim your attention under pressure and use it to your benefit. The reality is that stress isn't necessarily a bad thing. It has the potential to assist us in difficult times. The link between stress and attention is a complicated one.

Stress may be defined as a physical, mental, or emotional element that generates bodily or mental strain. I want you to think about what this means to you. Have you ever been under any of this kind of pressure? A large promotion, the pressure of a pending deadline, a fight with coworkers, the opportunity to make a keynote address, or a demanding manager are all examples of workplace stressors. Marriage, money difficulties, the coming of a new baby, relocating to a new house, or a death in the family are all examples of life pressures.

Your attitude toward yourself, your ambition to achieve, a bad diet, anxiety about what others think of you, not enough sleep, and self-talk, or what you say to yourself on a daily basis, are all examples of internally created stress. As you may have seen, not all of these tensions are terrible or negative. Something new, or even something pleasant, might cause stress. Change, opportunity, or anything else that forces you to leave your comfort zone might cause stress.

Researchers discovered that students who engaged in moderate physical activity before completing an attention span test scored better than those who did not. Although the researchers aren't sure why, they discovered that exercise improves our brain's capacity to ignore distractions. While there are sometimes contradictory scientific studies about many things, there isn't much argument about this: the physical, mental, and emotional advantages of exercise are immeasurable.

When we're stressed, our brain releases chemicals like cortisol and adrenaline, which, in the best-case scenario, activate us to deal with a short-term emergency, but in the worst-case scenario, create a continuing performance hazard. In that instance, the focus of attention narrows to the source of the stress rather than the work at hand. We fall back on unfavourable acquired behaviours when our memory reshuffles to promote thoughts most relevant to what's upsetting us. Our executive regions in the brain—our neuronal circuitry for paying attention, understanding, and learning—are hijacked by stress networks.However, one crucial component was missing from the equation: the attitude of the leader. Stress, conflict, worry, and negative emotions spread like a virus when a leader is loaded with them. Higher-ups' poisonous vibes will motivate valued team members to update their résumés rather than their to-do lists.

Stress can sometimes have a good impact. Stress, for example, may sometimes be a motivator. It might give you the energy you need to concentrate and complete your tasks. Consider how efficient you become under the stress of a tight deadline. Stress can also motivate you to go above and beyond what you previously believed was possible. Even the best athletes in the world feel the pressure of a big performance, but they know how to harness those sensations and the adrenaline rush that comes with them. When used correctly, stress may be a powerful tool for achieving peak performance. When you're performing in front of an audience, the appropriate amount of tension gives you that additional push to create the right conditions for the magic to happen.

In fact, research suggests that when your stress level rises, your level of performance rises as well, up to a limit. You know what I'm talking about if you've ever gone on stage and given a great presentation. It's something you perceive, and it's something the audience senses as well. Stress, on the other hand, has negative physical, emotional, and mental consequences. High blood pressure, cardiovascular disease, and other physical illnesses are all linked to stress. Stress may have a severe impact on your emotional and mental health. Stress might also impair your capacity to concentrate when it counts most.

I'd like to introduce you to a very useful tool that will help you gather, centre, and concentrate your attention, especially when you most need it. In this guided exercise, while you feel the inhale and exhale, I'll ask you to speak out the phrase, "Calm with the inflow and relax with the outflow." You will silently and repeatedly say these things to yourself.

Your sensation of serenity and ease will gradually increase as you mindfully and kindly record each breath. Even fleeting moments of serenity and relaxation will plant the seeds of an illness that will grow stronger the more you practice. Numerous stressors may be found during a regular workday, so finding ways to manage your stress is a surefire way to increase your efficiency and productivity. This does not imply, however, that you will always be able to focus and remain calm.

Even during a sitting, you will observe that the sense of focus and calm will come and go as you practise mindfulness of breathing. in the same way that you can feel calm and present for a minute during an ordinary day. Next, you'll likely feel anxious and distracted. This is normal and occurs during all phases of mindfulness training. Accept these shifting modes of experience. Just be aware of any judgement and keep your composure. Although you can't stop the waves, you can learn to surf, as one trainer put it. You may actually make it easier to achieve calm and steady focus by keeping a compassionate and interested focus on your breathing throughout all of the variations in your thoughts. The cornerstone of stability and presence, the breath serves as an anchor.

Then, at various points during the day, you may do a brief one-minute session, possibly while at your desk, in between meetings, or while getting ready for the subsequent activity on your to-do list. When that happens, consider pausing and taking a minute to breathe slowly and deliberately before opening the door and entering the office of the person you have an important appointment with. or, especially at these times, before you and your employee discuss the performance review. You might discover that returning to the present is made easier by mentally breathing in calm and breathing out ease.

You'll learn to apply your attention when and where it's needed, whether it's to stay productive throughout a long day at work or to finish a critical assignment on time. So, let's speak about concentration. First and foremost, it's critical to acknowledge that attention comes and goes. It has an ebb and flow to it. It's impossible to function at 100% concentration all of the time, no matter how strong your willpower. With this in mind, I'd like to give a few tips for improving and maintaining your attention during a hectic day. Reorganise your calendar and break it up into 20-to-30-minute work intervals.

You may resume working at the same job after a break if necessary, but take a short rest before doing so. These pauses will help you stay cognitively awake and re-energize your capacity to summon top-down attention when needed. Next, for each work segment, always have a precise goal in mind. Before you start working, write this down on your calendar or tell yourself this. While it may appear to be a simple task, goal planning is a powerful tool for achieving your objectives. You may use the time constraint to your advantage. Working in small bursts also aids concentration. Finally, when you've completed your work session, refresh, refocus, and depart. Stretch, stand up, roll your neck, or take a few deep breaths when you take a break to get the blood circulating and refresh yourself. As you can see, increased attention allows you to get more done in less time and with less effort. Analyse three distinct tasks that would benefit from increased attention as you consider your own focus patterns at work and at home, and utilise them to begin practising your focus.

You may have noticed that the breath varies in a variety of ways as you work on being attentive to your breathing. It may happen quickly. It might be sluggish at times. It changes depending on your emotions and ideas. It's possible to have shallow, short breaths when you're unhappy or nervous. The breath may be slow and soft while you're relaxed. By practising mindfulness, you can allow yourself to be present for whatever is going on. According to neuroscientific studies, mindful breathing balances the two branches of the autonomic, or involuntary, nervous system, resulting in a profound sensation of coherence in the brain itself. the one in charge of controlling our digestion, pulse, and breathing.

A lack of focus can be demonstrated by your attention occasionally drifting to other issues or feelings of anger, or even by quitting your task to hunt for food when you are not actually hungry. To improve stable presence and attention, use breath awareness as a focus.Being aware of your breathing provides you with a convenient anchor that will enable you to approach your task with more stability and clarity. It can aid in meeting concentration improvement, calmer presentation, increased work efficiency, and improved listening skills. The tension and anxiety of deadlines can be reduced with even a little period of attentive breathing. You may utilise the breath as the cornerstone of your mindfulness practise because it is always present and doesn't require any kind of belief. This makes the breath a great anchor that I may resort to both throughout and after our working life.

Is your work environment aiding or hindering your ability to concentrate? Meetings, queries from coworkers, emails, texts, alarms—these are just a few of the external distractions you may encounter throughout a regular work day. Internal distractions include odd thoughts, concerns, daydreaming, and internet surfing that lead to large amounts of wasted time. While mental discipline is essential, our immediate surroundings also play a significant role in supporting attention. I aim to assist you in altering your surroundings so that you may attract genuine attention. And it's all done in a few easy steps.

First, I'd like you to assess your work environment for any distractions. A modest amount of ambient noise might help some people concentrate. Background noise might be disturbing to some people. If you're bothered by background noise, invest in some noise-cancelling headphones. Certain sorts of ambient music might help you stay focused if you're working on something that demands your full concentration. Avoiding music that you can sing along to is a good rule of thumb. Close your door at particular times of day to avoid unexpected occurrences that take you off focus. To compensate for this, have open office hours. Assess your physical surroundings next. Do you have easy access to the tools, papers, and information you require in your workplace?

You may not know it, but being unable to quickly access what you want when you require it may be extremely distracting and cause you to lose attention or focus. Consider the furnishings in your office. If you have the option, a standing desk is a great way to stay attentive and physically active. Finally, be aware of how you interact with technology in the workplace.

Do you find yourself becoming distracted when working on your computer? Is your online research limited to news, social media feeds, and personal email? Using a website blocker is a terrific way to stay on track. Do you make use of your smartphone, or does it make use of you? If at all possible, keep your mobile device usage to a minimum throughout the workplace. Turn off noises and vibrations while you're working, unless you're anticipating something really vital and time-sensitive. If you're still tempted to check your phone on a regular basis, switch it off and stash it somewhere inconvenient. Switching between work and browsing takes you out of your zone of concentration.

Another wonderful tool for combatting wasted time and the internet is productivity monitors. Each day, week, or month, you can instantly check how much time you spend working vs. surfing the internet. Prepare to be startled if you've never looked at how much time you actually spend on your gadgets. It's almost always higher than you'd want to acknowledge. So, if you're ready to get started, here is what I'd want you to do. Take some time at the start of your next workday to evaluate your workplace with fresh eyes.

One of the most significant lessons I've learnt over my professional career is the importance of human connection. When it comes to connecting, whether it's to a group of 5,000 or a single person, focus and attention are essential. Making a personal connection is the key to leaving a lasting impression. Humans, on the other hand, aren't especially adept at staying concentrated. It is a tremendous problem that we live in a society where various stimuli fight for our limited attention all day, every day. With constant partial attention, we bounce from one item to another and back again. Because of these frequent fluctuations, it's difficult to stay focused on whatever you're doing, whether it's a business project, a tennis match, or a discussion. Your surroundings and behaviour are conspiring against your capacity to concentrate. So, what can you do about it, and how can you recapture your attention, especially when it comes to social interaction? It's all about returning to the present moment and remaining there. To begin, consider a recent discussion you had with someone. Consider these questions in the context of a specific conversation.

- Did you have the habit of interjecting throughout that conversation?
- Did your mind race ahead to see what they'd say?

- Did you keep your gaze fixed on the person or did your gaze wander?
- Have you ever found yourself staring at your phone during a conversation?

If you answered yes to any of these, you may be missing out on opportunities to interact with others. In the end, it's all about where you focus your attention. Now I'd want to take a moment to explain the relationship between attention and connection. The lens through which we direct our attention is called focus. You stay in the current moment while you concentrate. You're not totally present when your mind jumps around or races ahead. Your mind will remain focused on the job at hand if you maintain focus.

Focus allows you to perform one thing at a time, which in this situation is connecting. Your inner editor is kept at bay by focusing on the other person's words, gestures, and tone of voice. When you concentrate on listening, you neglect the others. It's not just about hearing, either. It's all about where you look. Because your concentration goes where your eyes go. The link between focus and eye contact is symbiotic. Visual input is thought to account for more than 70% of the information processed by a sighted person's brain. Your capacity to connect diminishes when your eyes are roaming and not attached to the individual or group. You're unable to understand subtle body language signs. Connectivity might be aided or hampered by eye direction.

Finally, decide to actively focus on the other person the next time you have a discussion. Concentrate all of your focus on them. Wait till they've finished talking before speaking. To establish a true connection, ask questions to ensure that you understand what they're saying and maintain eye contact with them. True connection is achieved through staying present in the moment and actively seeing and listening.

Have you ever been so anxious that you failed to save an essential document, or so frightened that you froze up during a job interview, or so disorganised that you missed notes at the start of a concerto you're playing? This is all about the mind-body feedback loop, and it has more to do with attention than you may think.

A basic lesson in biology In a complicated, strong feedback loop, your mind and body react to each other. Without your knowledge, your brain automatically activates a variety of physiological, mental, and emotional responses in response to your surroundings. To keep you safe, this mechanism has developed over hundreds of millions of years. But there's a snag. Under real or imagined danger, the mind-body feedback loop kicks in. That's one thing if your life is in jeopardy. It has the potential to be quite effective. The difficulty is that this stress reaction is frequently elicited in settings when it is ineffective, which is where distraction comes in. Your thoughts may become jumbled and forgetful. You may feel perplexed, and your performance may deteriorate as a result. You lose your ability to concentrate as well. By deliberately concentrating on your body and mind, you may tap into the power of this feedback loop. Because it takes practise to tap into your own mind-body loop, here's a simple exercise to get you started. Take a seat in your chair. Breathe a bit deeper and slower than usual. Feel your body's weight pass through your sitting bones, through your chair, and onto the floor. Now take a deep breath in. On the exhale, tense up any muscles you notice are tight. Exhale and let go of the stress.

Repeat this procedure a few times. Finally, set a goal for yourself for your next work session. This is your cue to concentrate.

A concentration cue is a concise statement of only a few words describing exactly what you want to accomplish throughout your work session. It will also assist you in focusing your mind and body on the task at hand. As an example, when you preparing any lesson, you focus on writing lecture as a focus cue. Make the concentration cue concise and obvious. Close your eyes, take a few deep breaths, repeat the attention cue to yourself, and then exhale. Rep this process numerous times to make yourself ready to return to work. Start by opening your eyes. When you do this over and over, your mind becomes more focused on the subject at hand. It's easier to get and stay focused on what you're going to do when you focus with clarity. At least once a day, before starting a work session or a specific assignment, do this.

How can you use mindfulness to fix your brain?

Paying attention to what's going on within and outside of you in the current moment is mindfulness. This starts with something really basic: a pause. Imagine yourself at a movie theatre, engrossed in a suspenseful thriller. The screen suddenly goes black. You become aware of where you are, the people around you, the noises and colours, the pulsating tension in your body, and what you're thinking and feeling because you're no longer swept up in the activity. This is what you can do during a pause. Learning to halt in the middle of your day brings you back to the present moment.

According to a Psychology Today article, mindfulness is defined as "the characteristic of being truly present in one's current experience, embracing the moment as it is, rather than doing what we typically do, which is get caught up in our thoughts and feelings." It can also have a significant impact on how individuals operate at work. When you learn how to practise mindfulness, you can pause, breathe, and instead of responding, you can reach a space of more clarity and empathy. You'll be able to reply with more dexterity, kindness, and balance. With mindfulness, you may pause after you finish writing an email before hitting send, pause before a challenging discussion, or even pause before getting in your car and driving to work. You may halt for a second or two in the middle of your regular workday duties and simply be present. Take note of how it feels to accomplish this.

Mindfulness enables us to recognise when the sea of distractions we swim through each day has drawn us in: here I am, perusing my inbox instead of finishing what I intended to accomplish. Our meta-awareness, or ability to follow where our attention wanders, improves as a result of mindfulness. When we find ourselves trapped in our inbox instead of completing that other vital activity, we might think to ourselves, "I don't need to do this right now," and return our focus to the task at hand. The cure for thoughtless multitasking is conscious awareness. We have the ability to focus on one thing at a time.

Being more mindful of what you do, the environment around you, and the ideas that enter your mind is what mindfulness is all about. Being more conscious allows you to concentrate on the areas where you spend the most of your time and energy, allowing you to make necessary changes. Keeping track of your activities, thoughts, and behaviour throughout the day can help you stay on track with your priorities. Being conscious as you settle in and set your priorities might help you stay on track. Many people assume that practising mindfulness is as simple as sitting down once a day to meditate.

Breath is vital because it ties you to the exhaling and inhaling of trees, the wild and chilly breezes that blow across the countryside, and everyone with whom you work and live. All that lives and breathes with us. Even in the middle of the commotion we sometimes encounter at work, becoming aware of our breathing helps quiet and settle our attention and increase our capacity to focus on whatever we're doing. You'll also realize that you don't need to retreat or limit your mindfulness practise to a dark room or a certain contemplative stance. You may practise mindful awareness at any moment, including during your workplace in whichever scenario you find yourself in. It's that easy to be mindful of your breathing, and yet it's revolutionary.

Simply said, mindfulness is the act of focusing one's attention in the present moment without passing judgement. Consistent physical activity has been shown to reduce the symptoms of a wide range of disorders, including anxiety, depression, substance abuse, eating disorders, and chronic pain, as well as improve overall well-being and quality of life! You don't need a spiritual belief, a religious inclination, or even one of those popular apps to participate (which are great, by the way). All you have to do is concentrate on your breath, body, or something in your immediate surroundings. When done on a regular basis over the course of eight weeks, you will notice significant changes-not just in your thinking, but also in the physical architecture of your brain!

This is because, rather than being distracted or spacing out for the rest of your life, you may sharpen your mind and master the ability to pay attention to exactly where you are. So let's get started with the breathing awareness practise. Take two deep, soothing breaths and notice how your breath fills and releases your body. Allow the breath to return to its normal rhythm. Take note of where you can most readily feel or perceive the breath in your body. It might be a sensation of coldness or tingling in the nostrils or back of the neck, or a sensation of warmth on the top lip.It might be the feeling of whole-body breathing, or it could be the rise and fall of the chest or belly. Rest your compassionate attention wherever you can most readily sense the natural breath rhythm. If any of these methods make it difficult to feel the breath, simply place your palm on your abdomen and note how it rises and falls with each breath.

Allow yourself to experience the next three in-and-out breaths, and while you do, allow your mind to settle and your body to relax. Try taking three more deep breaths. Continue to focus on the breath in this comfortable and tranquil manner for a while, and gently bring your attention back to it when you sense it has wandered. Even a few minutes of attentive breathing might help you relax and unwind from the stress of deadlines. You don't have to believe in anything to utilize the breath as the foundation for your mindfulness practise. This makes the breath an excellent anchor to which we can return in our work and life in many ways. Throughout these book, you'll learn to be more resilient and less worried in the face of whatever sensations occur in your body, emotions, or ideas. It might be the feeling of whole-body breathing, or it could be the rise and fall of the chest or belly. Rest your compassionate attention wherever you can most readily sense the natural breath rhythm. If any of these methods make it difficult to feel the breath, simply place your palm on your abdomen and note how it rises and falls with each breath. Continue to focus on the breath in this comfortable and tranquil manner for a while, and gently bring your attention back to it when you sense it has wandered.

What if you could make a significant difference in your life just by practising mindfulness? What if you could enhance your health by paying attention on purpose? My working definition of mindfulness is paying attention in the present moment on purpose, nonjudgmentally, as if your life depended on it. Actually, mindfulness is nothing more than awareness, which is the result of paying attention on purpose in the present moment, nonjudgmentally and as if your life depended on it. Now, awareness is something we're all familiar with but also completely unfamiliar with. So the mindfulness training we'll be doing together is actually just cultivating a resource you already have.

By the way, the first thing you notice when you practise mindfulness regularly is how thoughtless we are at the moment. Mindfulness goes hand in hand with generosity, compassion, and openness. So you must equally well comprehend what mindfulness is about when you hear the word mindfulness. When we hear the word heartfulness, we think of kind care or being gentle and compassionate with ourselves, because this isn't some sort of cold, harsh discriminating, witnessing, peeling back, you know, to uncover something that's kind of driving you to do things.

You may shift your focus from your ideas to your physiological sensations at any time, whether it's through the smooth stroke of your fingers on the keyboard or your posture in your chair. Over and over, say something wonderful about yourself. One of the key aims of mindfulness is to put a halt to the endless stream of ideas that run through your head every day. Surprisingly, choosing a brief, positive message about yourself and repeating it over and over with each breath is a terrific method to keep your thoughts on track. The simplicity keeps you focused on the task at hand and prevents extraneous ideas from creeping in.

Try this Harvard Business Review mindfulness exercise: concentrate on a specific target, such as your breath. When your mind wanders (and it will), be aware that it has done so. This necessitates awareness, or the capacity to watch without becoming consumed by our ideas. Then return your focus to your breathing. That's the equivalent of a single rep in weightlifting. This simple activity, according to Emory University researchers, really enhances connections in the attention circuits.

Through the day, practise mindfulness. Attention specialists advocate finding chances to practise mindfulness throughout the day, in addition to committing 10 to 20 minutes a day to mindfulness meditation. Simply put, mindfulness means focusing entirely on what you're doing, slowing down, and noticing all of the physical and emotional feelings you're having at the time.

When you eat, you may practise mindfulness by taking the time to chew your meal thoroughly and focusing on the flavours and textures. When you shave, you may exercise mindfulness by smelling your shaving cream, noting how nice it feels to apply a warm lather to your face, and slowly dragging the blade through your stubble. Short mindfulness practises throughout the day can help you build and increase your attention span for those moments when you truly need it.

Mindfulness can also assist you in overcoming distractions when they occur. "Be here now," think to yourself if you're working on a task and have a restless urge to do something else. Bring your attention to your body and your breath at that time. You'll notice that the distraction is gone after a few seconds of focusing on your breath, and you're ready to get back to work.Emotional intelligence includes the ability to self-regulate. People who are good at managing their emotions recover from stress arousal faster. This entails quieting the amygdala and other stress circuits at the neurological level, allowing the executive centres to function more effectively. The mind is more fluid, and the body is more relaxed as attention becomes more agile and concentrated. And performance is best when you're in a relaxed alert condition.

Think about it this way: don't think about it in terms of paying attention. This is just crap from a textbook. They informed you that you needed to pay attention in class. I was paying attention in class. I was quite focused, but nothing occurred. I didn't read because I was paying attention. They presented me with a textbook. I noticed a microscopic particle on the paper and spent the entire two hours staring at it. That isn't what they wanted me to do, though. They should have informed me that they wanted me to move my focus from one letter to the next, one word to the next, one phrase to the next. "Pay attention," they said. I was paying attention.

Don't give a damn about anything. There is a technique to increase the degree of focus that you have right now. Everything is in your focus if you become significantly more attentive. You'll lose your mind if you try to pay attention to everything. You should not pay attention to me if you are sitting here. All you have to do now is pay attention. Not only will my words flow into your ears if you are just listening, but much more will happen. People want to write it down because they are paying attention to the words and are afraid they will miss it. This is unlike anything you've ever experienced.

Life will never be the same for you. At most, you'll be able to pass a test. However, none of the world's finest beings, whom you revere, have ever passed a test. Krishna has never been known to take an examination. Gautama Buddha was never known to go to an examination. You've probably never heard of Jesus attending a medical examination. But you adore them simply because they learned to pay attention to life in such a manner that they saw more than you do. I also went for a test but didn't write anything down.

It's not about what you're paying attention to; it's about how you're acting. You just focus your attention on something rather than something else. Everything will now fall within your purview on its own. If you try to pay attention to everything, you will miss everything since there is far too much going on in the universe. Nobody has time to pay attention to everything. The mind is like a mirror. When you pay attention to something, you strive to catch one item. After a while, you'll turn into a filthy mirror that'll be worthless. It will become more of an annoyance than a benefit, as it has in most minds.

You won't have to make an effort to reflect if your mind becomes like a clean mirror. Everything you see in the mirror will automatically reflect back to you. Don't worry about this or that; simply concentrate on polishing the mirror. There's enough filth to last a lifetime. If you polish it incredibly bright and clean, it will now reflect the entire galaxy. What is it going to get away with? Is it possible for the sky to flee if you hold a mirror? It must, after all, reflect. As a result, don't try to focus on anything. However, there is a technique to train your attention to improve to greater and higher levels. Everything is now in your purview if you become hyper-aware; it cannot be avoided.

Taking charge of your own psyche indicates that you are in command.

Taking charge of your own psychology suggests that you are in command of your ideas, feelings, and actions. It's a purpose-driven perspective that reminds people that they have the capacity to create meaning in their lives and don't have to accept their current situation.

Managing your own psychology = Mindfulness + Metacognition + Reframing

Accepting that everything is a neutral stimulus is mindfulness. Nothing has an intrinsic good or negative quality. The only thing that makes an event charged is our judgement or perception of it. Metacognition allows us to see that our reactions are affected by our own thoughts and that we may take action to change them. Reframing aids in the control of our thinking. You may verify your thinking by reframing our experience to ensure you aren't engaging in any cognitive distortions and/or thinking mistakes.

This is a strong method that may assist leaders in accepting responsibility and taking action. Reframing aids in the control of our thinking. You may verify your thinking by reframing your experience to ensure you aren't engaging in any cognitive distortions and/or thinking patterns. This is a great method that can assist leaders in taking responsibility for their own psyche. The brain's capacity to comprehend all sensory stimuli available in the physical world at any given time is limited, so it relies on the cognitive function of attention to focus neuronal resources based on the demands of the moment.

Bottom-up attention refers to attentional guidance based solely on externally driven factors on stimuli that are salient due to their inherent properties relative to the background, whereas top-down attention refers to internal attentional guidance based on prior knowledge, willful plans, and current goals. In recent years, neurophysiological investigations have revealed new information about the brain circuits and mechanisms of bottom-up and top-down attention. The mean neuronal firing rate is also affected by attention. Finally, mindfulness, metacognition, and reframing can help us increase our internal locus of control, which relates to how much we believe we have control over the events that shape our lives.

- Individuals with a strong internal locus of control are more willing to accept responsibility for their actions.
- They are less swayed by other people's ideas.
- They usually have a high feeling of self-efficacy, tend to work hard to attain their goals, and have a higher rate of success at work.
- Be self-assured when confronted with difficulties.

The simple act of practising mindfulness increased both brain activity and brain tissue density in these brain regions: Self-control is controlled by the anterior cingulate cortex (ACC). It allows you to work effectively and make smart judgments by allowing you to fight distractions, focus, and prevent impulsivity. The ACC is also in charge of flexibility, and people with issues in this part of the brain are renowned for sticking to inefficient problem-solving tactics when they should be changing their approach. The hippocampus is responsible for resilience in the face of failures and hardships, among other things. Stress may easily damage the hippocampus, making it a high-need region for most people. In the picture shown, the hippocampus is red and orange.

Mindfulness is a basic yet powerful kind of meditation that allows you to acquire control over your erratic thoughts and actions. Even when they are not meditating, those who practise mindfulness are more focused. Because it helps you to stop feeling out of control, leap from one idea to the next, and ruminate on unpleasant thoughts, mindfulness is a good strategy for reducing stress. Overall, it's a terrific way to stay calm and productive during your hectic day. Practicing mindfulness improves the density of brain tissue where it counts, much like performing curls increases the muscular density in your biceps. Perhaps the only practise that can rewire your brain in this manner, resulting in a cascade of other great benefits, is mindfulness. Fortunately, mindfulness can be practised for as little as a few minutes per day to reap its benefits.

What mindfulness is not?

Mindfulness doesn't have to be practised in the Himalayan highlands or at a weekend retreat where you take a vow of silence. The technique's brilliance is that it's so easy that you can execute it almost anywhere and at any time. The act of mindfulness is simply concentrating all of your attention on the current moment. This necessitates objective, nonjudgmental observation of your thoughts and sensations, which allows you to awaken your experience and live in the now.

Life will not pass you by if you do it this way. I understand this may sound a little abstract and difficult, but spend several minutes focusing just on the process of breathing, ignoring all other thoughts. When you're upset, overwhelmed, or stuck on anything, mindfulness is the best thing you can do. Simply said, pause what you're doing, let go of your thoughts for a time, and engage in your preferred mindfulness approach (breathing, walking, or focusing on body sensations). Even a few minutes of this may go a long way toward calming your thoughts and lowering tension. Once you've taken a few seconds to clear your mind, you'll be astonished at how sensible things appear.

Mindfulness meditation may also boost motivation in other ways, such as by changing people's estimations of their chances of succeeding. A socially anxious person who practises mindfulness, for example, may feel less apprehensive and frightened before attending a dinner party and calmer and more focused once there. This boosts the individual's sense of effectiveness and expectations of social success, which increases their drive to attend additional social gatherings.

"A continuous flow of thinking and attention is defined as meditation. Concentration is like pouring water, whereas meditation is like flowing water. The mind gets quieter and more harmonious as the restlessness fades away. During meditation, the mind does not go blank, but the frequency of brain waves does. Meditation produces alpha brain waves, which are linked to intuition and creativity."

Take a stroll. You may meditate simply by taking a stroll. Putting Everything Together Nothing compares to the benefits of mindfulness meditation for your brain. Give it a go, and you might be surprised at where it leads. All you have to do now is concentrate on each step. Feel your legs moving and your feet landing. Concentrate completely on the act of walking and your surroundings' sensations.

When other thoughts begin to enter your head, concentrate much more on the experience of walking. It's invigorating to concentrate on something that comes naturally to you because it changes your mindset. It's pleasant to focus on something that's second nature since it shifts your mindset by turning off the never-ending stream of ideas that ordinarily consume your attention. When you wash your teeth, comb your hair, or consume a meal, you may do the same thing. Feel the sensations in your body.

To practise mindfulness, you don't even have to stop doing what you're doing. Simply focus your entire concentration on what you're doing without considering why you're doing it, what you should do next, or what you should be doing. You may shift your focus away from your thoughts and onto your physiological sensations by focusing on the soft strokes of your fingers on the keyboard or your posture in your chair. Flossing just one tooth is so simple and quick that it seems foolish not to do it. But once you get started, you'll find that flossing two or three teeth, or even your entire mouth, isn't that difficult.

When you're uninspired, time isn't on your side. That's why mapping out your time and effectively planning it is one of the best ways you can harness your motivation. You may do it in one of three ways. Number one, estimating the time it will take you to complete each task is a simple task that few people bother with. This is beneficial since it allows you to assess the challenge's scope. If you know you have 100 hours of work to do but only have 40 hours to do it in, you can go to your manager and request extra time or ask if another team member can be called in to assist.

On the other hand, estimating how long specific projects will take can help you locate little pockets of time that you can employ efficiently. That extra 15 minutes between meetings could have been wasted in the past, but now you know what to do with it since you have a 10-minute job to do. Second, it's a good idea to plan out your time ahead of time so you know how you'll spend it. You can plan things out once a week, looking ahead to the following week, or even at the conclusion of the workday to plan out the following day's activities. When you're not feeling well, you could choose modest duties such as responding to an email.

On other days, you can take it a step farther and complete a larger job. If you're uninspired, time might feel like an enemy, but by following these three steps, it can become your ally. When you're feeling unmotivated, going back to basics is one of the best things you can do. What is it that you desire to achieve? What difference does it make? When you reconnect with your mission and recognise the influence that your job may have, you are more likely to take action, even if it is difficult or unrewarding. Here are three thought-provoking questions to ponder.

First and foremost, how will what you're doing improve the lives of others? It might be long-term, such as when you're working on a project that will revolutionise your customer's business, or it could be short-term, such as when your modifications improve a colleague's presentation. Consider how you can make a difference, whether it's in a tiny or huge way. Second, for whom do you serve as a role model? You might not feel like doing anything some days. You can, however, refocus on those who look up to you. Perhaps it's your children, and you're showing them what it means to work hard. Perhaps it's your coworkers who need a wonderful supervisor who looks out for them. People are looking to you in one way or another to see what is possible in their own lives, and your achievements have enormous ripple consequences for them. Third, how far did I get today on important goals? One of the most important things we can do to generate a sense of forward momentum in our work life is to achieve even little progress on goals we find significant each day. Even on the busiest days, you may surely find a little method to advance the ball. That is significant. By asking yourself these three questions, you may connect with the reasons why your goal is important to you and enhance your drive to complete it.

A barrier to motivation may be that everything you need to perform appears to be difficult or dull. And we've all been there before. Nobody likes sitting for hours on end completing paperwork, yet it must be done sometimes. The idea is to find modest methods to motivate oneself to continue. Unpleasant duties may be made to appear more acceptable with a good reward, such as a lovely meal with friends at the end of the day or a midday walk outside. From time to time, we all confront opposition. You can get to the root of the problem and address it if you know what's driving you to postpone.You're always putting things off. But why is that?

There might be a variety of causes, and determining what is causing your procrastination is critical to resolving it. Here are three frequent roadblocks you could encounter and how to overcome them. The first stumbling block is that you have no idea what to do. Perhaps there are five items that might be considered priorities, and you're not sure which one is the most important. In that instance, ask your boss for advice on where you should concentrate your efforts.

You may also seek guidance from skilled coworkers or simply focus on one objective for a period of time, test it out, and see how much traction you receive. You can make changes as needed. Another potential stumbling block is knowing what to do but not knowing how to execute it. You may have a big objective in mind, such as increasing income by 50%, but you're stuck because you don't know where to begin. If that's the case, you'll need further information. Return to your boss and ask further questions if you were given the goal by them. Where should you begin, according to them?

Start small. The psychological barrier of getting started was the most difficult element. Second, aim for a swift victory. It's wonderful to have favourable comments right away. And it has a huge impact when you're in the beginning phases of taking action. It'd be so easy to attempt something and then abandon it if it proved difficult. Instead, concentrate on achieving instant results. And three, you are capable of accomplishing anything.

When you practise mindfulness, you can pause, breathe, and instead of responding, you reach a space of more clarity and empathy. Practicing mindfulness may help you increase your motivation, especially for achieving personally meaningful and genuine objectives.

CHAPTER TWO

Mindfulness Meditation Eases Stress And Anxiety

"When you have to make a choice and don't make it, that in itself is a choice."-William James

In order to lead a life that is meaningful, joyful, and content, it is crucial to understand how to detect stress and anxiety identify their sources, and find strategies to manage them.

You've learned how to focus your mindful attention on the breath, which serves as your body's home base thus far. While using the breath as the main anchor for the following two sections of this book, I will also broaden the experience of body mindfulness by directly and objectively investigating the world of physical sensations. A teacher of young children once asked her class what they believed the body's function to be. They responded by turning their heads. Realising how infrequently they are aware of what is going on within their body is one of the revelations that many individuals get at this stage of the everyday mindfulness. However, being conscious of your body while working might help you get a better understanding of your own lived experience.

Body sensations and emotions serve as sources of information and data for how you are feeling as well as for enhancing your emotional intelligence, self-assurance, and understanding.

You might be spending eight or more hours each day problem-solving, planning, choosing, and analysing in most workplaces, including offices, health clinics, and factories. Because of this, you rarely pay attention to your body's feelings unless they include extraordinary discomfort. Every one of your feelings, whether it be love, hurt, rage, excitement, or addictive behaviour, is fed by bodily sensations, even when you are not paying attention to them. When you become upset with a coworker for not performing their fair share of the job, physical symptoms also start to appear. Possible sensations include burning, tightness, and even a surge of energy that at first seems like power and strength but eventually becomes painful and unpleasant.

"Breathe. Let go. And remind yourself that this very moment is the only one you know you have for sure." – Oprah Winfrey

The notion of a stress-free life has grown to be a substantial roadblock on the way to effective stress management, which involves striking a balance between channelling stress constructively and reducing negative stress symptoms. Adding a smile to your daily routine will significantly enhance your life and help you deal with problems like stress, worry, and low self-esteem. Increased smiles can also improve your view on life and give you a positive outlook every day.

This chapter will examine the numerous ways that people experience and communicate stress throughout their lives. You'll be exposed to unhelpful thought patterns that you may not even be aware of, and you'll learn some useful methods you can use right away to help you change them.

The delicate balance that may cause a brief stressful experience to become a systemic overload and eventually cause inflammation, anxiety, depression, and other chronic health problems is being better understood via research. This useful and ground-breaking book outlines seven ways to combat stress and boost our body's natural defences to keep our thoughts fresh. This useful and ground-breaking manual explains seven ways to counteract the negative effects of stress and to fortify your natural defences so that, no matter what life throws at you, your bodies and brains stay robust.

This chapter will examines a typical stressor, such as inflammation, an out-of-tune body clock, cortisol levels, and emotional triggers, and offers straightforward strategies for reducing its negative effects through dietary and exercise changes as well as other daily routines. These strategies can include surprising tricks involving music, eye movements, body temperature, daily routine, and more. The perspective should be that the response is not determined by the stressor but rather by the individual's internal reaction, and stress should not be seen as a bad event.

As described below, people have both negative and good coping mechanisms for handling stress. Negative stress coping mechanisms include these, such as the use of drugs, alcohol, smoking, overeating, and other behaviours, many of which can result in dependency and addiction and actually exacerbate the disease we are attempting to halt or heal. This book is the ultimate user's guide for health, mind, and well-being because it transforms cutting-edge scientific findings into understandable, practical recommendations. The use of relaxation methods, effective time management, upholding strong relationships, engaging in physical activity, following a balanced diet, and other strategies are examples of positive stress coping approaches. Your body needs to be ready to handle it.

A little stress can spur you on, but too much can harm your relationships and health. The good news is that you may lessen the stress in your life by using the appropriate management strategies.

Learn how to recognise and evaluate your stress triggers, better control your reactions, and make wise personal decisions. Let's be real here. We all understand what stress is. It is commonplace. It can be brought on by a variety of factors, including strict deadlines, demanding coworkers, difficult clients, or self-imposed high expectations. Unchecked, it can lead to a variety of mental and physical problems that you'd want to avoid. The good news is that we have a lot of knowledge about proactive stress management and keeping it under control, so that you can continue moving forward. We can all definitely relate to stress. In fact, according to studies by the staff at stress.org, close to half of all employees eventually suffer from moderate to severe stress at work.

Life will always include some level of stress.

Even at low levels, stress makes it difficult for most employees to concentrate at work, and the expense is substantial. Recent estimates put the annual cost of missed production at as high as $300 billion. As a result, stress-related blunders, missed deadlines, relationship problems, tardiness, and absences from work are becoming more common. Although a little stress can be motivating, almost all top experts agree that the issue is that organisations have accidentally improved to a very high standard. Numerous typical outcomes are connected to stressful circumstances, according to the American Institute for Stress. For instance, bodily problems might be manifested as excessive weariness, back or neck pain, or recurrent headaches. Additional anxiety or wrath are examples of emotional effects.

Additionally, behavioural effects might take the form of overly defensiveness or social isolation. That is only a portion of the list. These kinds of characteristics also tend to deteriorate with time, occasionally reaching a far higher threshold of the mental and physical suffering we refer to as burnout. That kind of stress may ruin a career and lead to really dangerous diseases like depression.

When under the influence of stress, you may lose the capacity to connect with people. Other times, it might negatively impact your health. Having the appropriate knowledge can aid in preventing these problems. Maintaining excellent relationships with people, managing stress, preventing concern, and controlling anger are all important. You may discover all of these things here, along with many others.

Stress is characterised as a condition of mental or emotional strain or tension brought on by difficult or demanding situations.

It's normal to experience anxiety or tension; it's just a characteristic of being human. Whether a situation is important or not, stressing about it is an indication that you are feeling and that your heart is beating. Nobody in history can claim to have never experienced stress. More often than you would imagine, stress can be good for you. It can be a chance for you to increase your tolerance and endurance. Being able to rise again after a trying circumstance may make you more powerful, brave, and tough. Stress affects many of us, both at work and in our personal lives. Stress, like any other issue, necessitates a systematic strategy to overcome it, or at the very least manage it.

There will be days when you'll feel completely stressed out, regardless of who you are, what you do, or how happy you believe you are. That said, it still isn't any simpler! When you're under a lot of stress, it might be difficult to envision a way out. Stress can feel overwhelming. Sometimes, all you truly need to get through a stressful situation is a gentle reminder that the end of the tunnel is in sight and that light is just around the corner.

Getting what we want—such as love, admiration, cash, or support, among other things—is what makes us happy. But the majority of individuals prioritise the needs of others over their own satisfaction in their pursuit of happiness, which leads to sentiments of resentment, frustration, and wrath.

While it may be nearly impossible to avoid stress, this does not mean that you must accept the fact that you will always be under stress. Stress not only makes life difficult, but it also raises your risk of developing a number of illnesses, including heart disease, high blood pressure, and even stroke. This means that being able to manage stress well is crucial.

Life will always include some level of stress. Stressful events can help us learn and grow in ways that we otherwise wouldn't be able to if we respond to them constructively. However, excessive stress has a number of negative effects on our health, ranging from physical sickness to mental exhaustion. Stress is a normal and natural aspect of life. Promises of stress relief put individuals at risk of failure. The use of the term "stress-free" is still not recommended since the approach is permeated with an incorrect notion that will never materialise, even when utilised with the best of intentions and in conjunction with pertinent and advantageous thoughts and practises. Your life may be impacted by both people and situations that might create mental stress. Maybe these sayings serve as motivation for you to live the life of your dreams by removing tension from your life and thoughts.

Life is full of stress. It may be found in many of the things we do, especially at work and in problematic relationships. When under pressure, a small amount of stress may be beneficial for us and help us perform better. However, excessive stress can harm our general well-being, so when it begins to take hold, we must take swift and firm action to stop it. According to USA Today research, it now takes more adjustment to experience a friend's death, a job loss, or the birth of a child. The study contrasts how people perceive life changes now to how they did 40 years ago.

The present human condition sadly includes stress, sadness, and worry. According to statistics, more and more people worldwide are battling mental health problems. Thankfully, we're discussing these issues more freely than ever before. Workplace stress contributes significantly to overall mental health problems. Increased financial concerns and economic changes lead to pressure at work. According to data on workplace stress, deadlines, high workloads, and demanding managers all add to the issue. If left unaddressed, work-related stress can lead to major mental health issues for employees. Stress may cause significant declines in production, which end up costing both private businesses and governments a lot of money. These numbers on job stress have been gathered to demonstrate exactly how serious an issue it is.

On the globe, Americans are the most stressed people, and in recent days, our stress levels are rising daily. Life is stressful by design. Stress aids in our ability to learn, develop, and improve. When it comes to attempting to manage this mounting, debilitating stress, the savior hasn't abandoned us. In a recent study 40% of employees said their work was extremely or very stressful. 25% of people say that their jobs are their biggest source of stress. 75% of workers say they are more stressed out at work than they were a generation ago. 29% of employees reported feeling very or highly stressed at work.

Even if you enjoy your job, stress still affects you. All of us do. You should therefore think about developing your stress management techniques. The greatest place to begin is to identify the stress triggers that you experience clearly. The events that you experience that raise your stress and anxiety levels are known as triggers, whether or not you caused them. Sadly, we frequently put off dealing with our recognised triggers. It proceeds as follows: People go through one, manage to get out of it somehow, and then just forget about it until it naturally happens again. Take a piece of paper or your computer and spend a few minutes writing down your thoughts as you evaluate each of the following in order to discover your most frequent triggers at work and in your personal life. Then, let's confront the problem head-on. First, think about who. Who may act as a trigger? It may be one of your friends, your partner, your supervisor, or even an employee.

Most of the time, just one or two people are mostly to blame for your most stressful times. The task or subject that frequently raises your stress level is that which comes next. Perhaps there is a certain task or section of a project that you usually dread. By the way, I say with respect that if you can list several items here with ease, you could be in the incorrect position or line of work. Then, take into account the where, since geographic location might be a significant factor. You may be at someone's home or at your boss's workplace. You may start managing them once you identify the one or two sites that stand out as being the most pertinent. Finally, consider the timing.

Is it always during a certain meeting?

Perhaps it appears to occur every day at the same time. You may be more conscious of handling stress more successfully the more you are aware of it when it occurs. Refer to the list going ahead to make adjustments to your mental experience at work. I am aware that it is impossible to always avoid all stressors. But if you're aware of the key problems, you may try to steer clear of them whenever you can. If you can, control them, or at the very least, how you respond to them. Although stress can be reduced and managed, it will never completely disappear. You may handle your primary triggers far more successfully when you make an effort to stay aware of them rather than disregarding them.

Today, stress reduction is crucial for both our personal health and the health of the planet, as the root cause of stress in our lives is identification with the ego and its ideals. Our world is being destroyed by the ego-driven lifestyle that the majority of people lead. Fortunately, altering our minds—or, more specifically, our connection with our minds—is the major factor in changing both ourselves and our surroundings in this way. That is the main idea behind from "Stress to Stillness". You will learn how to detect stressful ideas, disassociate from them, and de-stress. You will also understand how stress affects the body and how we manage it.

How to alter your way of life to reduce stress?

People frequently wait until stress becomes unbearable before dealing with it; this is the incorrect course of action. You are more likely to develop one of the numerous ailments linked to stress. Have you ever thought that your obsession with perfection prevents you from getting work done? Did the prepackaged counsel from professionals really fail?

There is no such thing as a productivity strategy that works for everyone. The methods that your co-worker finds effective might not be as effective for you. Or maybe they don't function at all. Everyone has unique productivity quirks that enable them to work successfully and efficiently. They are just unable to break them. In this ground-breaking manual, I'll assist you in identifying your particular productivity profile and provide you with the structure to create a strong personal system. Your one desire is probably to have your life back if you're one of the 100 million Americans who wake up each morning knowing they will have to fight to survive another day.

Learn to say "no" when faced with demands, requests, invites, and activities that interfere with your personal time. I was constantly stressed out until I learned how to say no and mean it. When you choose to say yes, you'll quickly realise that you are a lot nicer, more present, and more productive person than when you first feel terrible and selfish for protecting your downtime.

Learn how to externalise your emotions, avoid thinking traps, focus more clearly, and other basic strategies. Included in mindfulness for stress management along with my concrete recommendations, so you won't have to spend weeks reading before you can start managing your stress.

Find efficient strategies to manage your stress, whether you're concerned about your kids, your career, or your personal life. By controlling your breathing and becoming aware of your body, you will discover how to stay in the now when things get crazy by controlling your breathing and becoming aware of your body.

In the middle of the daily commotion, find peace. This strengths-based book provides a special step-by-step method based on positive psychology to assist you in reducing chronic stress in a hectic world. If you're one of the many people who feel overworked, stressed out, and overwhelmed, you're not alone. This much-needed book provides a novel perspective that will help you relax and begin enjoying the life you really want to live.

Character and qualities are a special motivator for both pleasure and stress reduction. Since everyone has the potential for these qualities, including you, anybody can learn the techniques and exercises in this workbook.

- Are you feeling stressed out at work?
- Do you struggle with controlling your rage?
- Do your troubles ever consume you?
- Is work stress destroying your social interactions?
- Are you trying to find a solution to manage your stress and the effects it has on your life?
- Is stress a regular part of your day?

The sickness of stress can be lethal. It is crucial to remember that getting medical help remains the best course of action, particularly for managing chronic stress.

Do you want to develop effective coping mechanisms for dealing with stress in both your personal and professional life as well as in your business?

If you answered yes to any of these inquiries, then this book is the ideal remedy for you. You must be aware that mindfulness is made up of a variety of techniques that, when effectively incorporated into everyday life, may aid in severing the cycle of stress, worry, dissatisfaction, and weariness. Those searching for useful techniques they may use to raise their skill levels in the areas of anxiety, anger, workaholism, and self-control might consider mindfulness for stress management. These recommendations are the result of years of work in the work-life context, but they are applicable outside the workplace as well, given the importance of the ability to remain calm in many situations. It is significant to highlight that levels of job productivity may be greatly influenced by the quality of connections that are formed.

Your key to success is to set out with the intention of allowing yourself to stand out from the throng in people's memories. This may be useful, for instance, in the commercial sector or even in personal relationships if one is trying to establish a special connection with a group of people or an individual, as appropriate. Using mindfulness to strengthen relationships also raises overall life satisfaction levels. An increase in these skill levels will directly impact production on the bottom line in the context of business.

How far a person climbs the corporate ladder depends on the kind of relationships they develop there. The world's most stressed-out nation is America, and during the past several days, our stress levels have been rising steadily.

By design, life is stressful. We learn, develop, get stronger, and get more polished as a result of stress.

That isn't always the case, though. People of all caste levels worry about and endure perpetual trauma in various ways, and millions of people are living little lives as shells of themselves due mostly to stress—one of the shortest terms in the language. It's interesting to note that while some of the world's best minds have developed incredible technologies, cured complicated ailments, and produced significant advancements in other spheres of life, few, if any, have provided mankind with an efficient solution.

Focusing on bad experiences (especially through self-blame and rumination) might be the strongest predictor of some of today's most prevalent mental health issues, according to a new U.K. study of more than 30,000 people. How then, can we break the cycle of worry? You should start letting calm replace tension today. You may stop worrying and start paying attention to the present moment by applying the stress-reduction techniques for Stress Management.

It's normal to experience anxiety or tension; it's just a characteristic of being human. Whether a situation is important or not, stressing about it is an indication that you are feeling and that your heart is beating.

Nobody in history can claim to have never experienced stress. More often than you would imagine, stress can be good for you. It can be a chance for you to increase your tolerance and endurance. Being able to rise again after a trying circumstance may make you more powerful, brave, and tough.

According to a Gallup study, 83% of US workers are stressed at work. Stress at work costs US firms up to $300 billion annually. Every day, one million people miss work due to stress. Only 43% of US workers believe that their employers care about their ability to manage work and life. Depression results in $26 billion in treatment expenses and $51 billion in lost productivity. Each year, stress at work results in 120,000 fatalities and $190 billion in medical expenses. According to Statistics on General Stress during the day, 55% of Americans experience stress.

According to a Gallup survey on the prevalence of stress across different age groups, 65% of people in the 30 to 49 years age range experience stress. 64% of Americans between the ages of 15 and 29 are right behind them, while 44% of adults over the age of 50 reported feeling stressed. Stress seems to be another area where there is a gender discrepancy. On a scale of one to 10, women reported their stress levels to be 5.1, compared to 4.4 for males, according to the APA Stress in America 2016 poll. According to data from Everyday Health's United States of Stress study, 57% of people who encounter stress are rendered immobilised by it. The remaining 43%, on the other hand, claimed that stress gives them energy. Workplace Stress Statistics says, workplace stress affects 83% of US workers.

The stress levels of Americans are among the highest in the world. According to Gallup's 2019 statistics on emotional states, more than half of Americans report feeling stressed out throughout the workday. This is 20% more than the 35% global average. These stress statistics show that the US is rapidly catching up to Greece, whose people have been the most stressed-out in the world since 2012, with 59% of Greeks reporting daily stress. Stress affects many of us, both at work and in our personal lives. Stress, like any other issue, necessitates a systematic strategy to overcome it, or at the very least manage it. There will be days when you'll feel completely stressed out, regardless of who you are, what you do, or how happy you believe you are. That said, it still isn't any simpler! When you're under a lot of stress, it might be difficult to envision a way out. Stress can feel overwhelming. Sometimes, all you truly need to get through a stressful situation is a gentle reminder that the end of the tunnel is in sight and that light is just around the corner.

In terms of stress, there is a clear generational divide between baby boomers and Gen Z. Only 41% of baby boomers have received a mental health diagnosis, compared to 52% of Gen Z. According to a Korn Ferry study, the primary cause of stress for 35% of respondents was their boss. In a study of Signal Dynamic 2019 workplace stress statistics are discouraging. In a poll by Dynamic Signal of more than 1,000 US employees, 80% of them admitted to feeling stressed out as a result of their employers' poor communication techniques, a 30% rise from the year before. Stress has made 63% of US workers eager to abandon their jobs. Workers appear to experience a lot of stress from their managers and bosses in general. A little more than a third of US workers polled identified their boss as the primary cause of their job-related stress. Additionally, 80% of the workers surveyed stated that leadership changes have an impact on their levels of stress.

Life will always include some level of stress. Stressful events can help us learn and grow in ways that we otherwise wouldn't be able to if we respond to them constructively. However, excessive stress has a number of negative effects on our health, ranging from physical sickness to mental exhaustion. Stress is a normal and natural aspect of life. Promises of stress relief put individuals at risk of failure. The use of the term "stress-free" is still not recommended since the approach is permeated with an incorrect notion that will never materialise, even when utilised with the best of intentions and in conjunction with pertinent and advantageous thoughts and practises. Your life may be impacted by both people and situations that might create mental stress. Maybe these sayings serve as motivation for you to live the life of your dreams by removing tension from your life and thoughts.

Numerous employees are on the verge of abandoning their jobs due to stress, according to Dynamic Signal's 2019 State of Employee Communication and Engagement survey. 63% of the workers who participated in the study said they were prepared to leave their employment because of workplace stress. In 2017, 39% of workers reported that their primary source of stress was a heavy workload. The key factors contributing to occupational stress are highlighted by Statistical research from 2017. 39% of employees cited their workload as the primary source of stress at work, while 31% cited interpersonal conflicts, 19% cited balancing work and personal obligations, and 6% cited job security. In 2018, more than a third of people claimed that their employment was a frequent cause of stress.

Over 30% of respondents to Everyday Health's 2018 workplace stress survey identified their jobs or occupations as frequent sources of stress. This percentage rises to 44% among millennials and Gen Z, further demonstrating that stress is more prevalent than it was 20 or 30 years ago among younger generations. 54% of employees claim that their home lives are impacted by job stress.

According to 75% of workers, stress levels now are higher than in earlier eras. As NIOSH prior statistics have shown, younger generations appear to struggle with stress substantially more than older ones. The National Institute for Occupational Safety and Health (NIOSH) has conducted research on workplace stress statistics over the years, and the results indicate that 75% of employees believe they are under more stress than earlier generations. Employee assistance experts list depression as one of the top three workplace issues.

In 2018, 76% of US workers claimed that relationship stress at work had a negative impact. This additional figure from Korn Ferry highlights the extent to which professional stress has an impact on other aspects of our lives. According to a study by Korn Ferry, the majority of stressed-out workers said that job stress had a detrimental influence on their personal relationships. In 2018, stress kept 66% of American workers from getting enough sleep.

Stress has an influence on health, it goes without saying. In the Korn Ferry study, two-thirds of the participants reported having problems falling asleep as a result of their stress at work. Statistics on mental health at work clearly demonstrate that this lowers worker productivity and increases stress.

Stress has significant human and monetary implications for workplace mental health. According to statistics on workplace stress, almost 120,000 individuals pass away each year as a result of their jobs. The cost of working stress drains the US economy as well, costing the country $190 billion in medical expenses. Only four out of every ten employees who disclose their stress to their boss receive assistance.

What does job stress entail?

Workplace stress is a detrimental mental and physical strain brought on by a variety of workplace situations. When we examine statistics on stress in the workplace over time, we can observe that stress can cause anxiety, sadness, and other significant mental conditions when we examine statistics on stress in the workplace over time.

Workload and deadlines, as well as strained relationships between employees and supervisors, are the most frequent sources of stress at work. All of these raise the overall stress levels among employees. Stress can stimulate certain people, as evidenced by our statistics, but for the vast majority of workers, it lowers productivity. Employees who are under stress tend to waste valuable office time worrying about their problems, do inferior work, and occasionally need sick days. Taking sick days, asking for wage raises, and handling personal issues at work are all indications of stress, according to experts in employee aid.

In the office, relationships with peers, higher management, and the boss may all be stressful. As previously noted, the connection between an employee and their supervisor, as previously noted, is what stresses out employees the most. Find methods to relax, recognise your stressors, come up with professional and healthy answers to them, think about speaking with a health expert. When considering how to manage stress at work, we think these are your best alternatives. According to data on workplace stress, stress can result in decreased productivity, burnout, and conflicts at work. It can result in sadness, anxiety, and other severe mental health problems if left untreated.

The present human condition sadly includes stress, sadness, and worry. According to statistics, more and more people worldwide are battling mental health problems. Workplace stress contributes significantly to overall mental health problems. Increased financial concerns and economic changes lead to pressure at work. According to data on workplace stress, deadlines, high workloads, and demanding managers all add to the issue. If left unaddressed, work-related stress can lead to major mental health issues for employees.

Stress may cause significant declines in production, which end up costing both private businesses and governments a lot of money. These numbers on job stress have been gathered to demonstrate exactly how serious an issue it is.

According to statistics on workplace stress released by Wrike, 54% of employees feel that job stress negatively affects their personal lives. Stress at work has an impact on every aspect of our lives, including our jobs and how we feel and perform at work. The American Psychological Association carried out a poll in 2017 in order to ascertain Americans' levels of stress and the primary sources of their stress. In a study with many choices, "the future of our nation" came in first with 63% of respondents, followed by "money" (62%), and "job" (61%).

In addition to stress, depression is a significant issue when discussing mental health at work. According to Mental Health America's depression statistics, stress and family crises are the two other major issues that affect employee assistance workers. Depression is ranked third on this list. Stress was a factor in 16% of workers quitting their employment.

Some people's working conditions are made intolerable by rising levels of stress. A staggering 16% of workers have left their jobs due to stress at work. Because of a bad boss, 23.6% of workers have quit or plan to quit their jobs. According to a poll of US workers, the most stressful situation is when bosses are confused about their expectations. Around 46% of workers are considering joining the gig economy in 2019. According to employees, stress and anxiety have the greatest impact on their job productivity and relationships with coworkers.

The State of the American Workplace poll by Gallup examined how engaged US employees are at work. According to the report, stress causes more than 50% of workers to lose interest in their jobs, which reduces productivity. 41% of stressed-out workers claim that stress decreases productivity. Women are more likely than men to deal with stress by eating more (46%), interacting with loved ones and friends (44%), and using illegal substances (12%).

With stress levels rising, it's crucial to consider how we handle difficult situations. According to the ADAA's data on workplace stress, men and women handle stress in somewhat similar ways, but it's fair to argue that these approaches aren't always the best. The most popular strategy is increasing coffee intake (31%), which is followed by smoking (27%), and exercise (25%). On workplace stress, men and women handle stress in somewhat similar ways, but it's fair to argue that these approaches aren't always the best. The most popular strategy is increasing coffee intake (31%), which is followed by smoking (27%), and exercise (25%). Only 40% of employees who experience stress have discussed it with their employer.

The majority of workers don't feel comfortable disclosing difficulties connected to stress at work, according to statistics on workplace stress. Less than half of the workers who responded to the poll disclosed their stress at work to their bosses. More caffeine (31%), smoking (27%), and more frequent exercise (25%), among other coping mechanisms, are used by both men and women to deal with stress.

To make up for lost productivity or replace staff, businesses typically spend around 75% of a worker's yearly compensation. As was already said, stress decreases productivity and can even result in people quitting their employment. Stress has a significant negative influence on business finances, in addition to the obvious health expenses for employees. According to studies on workplace stress and lost productivity, it can cost up to 75% of a worker's annual compensation to pay for productivity expenditures or to acquire new employees. Those who take sick days due to mental health issues are seven times more likely to take additional sick days than those who take sick days due to physical health concerns.

Statistics on depression in the workplace from a 2016 UK Mental Health Foundation study show exactly how much stress impacts the workforce. A worker is seven times more likely to take subsequent sick days than a worker with physical problems if they take a sick day because of stress or another mental health problem. This accounts for 5% to 8% of all healthcare spending in the country.

Do you want to develop the abilities required to deal with the stress you deal with on a daily basis in order to live a better, more fruitful life?

Everybody has experienced stress. It may have been the morning traffic bottleneck, the incorrect ordering of your morning coffee, or even the unfavourable weather report. Perhaps your friend or coworker never arrives on time, or an unexpected medical emergency has struck a member of your family. Whatever the level of stress, whether it be acute or chronic, it can affect your relationships and quality of life. Mental health illnesses, including anxiety, sadness, and rage difficulties, are the more complicated effects of high stress. Along with breathing exercises, the significance of self-care, mindfulness, and meditation, these will be covered in detail through practical activities. As was already established, the major cause of stress at work is the boss. According to Randstad USA's data on workplace stress, more than half of employees have previously abandoned their jobs or would do so if their supervisor was abusive.

Gig economy usage is increasing. More and more employees these days desire to work independently, set their own hours, and act as their own boss. Given this, it comes as no surprise that many employees seek to transition to the gig economy in order to lower their stress levels at work. According to data from Randstad USA concerning workplace stress, over half (46%) of those polled are contemplating moving to the gig economy in 2019.

What do the statistics reveal? Well, the world is a nasty place. At work, we're feeling more and more pressure. There isn't enough time, our supervisors bother us, and there is too much work. The psychological and financial implications of work-related stress are horrifying when things spiral out of control. The upheavals in the global economy that have reduced financial and job security are intimately related to these growing levels of workplace stress. This explains why a large number of people are converting to the gig economy.

What can be done, then? Employee-employer connections must first be strengthened. Employees feel that their bosses put too much pressure on them and that they are unable to discuss their stress at work. Additionally, employers need to pay closer attention to employee mental health problems. Workers in the US and overseas face a bleak future if conditions don't change, as our data on workplace stress have revealed.

Do your life's responsibilities and obligations frequently make you feel worn out, unhappy, angry, or anxious? For you, is self-care just a fashionable buzzword? Do you always prioritise others? If you provided a yes or no response to any of them, you could be letting stress take over and nearly destroy your life.

The ADAA has conducted one of the most thorough studies on occupational stress and anxiety (Anxiety and Depression Association of America). The ADAA's data on workplace productivity shows that relationships with coworkers and peers (51%) and workplace productivity (56%) are the two areas where stress and anxiety have the biggest negative effects. According to a study was conducted by Gallup, 27% of US employees report feeling "checked out" while at work.

Men and women approach stress in the workplace in very different ways. Women typically eat more (46%) and converse more with friends and family (44%) than males (27%), respectively. Males, on the other hand, are more likely to engage in regular sexual activity (19% vs. 10%), and 12% of men vs. 2% of women use illegal substances to cope.

May the information in this chapter assist you in your quest to put an end to your needless suffering. Suppressing either happy or negative emotions can eventually result in physical and mental illness since your being craves integration.

We are pliable, squishy beings with emotional bodies that are permanently imprinted with the feelings we have encountered.

The antithesis of weakness is self-compassion, and in order to make any significant changes in our lives, we must be sympathetic and compassionate toward ourselves. Today, stress reduction is crucial for both our personal health and the health of the planet, as the root cause of stress in our lives is identification with the ego and its ideals. Our world is being destroyed by the ego-driven lifestyle that the majority of people lead. Fortunately, altering our minds—or, more specifically, our connection with our minds—is the major factor in changing both ourselves and our surroundings in this way.

On the other side, you react to the positive feelings, the lightness of excitement, happiness, and a swelling of the heart that you experience when you perceive success, whether you're enthused about a new project, find you've earned a bonus, or know you've been promoted. These feelings are neutral in nature. They are facts, knowledge that is necessary for making informed decisions. When you feel the sting of anger, you can choose how you want to respond thanks to mindfulness. Do you typically lash out, or do you focus for a time on the strong feelings of rage and allow them to pass so you can react appropriately? Can you actively observe the delightful flow of desire when it arises rather than fixating on the object of your desire? Instead of responding, you learn to be present with whatever sensations you are having via body awareness, and you observe that they come and go just like the breath.

Stress and anxiety are transient. Then, even when experiencing intense emotions like rage, fear, pain, or cravings, you can make better, smarter decisions regarding your actions and conduct. You may realise that the main obstacle with meditation is learning to stay, yes it is. Our brains frequently alternate between past regrets and recollections, as well as future aspirations and anxieties. Contrarily, the truth of our body is that it exists in the present. When you are in touch with your body, you are here and open to the direct, immediate manifestation of this enigmatic existence. So, let me tell you what it's like to have a completely friendly encounter with the body. Please take a moment to find a comfortable position for yourself. Take a few deep breaths. After that, let your breathing follow its natural rhythm. And use these initial seconds to gather your focus while relaxing your breath, experiencing the intake and outflow with calm and clear attention.

Now, while your eyes are still closed, lift one hand in the air in front of you at a distance of about 12 inches and slowly rock it side to side. Feel the feelings as you do this from the inside out. Let go of your preconceived notions of what the hand looks like and instead focus on feeling the tingling and aliveness of the energy. The immediate sensation in this hand is pressure, warmth, or cold. Put your hand down gently now, and pay equal attention to the hand that has been resting on your lap. Consider the two hands as a field of life. Is there a line that indicates the end of your hands when you feel them from the inside out? Can you imagine and feel what it's like to float in the field of awareness? Continue to feel each of these emotions from the inside out through your hands. Try focusing on your feet now to see if you can detect the same limitless dance of energy there. Allow yourself to feel the tingling, warmth, coolness, and pressure associated with this energy vitality. Examine the legs. Feel it in your torso and pelvis. your limbs You can feel it in your face, head, and neck. Rest in focused awareness while sensing your entire body's electric aliveness.

Bring your focus back to your breath, which serves as your main anchor, as you finish this exercise. Take pleasure in experiencing each breath as an intimate, responsive presence from the inside out. You might also focus on the feelings in your hands or feet if you've had trouble using your breath as an anchor. Similar to the breath, bodily sensations may act as a helpful anchor for the present, a place you can come back to time and time again. You can occasionally sit down to focus on your bodily sensations to help you become more attentive to your body while you go about your business. Any scenario you find yourself in may be handled more effectively with the support of this body awareness. Feel the chair's surface in touch with your sitting bones when you sit down. Additionally, you may feel your feet making contact with the ground. Check to see if you can relax your sitting bones as well as the soles of your feet to see if this improves your body's sensation of aliveness and presence as you work.

Last but not least, if you encounter any powerful emotions or bodily sensations while working, possibly as a result of interacting with people, let them be without passing judgement and observe how your experience changes. Your ability to respond intelligently rather than react to whatever scenario you meet will be further strengthened by mindful awareness of your body at work. There's a straightforward explanation for why practising bodily mindfulness increases your overall attentiveness.

The practise of mindfulness can help you manage your connection with the pressure you face at work in new ways. Your capacity to manage workplace stressors that may have a detrimental influence on your physical, mental, and emotional well-being is strengthened by mindfulness. Learn techniques in this book to recognise what makes you feel pressure, how your body responds to it, and how to lessen its negative consequences. Learn strategies that will enable you to manage your responses and avoid stressful situations in your life. Learn to free your mind and body from anxiety's symptoms to have a better relationship with it. Learn how to develop meditation as a habit and how to prevent the ongoing stress of rumination. Understanding how stress manifests in the body and understanding how to step back from the edge of the stress are both necessary for managing the tension that is always rising and falling in our life.

Another crucial concept is that in order to handle stress, I must meditate to develop the ability to relate to it. And finally, the significance of persistently practising on a regular basis. Many people believe that meditation requires time, but the first step is to establish a regular practise, so let's start there. To understand what stress is and how it manifests. An object is under stress when tension or pressure is applied to it. There may have been too much pressure placed on something, causing it to become strained and break. However, the stress I'm referring to today is the strain and tension brought on by demanding situations and difficult times that have an affect on our mental and emotional health. Whatever the difficulty may be, mindful meditation may not always result in a solution or resolution. However, it will give you a talent and a method to relate to the stress. The effects it has on your bodily and emotional health are also very essential.

The first step in overcoming stress is to acknowledge its presence. And on that, today's practise is concentrated.

The only thing you need to do is pay attention to the cues, then transfer your focus to different parts of your body to observe how they feel and other parts of your emotional field to see how they feel. Focus on the mind and take note of its sensations. And the key is to recognise what is there rather than trying to change it.

Therefore, let's begin. Inhale deeply through your nose, then let out air with your mouth open. I'll take another big breath and exhale. A second full, deep inhale expands the abdomen and fills the chest. Lastly, when you breath, softly close your eyes. If closing your eyes entirely doesn't seem comfortable, let your gaze fall downward toward the ground so that you're not paying attention to anything in particular. Afterward, take three independent slow breaths. Keeping your focus on the breathing sensations to the best of your abilities. The foundation of mindful meditation is the idea of being present in the moment. This is how it is done. This is the guiding idea. This is the mindfulness way of thinking.

In the present, let's allow the physical body be that item to which we must pay attention. Allow your awareness to expand so that you can observe your entire body, from head to toe. You most certainly already are aware of the precise locations where stress, tightness, and tension manifest themselves. Perhaps it's a tightened fist, a raised shoulder, or clinched teeth. You can tuck your tummy in or tighten your gluteal muscles. Now, take a moment to scan your entire body with your mind's eye, your attention, and your awareness. To observe how the body is now feeling, start with the feet and work your way up through the legs, hips, and pelvis, until you reach the abdominal wall. the lower back, the chest, the shoulders, the upper back, the arms, and up to the face.

- Does the body feel flexible or tight?
- Is there a feeling of holding or squeezing?
- Does it have a loose, supple, open feeling?

Again, nothing needs to be altered. Just check in with your body, and take another deep breath. As you exhale, accept what some refer to as the emotional body or the emotional field and let the body be.

In general, I can tell whether someone is feeling happy, neutral, or negative emotionally by giving them a plus, neutral, or minus here. The feelings and experiences of pleasure, happiness, and satisfaction are considered positive. Neutrality can seem as emptiness, evenness, and negativity, as well as as dread, rage, concern, and doubt. Right now, where do you land? No need to alter; simply take note. Take a slow breath in and let the emotional field be what it is as you exhale. This will focus your attention on the mind. Our aim is to become familiar with the activity and how it feels rather than trying to block our natural urge to think. What's the mental weather, if you will? Is it clear or stormy? Is it hot or chilly outside? Are the ideas hard or fuzzy?

Removing ourselves from the edge of the experience is a critical component of stress management. Stress develops rapidly. Many people believe that stress management involves preventing stress from entering our lives. The actual stress management is the replay we perform in our minds. Those stressful times happen quickly, whether it be a text message or a phone call that is interrupted by traffic. After it has happened, I frequently replay it over and over again.

Chronic stress is the result of such mental suffering. The real stressful incident and its repetition are indistinguishable to the mind and body. It reacts as though stress is there all the time as a result. It reacts as though stress is there all the time as a result. It is possible to allow some space, some distance, and give yourself an opportunity to have some resiliency around the stress that is continually present by stepping back from the edge of that rumination, that repetition in your mind. So let's now take a step back from the brink. Breathe in deeply through your nose. Exhale with your open mouth. (exhales) Take another deep breath. letting the air out gradually. Take one more deep inhale and let it reach your gut. And as you let out a breath, you felt my eyes slowly close. Return to whatever simple and natural breathing pattern seems right for you right now, allowing the body to become conscious, detecting any lifting or squeezing, and inviting the muscles to extend, relax, and soften. It's acceptable if your mind is currently dwelling on a difficult event in your life. The goal of this technique is to step back from the edge of our tension by concentrating and focusing on anything right now.

You may do this exercise is stroking your thumb and index finger together. Make the word "okay" with your thumb and index finger, then gently start rubbing your fingers together in a circle. Nothing about this has to be rationally understood; instead, focus on the sensation of the fingers gliding over one another. the minimal friction being felt. Two breaths in, two breaths out. Three in, three out. Four out of four. out of five, in five. up to number 10, with the final five repetitions at your own pace. Spend a few more counts concentrating on your inhalation and exhalation. And with each subsequent exhalation, let go of the count, wherever you are in your counting. And in the last seconds, shift your attention to being open rather than concentrating on a bodily experience or an accounting of your breath. observing, listening, and just being there while taking note of noises, scents, emotions, and experiences. Deeply but comfortably inhale. With this exhale, elevate your gaze, allowing your eyes to relax and start to blink open. Taking two breaths in and two breaths out. Three down, three to go. Four in, four out. Five out of five. Continue until you reach 10, finishing the final five at your own time. For a few more counts, shift your attention to the inhalation and exhalation. Wherever you are in your counting, let go of the count with your subsequent exhalation. Finally, shift your attention from being focused on a bodily experience or an accounting of your breath to being open. watching, listening, and just observing noises, scents, emotions, and experiences. Taking a good, leisurely, complete breath in. After this, exhale while allowing your eyelids to relax, start to blink, and focus your attention. I appreciate you practising taking a step back from the tension you are feeling right now. a vital technique for reducing stress in your life.

"Many people struggle with chronic stress, which can cause a variety of physical and mental health issues, including heart disease, anxiety, and depression. If you're one of the many people who feel overworked, stressed out, and overwhelmed , you're not alone."

Many of us have truly struggled to get to sleep at night because of unresolved issues that torment our brains. Most people make decisions and say things they later regret while acting impulsively. We frequently find ourselves in uncontrollable situations, which makes us vulnerable and upset. Stress management is one of the best ways to maintain your health and happiness. Stress may have a very negative impact on a person's happiness and health.

You can either learn to deal with it and put it on your own in a happier and healthier area, or you can ignore it at your own risk. You can either deal with it and relocate it to a happier and healthier location, or you can ignore it at your peril.

According to the majority of experts, stress is the single biggest cause of all illnesses. We are continuously at war with this enemy in today's fast-paced society as a result of our anxiety to achieve more and more. Even though not all stress is negative and being worried or tense may sometimes be helpful, when it overwhelms only your stomach's butterflies or your brain's processing speed, it causes more strain than your heart can tolerate. I don't mean the heart in a literary or artistic sense; rather, I'm referring to the fundamental physics behind it all—your heart's pounding.

Stress burnout is more probable when there is a chance that your contributions won't be acknowledged. Uncertain expectations and goals might also arise, which is stressful.

Don't worry, this chapter will provide you with skills and strategies to combat stress and will get you closer to self-accomplishment and pleasure. Some techniques and procedures to alter and develop yourself will be difficult to use, and few individuals have what it takes to achieve what is necessary.

- How to recognise the sources of your stress?
- How does your diet affect how much stress you feel?
- How to give yourself some alone time?
- How to release everything?

- Why your worries are unimportant?
- Why it's vital to say no?
- How to express gratitude?

Stress burnout has a variety of reasons. Ironically, even though so many of us aim for professional success, it can occasionally cause serious issues. For instance, our work schedules may be the most important component in this situation. The Organisation for Economic Cooperation and Development reports that Mexico, South Korea, and Greece are the top three countries in the world for the number of hours worked annually per person, all of which exceed 2,000. Among the main industrialised nations, US workers put in the most hours—more than 1,700 hours a year. Of course, a sizable fraction of them work several jobs and put in an average of over 40 hours every week. Thus, burnout is probably not all that surprising.

Let's consider the work you are doing right now. Taking your level of responsibility as an example. Naturally, with increased responsibility comes more stress. Additionally, you must think about the overall impact of all of your significant professional connections. The one with your immediate boss is by far the most important. Stress can quickly build up if a relationship is generally more negative than pleasant. Let's also consider how your manager treats you. You can have a severe lack of control, which is challenging.

The fit between jobs, or how well your interests and talents correspond with what you really do, is the last work-related aspect to think about. You guessed right. High stress is caused by low fitness. In order to find positions that truly reflect who you are, you must take action over the long term. Continuing with the non-work portion of the equation I want you to start by considering the calibre of your most important connections. That mostly consists of family and close friends. The tough sensation it produces when those relationships are strained will accompany you to work and weigh on how you feel. The robustness of your identity outside of work is another consideration. Your sole identity, though, cannot be that one.

People who are successful and in good health always have a variety of compelling non-work-identities to aid with balance. A father, wife, coach, and volunteer are a few examples of this. Who knows, but don't ignore your identity outside of work.

Finally, I have to emphasise your physical health. I won't go into great detail on this topic beyond stating that food, exercise, and sleep all have a significant impact on possible burnout. This entails consuming more fresh meals and fewer unhealthy fats; engaging in regular exercise to keep one's energy levels up; and getting at least seven to eight hours of sleep each night.

Excessive anxiety may be brought on by a major incident or a pile of less stressful life circumstances, such as a loss in the family, work stress, or persistent financial worries. personality. Anxiety disorders are more likely to affect some personality types than others. Each person has unique stressors.

According to polls, workplace stress takes the top spot. One-quarter of American workers believe their jobs are the main source of stress in their lives, and 40% of them admit to suffering from office stress. Workplace stress factors include: Being dissatisfied with one's job because it is overburdened with work or responsibilities. You had a long workday. Experiencing inadequate management, ambiguous job objectives, or being excluded from decision-making. Working under hazardous circumstances being concerned about your potential for advancement or the possibility of being fired.

Do you want to achieve your goals less anxiously and heal your scars so you can live without depression?

Continue reading if so. Anxiety may be a debilitating condition that permeates all aspects of a person's life. It can affect a person's relationships, academic or professional performance, change their overall happiness, make them feel alone in the world, and even trigger suicidal thoughts. This is why it is so important to work hard to get the situation under control. It's typical to worry about a demanding circumstance.

I have to speak in front of coworkers. encountering harassment or discrimination at work, especially if your employer isn't supportive. Stress from daily life can also be quite damaging. Life pressures include, for example, the loss of a close relative, divorce, increased financial responsibilities due to losing a job Getting hitched relocating to a new house chronic damage or disease emotional difficulties (depression, anxiety, anger, grief, guilt, low self-esteem), taking care of an ill or elderly relative traumatic experience, including a natural disaster, theft, rape, or violence committed against you or a loved one stress can occasionally originate within rather than outside. Just wondering about something might make you anxious. These elements all contribute to stress: Fear and apprehension. Stress can result from hearing on the news frequently about the potential of terrorist attacks, global warming, and harmful chemicals, especially if you believe you have little influence over these occurrences.

It becomes a different issue if the unemployed individual finds work but is nevertheless plagued by the fear of being fired once more. Their fear has taken over their life and has become chronic. Perhaps they are afraid of losing their jobs and feel the need to preserve money, which makes them no longer want to go out with friends. Perhaps they insist on leading such a simple life that it borders on the absurd and damages their relationships with others around them.

When compelled to pay all of their payments at the beginning of the month after being newly unemployed, a person may likely feel more stressed. They may have trouble sleeping and functioning until the problem is resolved, but if their worry disappears when the problem is fixed, they have only experienced a typical response to a stressful scenario.

If it develops into a chronic problem that is impairing your quality of life, you should get care. To overcome anxiety, the many anxiety-related branches must be addressed separately, and the anxiety's underlying causes must be found. Prior to benefiting from the measures to assist in relieving sadness and anxiety, a person with a panic disorder will gain the most from having the precise source of their fear identified. The symptoms of extreme shyness can be similar to those of generalised anxiety disorder, but before taking such actions, a person with severe shyness must first address the causes of their shyness. As a result, it's important to accept the disease for what it is.

Furthermore, despite the fact that catastrophes are normally extremely infrequent occurrences, the media's vivid portrayal of them may give the impression that they are more common than they actually are. Fears may also be more personal, such as worrying that you won't complete a task at work or that you won't have enough money to cover this month's expenditures.

Do your life's responsibilities and obligations frequently make you feel worn out, unhappy, angry, or anxious?

Clearly, there are several variables that might lead to burnout. This is your request for action. Can you now start to list the key influences affecting you, regardless of how stressed or burned out you may be right now? I certainly hope so, as you are far more likely to address issues and become better if you keep these things in mind.

For you, is self-care just a fashionable buzzword? Do you always prioritise others?

If you provided a yes or no response to any of them, you could be letting stress take over and nearly destroy your life. This chapter will examine the numerous ways that people experience and communicate stress throughout their lives. You'll be exposed to unhelpful thought patterns that you may not even be aware of, and you'll learn some useful methods you can use right away to help you change them.

Perhaps your friend or coworker never arrives on time, or an unexpected medical emergency has struck a member of your family. Whatever the level of stress, whether it be acute or chronic, it can affect your relationships and quality of life. Mental health illnesses, including anxiety, sadness, and rage difficulties, are the more complicated effects of high stress. Along with breathing exercises, the significance of self-care, mindfulness, and meditation, these will be covered in detail through practical activities.

Everybody has experienced stress. It may have been the morning traffic bottleneck, the incorrect ordering of your morning coffee, or even the unfavourable weather report.

When it comes to attempting to manage this mounting, debilitating stress, numerous teachings, techniques, tips, and recommendations about how to handle daily stress and deal with the stress that is unavoidable have been given to you. I have also given you advice on how to find peace in a hectic environment. The current way of life is rife with pressures of many kinds, from trying to fulfil work deadlines to working several jobs to taking care of your family while also attending school.

The fundamental blood flow should be evenly dispersed throughout your body, assisting in the transmission of all messages necessary to maintain the efficient operation of all organs. When the heart is overworked for an extended length of time, imbalances are created that change how the body functions. Different chemicals are created and react in unusual ways.

The hormone cortisol, which has receptors in practically every cell in your body, is what causes this stress. It triggers a variety of behaviours, from giving you a kick in the butt to get moving while you're being followed down the street by your girlfriend's father to having a panic attack.

This stress hormone is necessary to get up every morning since it triggers the cells' normal processes.

However, when you consistently, or in significant amounts, respond involuntarily to events, situations, or circumstances, you inevitably increase the amount of glucose coursing through your bloodstream. In fact, Type 2 diabetes, the majority of weight gain and obesity issues, and cardiovascular issues can all be attributed to cortisol.

Even joyous events like getting married or getting promoted at work may be stressful big life changes. Even worse occurrences like divorce, huge financial setbacks, or death in the family can be big sources of stress. Depending on your personality and how you react to circumstances, your degree of stress will change. Some individuals let things slide. Your nervous system goes into overdrive, producing hormones that either get you ready to fight or get you ready to flee. The "fight or flight" reaction causes your body to stiffen up, your respiration to quicken, your muscles to tense up, and your body temperature to rise when you're in a stressful environment. This type of stress is brief and transient (acute stress), and your body often recovers from it rapidly.

- What are the typical causes and effects of stress?
- How does it manifest as mental health disorders and how to treat them (depression, anxiety, and anger issues)?
- How to treat stress and addictions, cognitive-behavioral techniques and strategies, effective methods for developing a rational mind?
- How to manage negative thinking in relationships?
- How to develop stress-relieving habits?
- How to prepare for unexpected stress?
- How to prioritise yourself?

While it may be nearly impossible to avoid stress, this does not mean that you must accept the fact that you will always be under stress. Stress not only makes life difficult, but it also raises your risk of developing a number of illnesses, including heart disease, high blood pressure, and even stroke. This means that being able to manage stress well is crucial. Every single one of us has experienced stress at some point or another. Stress actually comes and goes in our lives frequently, maybe even without our notice. When stress is at its worst, it may completely upend our lives and cause significant problems like mental breakdowns and even deadly heart attacks.

You can stop stressing yourself out by evaluating your thoughts and changing how you interact with them with the help of this book. I would offer numerous practises that will help you achieve greater peace and tranquilly, even in a hectic and stressful world. It does this by drawing on the wisdom traditions; mindfulness meditation; psychology; new thoughts; and my own experience as a spiritual teacher and counsellor.

Our culture is plagued by stress, which leads to problems with relationships, physical disease, addictions, errors, inefficiency, lack of satisfaction, and unhappiness.

Your body can get severely damaged by the persistent surge of stress hormones, age more quickly, and become more prone to sickness. Following a brief period of stress, you could start to experience some of these physical symptoms: headache, fatigue sleeping issues, concentration issues, stomach discomfort, irritability, Long-term stress that is not effectively managed can result in a number of more significant health issues, such as: Depression, elevated blood pressure, an irregular heartbeat (arrhythmia), the arteries become harder (atherosclerosis). poor heart condition, irritable bowel syndrome, heartburn, gastrointestinal distress, diarrhoea, constipation, and cramps loss or gain of weight changes in sex drive infertility issues, flare-ups of arthritis or asthma, irregular skin conditions, including psoriasis, eczema, and acne etc. Your health can be significantly improved by learning to manage your stress.

Stress can inhibit the production of insulin, resulting in a condition of elevated glucose levels. Additionally, it causes artery narrowing in order to force the heart to pump more oxygen-rich blood, raising the heart rate. A cortisol crash frequently occurs when stress takes over your body's operations. Many of the medical issues we encounter today are really sparked by this dysfunction. The first piece of advice that physicians will provide is to minimise stress levels. This is true for anything from stomach problems, migraines, and sleeplessness to even more dangerous diseases like cancer.

However, many perceive stress as a psychological issue that has to be handled individually because they are unaware of the scientific impact that stress has on how our bodies work. Our daily lives produce stress as a byproduct. If we want to stay healthy, we must develop a strategy of relaxation based on individual needs. Numerous methods have been developed to help us live stress-free lives, including yoga, music therapy, colour therapy, pranayama breathing techniques, and meditation. It is crucial that we take advantage of this as part of our daily wellness regimen. Your body needs rest and relaxation in order to function at its best, just as it needs nutrient-dense diets, exercise, and sleep. Some individuals are said to perform better under pressure. I would advise them to use the tension to build, not destroy. Use it sensibly and in moderation to increase metabolism, alertness, and attention. Be the boss, not the underling.

According to one study, women with heart disease who participated in stress reduction exercises lived longer. The majority of tension is brought on by the way we think. These problems are all the result of being cut off from our source, from our innate knowledge and tranquilly. How to confront and alter a basic belief that is no longer in your best interests; how to use treatments when stress and anxiety are draining your energy; the long-term dangers of not treating your stress and anxiety, as well as the health advantages of doing so.

- Why is it necessary to be optimistic every day?
- How does the task list address the issue?
- How to relax and relieve tension tips for implementing mindfulness?
- Where do you find bad ideas?
- Does stress make you feel weak?

Now you can rapidly discover how to lessen stress and anxiety without having to wade through a tonne of psychiatric lingo. These tried-and-true techniques are effective for lowering anxiety, fear, and tensions associated with a range of circumstances that you will come across in your daily life.

We all go through challenging situations in life that lead to high levels of tension and worry. When our circumstances are unexpected and we have little control over how they play out, it is totally reasonable to feel overwhelmed. Unfortunately, there isn't a cure that will make things better; you just have to carry on till the problems are fixed. The good news is that we have tools at our disposal to manage those times of ambiguity. On the globe, Americans are the most stressed people, and in recent days, our stress levels are rising daily. Life is stressful by design. Stress aids in our ability to learn, develop, and improve.

The ideas and approaches in this chapter, which were developed for readers from all walks of life, can help you not only manage stress but also lessen the potentially harmful effects it can have on your life. This chapter is for you if you want to be prepared to control your body and mind in any circumstance. You will face numerous obstacles, and there is no quick fix, but you have the power to overcome any challenge, so stop leading an unpleasant and miserable existence.

Do you want to manage your stress and create the kind of life you deserve and want?

You may better handle stress in your life with the aid of the useful knowledge in this book. The information era has made life more challenging than we could have ever anticipated.

Nowadays, people are under greater stress than ever. According to 2017 American Psychological Association research, 63% of Americans experience stress due to future uncertainty. Numerous additional concerns, including employment, money, information overload, health, crime and violence, and much more, are causing stress for large numbers of individuals. Because of this, I decided to create this book to aid those like you and me in battling what has recently grown to be a serious issue. Since stress is such a widespread issue, I'm going to presume that you are already well-informed about it.

No, it is not all in your brain; everyone experiences stress in different ways. However, different people respond to the same circumstances in various ways. Recognising what we can and cannot control is essential for stress management and is an awakening in and of itself. This useful book aims to apply the stress-reduction advantages of mindfulness meditation practise. A frightening 88% of Americans list antagonism, office fury, and rudeness as their top workplace worries.

The phone is constantly ringing. You have an overwhelming inbox. Your boss knocks on your door to inquire how your most recent project is doing since you are 45 minutes past the deadline. To put it mildly, you're stressed. All of these are instances of acute stress. They are only temporary, won't last more than your workday, and could even be good for your health in some aspects. But if this is how every day of the week feels in your life, you could be dealing with chronic or long-term stress. If you don't make an effort to deal with it or overcome its consequences, this kind of stress might be harmful to your health. Large-scale stresses include financial difficulties, work-related problems, marital problems, and significant life upheavals like the death of a loved one. Smaller stresses might also accumulate over time, such as long daily drives and busy mornings. The first step in managing stress is learning how to identify its causes in your life.

Health stress can be exacerbated by ageing, a new medical diagnosis, symptoms of an existing sickness, or its repercussions. Even if you don't experience any health issues yourself, a family member or friend may be dealing with an illness or disease. That may also make you feel more stressed. The American Psychological Association (APA) reports that more than half of carers feel overwhelmed by the quantity of care that their loved ones require.

Arguments with your partner, parents, or kids might make you feel more stressed. It might be considerably more difficult if you share a residence. Even if you are not directly engaged, issues inside your family or home might still make you anxious.

Arguments over political, religious, or personal convictions might be difficult for you, particularly when you can't escape the battle. Stress can also be brought on by significant life experiences that make you doubt your own views. This is especially true if your ideas diverge from those of your closest friends and family.

Stressful situations involving money are not uncommon. You may experience severe stress due to credit card debt, unpaid rent, or a lack of capacity to support your family or yourself. Financial stress is something that almost everyone can relate to in this world when so much emphasis is placed on what you have and what you can buy. Almost three-quarters of Americans, according to the APA, report that their financial situation causes them stress in their daily lives.

According to occupational research, the demands and conflict of the workplace may be a significant source of stress. According to the American Psychological Association (APA), 60% of Americans experience work-related stress.

Long-term stress can be brought on by discriminatory feelings. For instance, you could encounter prejudice based on your colour, ethnicity, gender, or sexual preference.

Discrimination and the stress it brings are a daily reality for some people.

Chronic stress may be brought on by unsafe neighbourhoods, dangerous cities, and other safety worries. People who have gone through a traumatic incident or a circumstance in which their lives are in danger frequently have long-term stress. For instance, if you have endured a robbery, rape, natural disaster, or war, you may feel long-term stress. You could truly have post-traumatic stress disorder in numerous circumstances (PTSD).

A traumatic incident or a succession of stressful experiences can cause PTSD, a persistent anxiety disorder. The National Center for PTSD of the United States Department of Veterans Affairs estimates that roughly 7% of Americans will get PTSD in their lifetime. The illness is more prevalent among women, veterans, and trauma survivors.

Feeling like you can't relate to someone or that you need to express your emotions but can't may be distressing. Only two mental health illnesses that worsen emotional stress are depression and anxiety. Both the treatment of mental health conditions and constructive emotional outlets are necessary for effective stress management. Losing a loved one, changing professions, moving, and sending a child off to college are all significant life events that can be stressful. Even positive life events like retirement or marriage can cause a lot of stress.

Everybody experiences stress from time to time. Acute stress may provide you with the motivation you require in the short term to overcome a trying situation or meet a looming deadline. But over time, long-term (chronic) stress may negatively affect your health. If you constantly feel worn out, overworked, or nervous, you may have chronic stress.

The first step in successful stress management is determining the sources of stress in your life. You may take action to lessen or minimise your stresses once you've identified them. To control the impacts of stress, you may also include healthy lifestyle practises and techniques. You could feel more at ease, invigorated, and focused if you consume a healthy diet, exercise frequently, and get adequate sleep. Using relaxation techniques like yoga, meditation, or rhythmic breathing can also help reduce tension and anxiety. Speak to your doctor or a mental health expert to find out additional stress management techniques.

"The more tranquil a man becomes, the greater is his success, his influence, his power for good. Calmness of mind is one of the beautiful jewels of wisdom."

To understand stress disorder, you must learn how to deal with or go through the most trying circumstances you'll ever face. This chapter will teach you how to confront your stress, dismantle it, and recognise it for what it is: an impediment to your happiness that you can go over, around, or through. All of the stress-reduction methods described in this chapter have been tried and true and have been shown to be very effective.

- Are you feeling stressed out at work?
- Do you struggle with controlling your rage?
- Do your troubles ever consume you?
- Is work stress destroying your social interactions?
- Are you trying to find a solution to manage your stress and the effects it has on your life?

You are more likely to develop one of the numerous ailments linked to stress. Here is an example of what you will learn from this book: How to recognise the sources of your stress? How does your diet affect how much stress you feel? How to Give Yourself some alone time? How to release everything ? Why your worries are unimportant, why it's vital to say no, how to express gratitude, and much more.

Many people struggle with chronic stress, which can cause a variety of physical and mental health issues, including heart disease, anxiety, and depression.

How to recognise stressors in our lives? How to take charge of stress? How to show yourself compassion? How to stay upbeat while under stress? How to manage stress and stay healthy?

The current way of life is rife with pressures of many kinds, from trying to fulfil work deadlines to working several jobs to taking care of your family while also attending school. While it may be nearly impossible to avoid stress, this does not mean that you must accept the fact that you will always be under stress. Stress not only makes life difficult, but it also raises your risk of developing a number of illnesses, including heart disease, high blood pressure, and even stroke. This means that being able to manage stress well is crucial. Every single one of us has experienced stress at some point or another. Stress actually comes and goes in our lives frequently, maybe even without our notice.

When stress is at its worst, it may completely upend our lives and cause significant problems like mental breakdowns and even deadly heart attacks. In order to lead a life that is meaningful, joyful, and content, it is crucial to understand how to detect stress, identify stress sources, and find strategies to manage it.

The tactics for dealing with stress are covered in this book, along with some of the sources of stress, so that you may manage your stress while also knowing how to avoid specific stressors. Given that stress is a normal mental and physical response to both positive and negative situations, it is a given that as long as you are alive, you will feel stress. Keeping our lives' stress levels in check and much more. It's normal to feel a bit stressed out. Given that stress is a normal mental and physical response to both positive and negative situations, it is a given that as long as you are alive, you will feel stress. At times, balancing the stress in our lives may seem like an impossible undertaking, but it is attainable. At some point in our lives, we all experience excessive stress.

When your thoughts are racing out of control, you're worried about the daily tasks you have to complete, or you simply want to quit thinking about life. Your problems can be solved by reading this book. The truth is that we all have negative thoughts from time to time. However, if you are prone to feeling overwhelmed, you should carefully analyse how these concepts are affecting your way of life. The solution is to practise certain mindfulness techniques that provide your mind more "space" so that you may feel inner peace and fulfilment.

These problems are all the result of being cut off from our source, from our innate knowledge and tranquilly. How to confront and alter a basic belief that is no longer in your best interests; how to use treatments when stress and anxiety are draining your energy; the long-term dangers of not treating your stress and anxiety, as well as the health advantages of doing so.

Suppressing either happy or negative emotions can eventually result in physical and mental illness since your being craves integration. We are pliable, squishy beings with emotional bodies that are permanently imprinted with the feelings we have encountered. The antithesis of weakness is self-compassion, and in order to make any significant changes in our lives, we must be sympathetic and compassionate toward ourselves.

Can you relieve your stress right now without using any medications, acquiring any skills, or giving up contemporary life? The typical response is, "No, but I'm working on it." They believe that a particular person, their job, their financial status, their health, etc. is to blame for their stress.

You may call it anything you want: pondering, worrying, stressing, or even freaking out. I refer to it as a busy mind. How about that? You waste 99.9% of your ideas. One of the founders of the philosophical school of pragmatism and former top psychologist in America, William James, said it best: "A great many individuals think they are thinking when they are only rearranging their biases." The intellect is viewed as a tool in pragmatism.

People who have trouble controlling their minds don't think it's feasible. "I can't help but think these things," they confess. Well, with enough practise, you can take control of your thoughts. It just takes a few minutes to read, and you can apply it right away to sharpen your thinking. You have the power to choose your thoughts. You might also decide not to think. And that is among the most significant and useful lessons you may acquire in life. I used to spend a lot of time in my thoughts before I mastered that talent.

Just consider how much you think. I wonder what my supervisor thinks about this. "What happens if I make a mistake and get fired?" What if my company never becomes successful? Is she in love with me? "Why is my life so miserable?" What if I develop cancer? " I'm unable to complete anything.

A frightening 88% of Americans list antagonism, office fury, and rudeness as their top workplace worries. Executives, supervisors, and managers will benefit from reading. How to reduce workplace conflict and stress? Because it will show them how to shield productivity, profit, and pride from these crippling feelings. Most people's reactions to job annoyance are almost imperceptible behaviours that exacerbate interpersonal conflict. And since workplace irritants are constant, even a small number of irritants per day adds up to thousands of dollars per employee per year! It is not in the nature of humans to react to frustration with blame and defensiveness, but it is a reflexive reaction that can be altered.

Avoid conflict and cynicism since they deplete relationships, resources, and financial success. Learn how to rapidly soothe irate coworkers and customers as well as why anger makes individuals illogical, lonely, and miserable. Take advantage of the financial and personal advantages of "hard on the issue, gentle on the people." Shared accountability for the future should take the place of past resentment. It produces a workforce that is emotionally strong and resistant to blame.

The advantages and statistics will astound you. In any given month, 75% of Americans claim that stress in their life results in at least one physical or mental symptom. There is hope for individuals who desire to solve this issue without using medicine, so you are not alone. Don't allow worry drag you down and negatively impact the people you care about. If you wish to manage stress without using medication, this book covers the key topics to get you started. I have complete faith in you to take the next steps toward becoming a healthier, happier, and more peaceful version of yourself if you have taken the initiative to locate this book and read this description.

How to handle stress triggers in relationships, the workplace, and other aspects of daily life. Take a moment to relax and start using this mindfulness workbook based on scientific facts right away. Although stress is a natural part of life, it doesn't have to rule your existence. With the guidance of this manual, you'll learn the abilities you need to deal with challenging emotions, cultivate self-compassion, form healthy physical and emotional habits, increase resilience, and align with your core beliefs. Everybody encounters stress. Our days are filled with stressful situations, both major and minor, from the time we wake up in the morning until the moment we finally get into bed at night. These situations may rapidly accumulate and feel overwhelming. Unfortunately, stress is unavoidable.

However, you may alter how you view things. This crucial book will demonstrate how. In today's fast-paced society, stress is an inescapable side consequence of being human. But with the help of this book, you'll develop the abilities required to manage stress and lead a more active life!

- Do your thoughts sometimes race and your chest feel tight?

- Do you feel powerless to make changes to your life because it has overtaken you?
- Do you frequently hear comments from others that you "overthink" or "overreact" when you're upset?

Then you should continue reading. If this describes you, you are by no means the only one. According to the Global Organisation of Stress, 450,000 employees in Britain alone think that stress is causing them to get unwell, and 75% of Americans reported moderate-to-high levels of stress in the preceding few months.

In today's chaotic and fast-paced world, experiencing stress and anxiety is becoming more and more prevalent. There is much more to stress than just a feeling. It can make you physically unwell and have a bad impact on your mental health or your capacity for clear thinking. It may leave you feeling completely alone and overburdened, and it may even prevent you from being able to think clearly enough to handle the issues you are now facing. But remain calm; there is still time. You won't have to worry about having restless nights or a tightness in your chest if you know the most recent information on how to manage your stress and anxiety, because stress management and anxiety alleviation are fortunately well-researched and predictable.

What causes stress in you and why do we react to it?

Rearrange your life to better manage your stress and the stress of those around you. How to deal with common life-stressful situations that you can comprehend and resolve successfully. How to develop effective habits that will support effective stress management and much more. Hans

Selye, who is renowned for his research and beliefs on the effects of stress on the human body, said, "It's not stress that kills us, it's our attitude to it." You've come to the right place if you're looking for easy-to-implement solutions to help you cope with stress. This chapter offers a straightforward stress management practises for those wishing to improve your lives. No matter who you are or what your circumstances may be, the medical and psychological principles in this chapter are discussed in simple, understandable language and will lead you through procedures that you can immediately apply to your daily life. Even if you have tried and failed with other stress management books, you will succeed with this one because it is so easy to follow.

Two of the most prevalent adverse impacts of contemporary society's fixation on rapid pleasure are stress and anxiety. In 2018, more than 77% of American adults said they often go through extended periods of intense stress, and more than 40% said they had an anxiety illness of some kind. Unfortunately, both conditions have the potential to result in severe, maybe permanent, mental and bodily harm if left untreated.

According to the report, 80% of workers think there are no programmes to reduce stress at work, and as a result, close to 60% of them desire to quit their employment due to their stressful work environments. According to a recent TimesJobs poll, 80% of employees say that their companies do not provide corporate stress management programmes, despite the fact that 90% of them are interested in taking part. Additionally, it stated that 60% of workers believe workplace stress to be so severe that they want to leave their positions, which is frightening news for many firms. According to the survey, every working professional has experienced the burden of work-related stress at some point in their career, regardless of age, experience, gender, or profile.

What is stress at work?

When there is a tension between an employee's job expectations and their level of control over satisfying those needs, it can lead to workplace stress, a damaging physical and emotional reaction. Surprisingly, stress may actually boost creativity and productivity, so it's not all negative. Humans typically respond to stressful situations or events by tensing up, then calming down and returning to their regular, relaxed condition. The issue arises when stress levels are so high or so persistent that this rhythm is disrupted, resulting in both mental and physical sickness. Stress at work is an expensive pandemic. Although the health ramifications of this disease are frequently highlighted, the economic repercussions are equally worrisome.

Absenteeism, decreased productivity, employee turnover, workers' compensation, health insurance, and other stress-related costs are all caused by workplace stress. According to the survey, employees of small-sized firms express a substantially greater degree of workplace stress than do those of large organisations. About 50% of employees in small firms and 30% of employees in large organisations claim to experience significant levels of stress at work. As it was already said, the report shows that 80% of workers complain about stress at work, to the point where over 60% desire to abandon their employment due to excessive stress levels.

As it progressively spreads throughout many firms, workplace stress may one day be referred to as a "Global Epidemic." According to the most recent worldwide workforce data from Gallup, stress levels are at an all-time high. Work "sucks," as the saying goes, everywhere. According to Gallup's State of the Global Workplace 2022 study, employees are more stressed than ever. 60% of workers questioned say they feel "emotionally distant" at work, while 19% say they always feel "miserable." These numbers surpass those from 2020, which established a new record for the percentage of workers who reported experiencing daily stress.

According to the research, employee engagement and well-being are still relatively low globally and are preventing businesses from realising their full potential for growth. Globally, just 9% of employees are "thriving and engaged," while 57% of workers are "not engaged and not thriving." The general well-being of employees in South Asia and Europe has significantly decreased. Only 11% of South Asian employees and 47% of European workers report "thriving" overall life quality. The "most engaged" workers are those in the United States and Canada, where 33% of survey participants reported feeling involved at work. Despite having a high level of involvement, American and Canadian workers are the most stressed out in the world.

The best quality of life is reported by employees in Australia and New Zealand, where 63% of respondents claim they are "thriving." A recent LinkedIn Learning poll found that 52% of professionals—more than half—are stressed at work. Additionally, we discovered that stress tends to rise when your profession develops and your income rises. That much pressure is a lot. How are people handling everything? Here are the top suggestions for dealing with workplace stress: Have you ever had the thought, "I have the same number of hours in my day and look at how much they do!"? Some use this line of reasoning as motivation to work harder and more quickly than their contemporaries, to push themselves fiercely, and to embrace the hustle. The issue is that this way of thinking is crippling, counterproductive, and when we're feeling overwhelmed, it may result in burnout and negative avoidance.

In the short term, comparing yourself to others could help you finish a sprint, but in the long run, it won't benefit you much. Keep in mind that you never truly know what another person is going through or what resources they may have available to them on a daily basis. There is no stress alleviation in comparing oneself to a fictitious world, is there? According to 71% of respondents in the U.S. and Canada, it's a good time to seek a job right now. The Commonwealth of Independent States (35%), the Middle East and North Africa (28%), and East Asia (27%), are the regions with the least promising job prospects. Organisations must consider the entire person, not just the employee. Well-being data must be included in executive dashboards. According to the study, leaders should emphasise employee well-being as a component of their employer brand promise.

I divide up my day. I put incoming calls on hold until noon so that I could concentrate on my top priorities and finish the majority of my scheduled outbound calls. My clients are aware that I'm now concentrating on finding solutions to their recruiting or training problems. Three times a day, in the morning, midday, and afternoon, I also respond to email. Clients are aware that they may phone and ask to be interrupted if they need to contact me. An avenue to a life that is more in focus is writing.

Each morning, I start by writing 750 words in journal. It helps me to relax and prepares me for the day. A fantastic method to help yourself genuinely overcome stress is to picture yourself in a situation where you can do so. I do it using music from movies. I'll put on one of my favourite movie soundtracks when the protagonist is confronted with a choice while I'm under pressure at work. The strain and stress are audible in the song. The hero then succeeds in overcoming the difficulty via will, good fortune, or cunning. You can hear the musical flourish that denotes their achievement, and I let that uplift my mood.

Throughout history, great thinkers and doers have frequently shared a passion for walking. Your amygdala is activated while you are moving through space in a way that is different from when you are stationary. To schedule a 15-minute slot to see your campus, open your calendar. A bad day may be turned around by feeling the sun on your back and the breeze in your hair. If your calendar is already full, find a meeting you can attend online.

Meetings with only one person are a terrific place to start. Every other meeting should be a walking meeting, so ask the person you are meeting with whether this is possible. You sometimes simply need to leave the office. When the tension of the workplace got too great, I used to work in Mumbai City and walk outside. Of course, there are horns, sirens, and all other kinds of noise on the streets, so I would walk to a peaceful park in Mumbai city and take a brief break from the commotion. I could unwind, refocus, and reenergise there for the remainder of the day. A great strategy includes adding high intensity to the combination of a brief trek, brisk stroll, mind-clearing music, or meditation session. Take a break and engage in something physically and mentally stimulating if you start to feel stressed. You won't regret doing it!

Middle class income syndrome has become more prevalent. Here are some options for you. Hiren, a young professional employed by one of the top MNCs, has a highly busy schedule. Working hours extend throughout the weekend, with him always having his laptop and mobile device nearby. Meetings, product launches, professional goals, and travel have a cost. Add to this, the lack of exercise, poor eating habits, and ample time for leisure activities. Do you identify with Hiren? His situation is hardly unique. Working long hours and meeting strict deadlines can be difficult. Additionally, Hiren has a devoted family, for whom he has a limited amount of time remaining. How exactly does one survive? This is the story of India's syndrome of the rising middle class.

Let's acquire some perspective now. India is positioned to have one of the strongest economies in the next few years. Our nation takes pride in having the youngest workforce in the world. This demographic dividend undoubtedly has unfavourable effects of its own. India is a growing nation with an aspirational rising middle class that places a strong emphasis on education and skills. There are many career choices available today that are both tough and difficult. The path to new heights is not an easy one and is not without its problems. One of them is "stress," and it is imperative to assume control before it is too late.

The Cigna 360-Wellness Programme A study published in May 2016 that involved more than 3000 respondents and 10 Indian cities indicated that 62% of working Indians experience stress. In some industries, like the retail industry, the stress levels are higher. The poll also showed that stress levels among women were higher than those among men. Usually, people work longer than 50 hours each week. According to the aforementioned report, 62% of workers exhibit some physical and mental signs of stress. The body's natural response to any demand that interferes with daily living is stress. Hours, days, and even months might pass during times of stress. Stress acts as a bodily and emotional alert, much like a warning signal. Observe the following signs closely: Sleeping difficulties, emotional symptoms such as forgetting when you were happy, workplace rage like fatigue, headaches etc.

Today's workers have decreased energy, irritability, and sleep loss, which negatively affects their personal health. Additionally, organisations are seeing a decline in production and effectiveness. Stress may be beneficial, but only in tiny doses. According to studies, stress is not all negative. A difficult paper before a test comes to mind. You worked harder to study because of the pressure, and it paid off. You scored a perfect score. This is one perspective on stress that is distinct. So even at work, feeling stressed out before a review meeting is beneficial. If the review goes well, you could get the job. Unmanaged or poorly controlled stress has been linked to high blood pressure, heart disease, obesity, diabetes, and even suicide. Therefore, be alert and act quickly before it's too late. There are ways to deal with stress rather than having to endure it. Here are some actions one might take: Aim for a "blended work-life" balance: All of us operate in a globally localised workplace. Due to the pressure to perform brought on by Indian companies' going worldwide, the idea of work-life balance is unfounded. So let's not waste our time chasing after an impossibility.

Use the "Blended Life Approach" instead. Utilise technology to ensure that your job is not jeopardised and that deadlines are met while still allowing you to have a personal life and be accessible to your loved ones. Invest in Exercise: Making a financial investment in one's physical well-being pays off handsomely. The workplace is extremely demanding, and in order to succeed professionally, one must be both physically and intellectually healthy. Through a variety of consumer and staff engagement programmes, we also recognise "Yoga Day." Such activities promote health, happiness, and well-being. Save your time: As corny as it may seem, time management is a skill that must be well-honed.

Create a task list and learn how to prioritise your tasks to increase productivity and cut down on wasted time. Use your phone to set reminders and keep track of your progress as each day passes. Why worry if the task is adequately planned and carried out? In reality, if time is used correctly, it is simple to organise a holiday that really aids in rejuvenation.

Modern businesses strive to foster a culture of "rewards and recognition." This is critical because it is crucial to reward people that put in a lot of effort, add value, and help the business expand. Employees who feel valued and are consequently driven cannot work under stress. Increase your intellectual capacity by making use of the numerous options that businesses currently provide for their employees to advance their knowledge and abilities. In reality, on-the-go, anytime, anywhere learning has altered due to online education. For instance, businesses encourage staff members to enrol in "Advance Management Programs" at prestigious universities like Stanford, INSEAD, and Harvard Business School, among others.

These classes are excellent venues for stimulating and testing your brain with like-minded others.

As a result, keep learning and managing your stress. Giving supports In the midst of our hectic lives and quest for professional achievement, selfishness occasionally rules. We frequently overlook counting our blessings. Giving your "time" to teach a needy kid, plant trees in your neighbourhood, or simply play with the less fortunate may be soothing. Organisations now go above and beyond to improve the world in a variety of areas, including teaching, cleanliness, sanitation, and the environment, among others. Trying it out will help!

Workplace stress is commonplace nowadays, but it doesn't have to be that way with a little cooperation from the employee and the company. The nature and environment of the job we do now invite stress, as one might assume. Some people think stress is beneficial, even required to promote growth and greatness. Others think that a relaxed setting accomplishes the trick. Some jobs are considered to be more stressful than others, or some jobs see seasonal increases in stress. For instance, a tax accountant's job is likely to be stressful at the end of the fiscal year, but a TV or newspaper journalist's job is likely to be difficult throughout. The fact that various people respond differently to stressful conditions means it is incorrect to believe that working under continuous pressure will necessarily be harmful or beneficial.

While a small bit of stress or pressure may serve as a stimulus, if it becomes excessive, stress may manifest as a physical or psychological illness and negatively impact relationships and professional performance. Only when we stop to consider how frequently we romanticise the concept of doing a demanding job do we begin to understand the intricacy of how working under pressure has evolved into the new norm. It almost seems as though it is assumed to be a sign of significance, success, or that it comes with the position.

Employees are frequently the focus of conversation on the subject of workplace stress and pressure because they are motivated and urged to achieve a better work-life balance. This book will go off topic and focus on managers, supervisors, and employers, offering advice on how to support their staff during trying times.

- Find the source of the stress.
- Don't assume that employees or a subset of employees are just under strain because of the sheer volume of work.
- Investigate further to see whether the source of the stress is a disagreement with a teammate, uncertainty about the position and their career in general, uncomfortable working circumstances, etc.
- Events outside of work, such as the death of a loved one, a divorce, or poor health, can be quite stressful.
- It may not always be obvious whether the stress is connected to work or is the result of personal circumstances, but it is always good for you to do what you can to alleviate the situation.
- Talk to your employee sympathetically and ask what you can do to improve the situation.
- Given that the employee would be preoccupied at work and perform below optimally, it is preferable to grant some time off for private matters.
- Recognise more than you often do.
- Make sure the praise and awards for the job are commensurate with the extra effort put forth by your

department or organisation if you are aware of it.

- Give your employees greater and more frequent thanks than you normally would.
- Recognise that they have been under strain and that they have been performing well.
- As a team, express your gratitude to the workers for their weekend commitments and all-nighters.
- Make these acknowledgements and recognitions in both public and private conversations.
- Ensure that everyone receives overtime compensation in accordance with corporate rules as well.
- Build a network of support.
- While some people may do well under pressure, others may make a few mistakes.
- Create a support structure for the latter that includes a time-management strategy, which may involve assisting them in determining priorities, establishing objectives, making future plans, and delegating work wherever it is feasible.

Training in self-management and assertiveness might be given to help individuals manage stress better. They will adapt to the task more quickly if a mechanism is created where they can get in touch with other managers, HR, or upper management for support. If they are merely unable to handle the burden, particular effort must be taken to develop and train them in smaller jobs until they are capable of handling greater projects on their own. All employees who are working under pressure need to get regular feedback on how they are performing and suggestions for improvement.

In high-stress situations, systems and procedures are put to the test, so it is beneficial if the management is willing to alter them—even temporarily—to meet the demands. Even on hectic days, someone could have a good reason to miss a few hours of work. If it won't have a significant influence on the bigger team goals, let them take the time off. Allow staff to submit creative recommendations and ideas for meeting the deadline more quickly and effectively, and then use the best ones.

Be accommodating to the employees's demands, even if it means only providing them with consistent, high-quality coffee. Start a wellness programme from scratch if you don't already have one. Any organisation may implement a multifaceted wellness programme; it doesn't matter how big or small it is. Set up some yoga mats in the lunchroom; play some simple yoga videos on the LCD instead of the news; switch to green tea from coffee; serve dry fruits and nuts with tea as a snack; schedule a 15-minute time-out de-stress meeting at a set time and perform a fun exercise during it; or even if you don't, just avoid talking about work during that time.

There are several solutions available; all you need to demonstrate is a genuine dedication to your employees' wellbeing. People who work there must be at their best for a team and an organisation to succeed. Stress doesn't bring out the best in individuals; on the contrary, chronic illness and poor health can significantly lower productivity. Continuously stressful conditions at work can eventually lead to people losing motivation, being more prone to errors, and just losing interest in the organisation as a whole, but managers and employers can prevent this by implementing simple yet effective measures. Workplace stress is a normal part of modern life, but with a little cooperation from both the employee and the company, it doesn't have to be.

Employers must take some steps to ensure employees' mental wellbeing at work. Every employer's top priority as the leader of the pack is to maintain regular and transparent communication with the workforce. Many fights are reportedly won or lost in the head. Therefore, having a psychologically healthy staff is crucial for the success and development of any firm. The World Health Organization (WHO) estimates that depression and anxiety cost the world economy close to $1 trillion annually. If left uncontrolled, this loss of production caused by mental diseases will inevitably rise at times of global crises like the epidemic. We have seen unheard-of changes to how we live and work over the past 15 months.

The epidemic caused shutdowns and remote working in an unprecedented fashion since change is always accompanied by uncertainty about what will happen next. There are still serious concerns about things like a third wave even after the epidemic has been going on for more than 18 months. Every employer's top priority as the leader of the pack is to maintain regular and transparent communication with the workforce. It is always possible to express that we are all in this together, even though it is impossible to predict how things will be in April 2023. People who work remotely can feel isolated since they don't regularly connect with the upper management or the HR staff. A CEO, founder, or HR Director may hold monthly town hall meetings, send out emails, or post recorded messages that discuss the company's performance, present strategy, evaluations, and future goals, depending on the timetable. Periodic dissemination of such information to every employee may reduce stress and guarantee that everyone is aware of the organisation's overall goals.

Allowing workers to work flexible hours is crucial, even if a company has resumed operating in-person or remotely. Flexibility may do wonders for productivity as long as there is output and the company's overall work performance is not impacted. The majority of businesses today provide staggered hours, in which there are some times when all shifts overlap. As a result, even when they work different shifts, all employees are required to collaborate for at least a few hours. This helps to ensure that there is appropriate support for collaborative effort. Physical fitness has not often been a concern for companies. Long workdays at the computer are necessary for careers in the IT and software industries. In such a situation, implementing novel work practises might help the company's employees stay physically fit. Examples include incorporating gym, yoga, and meditation areas, as well as going on walks during working hours. In addition to physical stimuli, providing a cheery and well-lit environment at work can help keep people engaged and focused.

Artificial intelligence (AI) and conversational analytics are two technologies that might fundamentally change how workplace mental wellbeing is promoted. Beyond fitness trackers, it is also feasible to create AI-chatbots and other digital tools that may communicate with staff members about various aspects of their behaviour and mental health. The AI therapists demonstrate that they are practical, quick, simple to use, completely anonymous, and the greatest thing is that they are accessible from anywhere, at any time. Therefore, for businesses with large and dispersed workforces, such digital solutions may address wellness problems on a large scale. Every company leader has to pay attention to these and other developments affecting employee mental health, whether they are caused by technology or not.

According to a survey, 55% of professionals in employment in India feel stressed. The research is based on a survey carried out by a professional network. 70% of Indian employees report feeling stressed. Survey In a poll of 1,908 Indian workers, 70% of them claimed to regularly experience stress at least once throughout the workweek. Indian workers have stress levels that are much higher than the Asia-Pacific average of 60%. According to new research released this week by global payroll and HR giant ADP, seven in ten Indian employees report experiencing stress at work at least once each week. The information was gathered for ADP's Global Workforce View 2020 research, which examined employees' views and opinions on the current workplace as well as what they anticipated and hoped will be different in the workplace of the future. In a poll of 1,908 Indian workers, 70% of them claimed to regularly experience stress at least once throughout the workweek. The percentage of stressed out employees in India is much greater than the Asia-Pacific average of 60%. Indians, on the other hand, were among those in APAC who were most inclined to disclose mental health issues at work, according to the report. 89% said they would feel comfortable discussing their mental health with a coworker. There is a responsibility of care for company owners, executives, and managers to establish a work environment that prioritises its employees' mental health and welfare. Even while facing pressure is a natural part of life, the proportion of Indian employees who say they often feel stressed implies that we are failing short. It is well known that mental health issues like anxiety or depression can be brought on by stress or made worse by it.

Mental health has a significant influence on individuals, groups of people, organisations, and the economy. We are aware that there is a compelling commercial argument to be made in favour of building a helpful and productive work environment, in addition to the ethical ones. Anxiety and depressive disorders cost the global economy $1 trillion in lost productivity annually, according to a 2019 WHO study. The study stated that workforces with lower incidences of mental stress are likely to be more productive, have higher levels of employee retention, and report fewer days of workplace sickness absence. Improving our teams' mental health is truly in everyone's best interests, both as employers and as workers. The new ADP data suggests that the advances made in recent years to talk about and educate about mental health are taking effect, which is a healthy development. The likelihood of Indian employees discussing mental health difficulties at work with their coworkers or bosses is among the highest in APAC. "The first step in treating mental health difficulties is having an open and honest conversation; by expressing concerns, strategies and procedures may be implemented to help address the root causes of stress.

According to the data, India has made great strides in this area. According to the data, India has made great strides in this area. In order to duplicate India's success in other areas where advancement in the conversation around mental health in the workplace remains sluggish and stagnant, we must swiftly and thoroughly grasp how India has accomplished this. Work-life balance is frequently a reliable sign of workplace mental health. According to the same ADP poll, nearly half (46%) of Indian workers put in between 6 and 10 hours per week of unpaid employment.

Employers must take some steps to ensure employees‘ mental wellbeing at work. Every employer's top priority as the leader of the pack is to maintain regular and transparent communication with the workforce. Many fights are reportedly won or lost in the head. Therefore, having a psychologically healthy staff is crucial for the success and development of any firm. The World Health Organization (WHO) estimates that depression and anxiety cost the world economy close to $1 trillion annually. If left uncontrolled, this loss of production caused by mental diseases will inevitably rise at times of global crises like the current epidemic. We have seen unheard-of shifts in how we live and work over the past 15 months. The epidemic caused shutdowns and remote working in an unprecedented fashion since change is always accompanied by uncertainty about what will happen next. There are still serious concerns about things like a third wave, even after the epidemic has been going on for more than 18 months.

Every employer's top priority as the leader of the pack is to maintain regular and transparent communication with the workforce. It is always possible to say that we are all in this together, even though it is impossible to predict how things will be in April 2022. On a regular basis, the senior management or the HR staff A CEO, founder, or HR Director may hold monthly town hall meetings, send out emails, or post recorded messages that discuss the company's performance, present strategy, evaluations, and future goals, depending on the timetable.

Periodic dissemination of such information to every employee may reduce stress and guarantee that everyone is aware of the organisation's overall goals. Allowing workers to work flexible hours is crucial, even if a company has resumed operating in-person or remotely. Flexibility may do wonders for productivity as long as there is output and the company's overall work performance is not impacted. The majority of businesses today provide staggered hours, in which there are some times when all shifts overlap.

As a result, even when they work different shifts, all employees are required to collaborate for at least a few hours. This helps to ensure that there is appropriate support for collaborative efforts. Physical fitness has not often been a concern for companies. Long workdays at the computer are necessary for careers in the IT and software industries. In such a situation, implementing novel work practises might help the company's employees stay physically fit. Examples include incorporating gym, yoga, and meditation areas, as well as going for walks during working hours. In addition to physical stimuli, providing a cheery and well-lit environment at work can help keep people engaged and focused.

Artificial intelligence (AI) and conversational analytics are two technologies that might fundamentally change how workplace mental wellbeing is promoted. Beyond fitness trackers, it is also feasible to create AI-chatbots and other digital tools that may communicate with staff members about various aspects of their behaviour and mental health. The AI therapists demonstrate that they are practical, quick, simple to use, completely anonymous, and the greatest thing is that they are accessible from anywhere, at any time. Therefore, for businesses with large and dispersed workforces, such digital solutions may address wellness problems on a large scale. Every company leader has to pay attention to these and other changes, whether they are caused by technology or not, to employee mental health in the new normal.

The significance of mental health at work Over 40% of workers in the private sector suffer from depression or general anxiety disorder, according to a pre-pandemic poll by The Associated Chambers of Commerce and Industry of India (ASSOCHAM). According to the World Health Organization, health is not just the absence of sickness or infirmity but also a condition of full physical, mental, and social well-being. Not only has the COVID-19 epidemic affected people's physical health but also their emotional well-being. An estimated 264 million individuals throughout the world experience sadness and anxiety.

An estimated 264 million individuals throughout the world experience sadness and anxiety. The global pool of professionals was already struggling due to work stress and burnout when the economic downturn and the job insecurity brought on by the pandemic compounded their problems. Although stress by itself is not a disease, it raises the risk of mental health issues like depression when it is experienced regularly. Workplace stress can contribute significantly to occupational ill health, lower levels of performance and productivity, and even the emergence of different illnesses and lifestyle disorders.

Additionally, psychological side effects include difficulty concentrating, poor decision-making abilities, anxiety, and despair may accompany this. Data from several nations show that mental health issues are a global phenomena that significantly impacts business personnel. According to a pre-pandemic poll conducted by The Associated Chambers of Commerce and Industry of India (ASSOCHAM), over 40% of employees in the private sector suffer from depression or general anxiety disorder, making the Indian corporate sector comparable to its international counterparts.

In order to predict the psycho-social factors that contributed to distress among the Indian population after the implementation of COVID, an online survey was conducted in 2021. It also revealed that the age range of 21 to 35, which makes up a sizable portion of the working-age population in India, was the most vulnerable.Employees encounter discrimination at work and even while applying for employment due to the stigma associated with mental health difficulties, in addition to the physical and psychological repercussions they must endure in the workplace.

Without assistance, many workers struggle to live in a hectic workplace, which affects their performance and attendance. Many of them eventually quit their jobs as a result. As a result, it makes sense for businesses to prioritise promoting mental health from both an economic and social standpoint. An organised "employee support programme" on mental health is needed to address this problem, and it must include both preventative and corrective steps. Most Indian corporations lack this, despite the fact that many of them might hold a few workshops or provide services like counselling. There are a few measures that smaller businesses may do to assist their employees have better mental health, however it may not be simple for them to establish such comprehensive programmes.

Establish stringent guidelines against harassment and discrimination to create a healthy work environment. Relationship problems with bosses and coworkers, an excessive workload, high expectations for performance, a lack of work-life balance, and job security are some of the most frequent causes of stress in the workplace. Unrealistic expectations, putting one employee against the other, and failing to strike the correct balance between work and family obligations, to mention a few, are common problems with managers.

Having a well-structured goal-setting process, reducing work role ambiguity, regular check-ins with the employee by the line manager to help facilitate deliverables, and a well-defined employee communication framework that leaves no doubt as to where the company is headed and what their role is in it; a structured employee grievance mechanism that will look into any type of discrimination and harassment; policies and guidelines that keep a check on eAccepting a job offer.

Accepting and incorporating employee wellness initiatives that address mental health and wellbeing Indians feel at ease disclosing and talking about their physical concerns, in contrast to many western nations where health matters are regarded as private and shared only with pertinent parties. Accepting or talking about mental health difficulties, however, is still fraught with stigma.

Organisations should take action to address workplace mental wellbeing through a clearly stated mental health policy. They should be able to clearly describe the steps they would take to prevent employee burnout or how to deal with it in the same manner that someone would deal with a medical illness: by giving them time to recover and using the organisation's support system to help them return to work. This makes it simple for the staff to feel confident that they can accept, talk about, and ask for support safely without fear of being judged or treated unfairly.

Address mental health concerns at the leadership level by expressing and showing that you are committed to creating an environment where employees' mental health is valued. Approach employee mental health and wellbeing holistically. The first step in boosting workers' mental health is to provide a work atmosphere free of excessive fear and persistent worry. Promote a balanced lifestyle among employees and support it with rules that make it easier to do so.

Spend money on educating employees and managers about mental health issues, such as how to recognise warning signs before they become illnesses, how to show empathy for affected workers, and how to refer them to professional care. Employee assistance programmes (EAP) that would address mental health holistically by assisting employees in focusing on their mental health, holding workshops on how to recognise early warning signs and preventative measures to stop it from getting worse, and providing counsellors to assist those in need, as well as access to clinical psychologists for those who are having problems. We need to deal with the problem of mental illness, treat those who have it, and establish places where people can get the support they need. We must bring it out into the open, out of the shadows, and out of the closet.

According to a recent study, mindfulness exercises like meditation won't immediately alter the structure of your brain, but they may help you pay more attention. Many businessmen practise meditation. It can be because doing so can prevent mistakes from occurring. Bill Gates, Marc Benioff of Salesforce, and Arianna Huffington are among the business titans who practise meditation. Blood pressure and anxiety are reduced as a result of meditation. According to research by Michigan State University, it also aids in reducing errors.

According to a recent study, mindfulness exercises like meditation won't immediately alter the structure of your brain, but they may help you pay more attention. Many businessmen practise meditation. It can be because doing so can prevent mistakes from occurring. Bill Gates, Marc Benioff of Salesforce, and Arianna Huffington are among the business titans who practise meditation. Blood pressure and anxiety are reduced as a result of meditation. According to research by Michigan State University, it also aids in reducing errors.

What causes anxiety and how to deal with it?

What about the self-conscious, uneasy, or apprehensive sensations or thoughts you could have while you are relaxed and your superego isn't in charge? What is their origin? When I ask people where their feelings of fear, anxiety, or other negative emotions come from, they typically respond that they originate from whatever it is that they are afraid of, including strangers, snakes, the audience watching them give a presentation, or that ominous person interviewing them for their dream job. But things don't quite operate that way. It's not as though an audience beams forth terror, which your body then absorbs. If that were the case, then everyone would have the same fears. If that were the case, then everyone would have the same fears. One of my clients complained when I explained this to her, saying, "So you're telling me that if a snake walked into my room right now, it's not the snake that makes me terrified, but my own thoughts?" Yes, that was what I was saying; I can attest to that. But she said that if the snake weren't around, I wouldn't be afraid. Yes, I said, but the source of your apprehension isn't the snake. It starts with how you see the snake.

For instance, I enjoy snakes; therefore, my reaction if I unexpectedly discovered one in my workplace would depend on a variety of factors. If I knew the snake was harmless, I would probably be more interested in learning where it came from and finding it amusing. I'd probably feel a bit afraid and uneasy if I could tell it was harmful. Furthermore, if I mistook the snake for a harmless one when it was actually rather poisonous, instead of being terrified, I could be fascinated and amused. My feelings aren't being caused by the snake, because if a hazardous snake causes fear in me, even if I know it's harmless, I should feel terror.

So it's not like the outside world has no impact. Our experiences and observations can spark a variety of thoughts. But such ideas are not determined by the outer environment. I used to be so frightened of public speaking that if I had a presentation to give in class, I would skip it. However, one of my favourite things to do these days is take the stage and instruct a crowd. Public speaking or rooms full of people didn't change anything; only my thoughts about those things changed, and when they did, so did my feelings about them. And understanding this is crucial because, if you think that the outside world is what shapes your inner experience, you will be forced to try to alter it in order to alter how you feel, which will inevitably alter your confidence. However, things get a lot simpler when you realise that all that has to change for your sentiments to change is the way you think, since this removes the need for anything else—like approval from others or anything else—to boost your confidence. All that needs to happen is a positive shift in our perceptions of who we are and what we are capable of. Of course, this training aids you in doing just that. Follow the exercises you've already mastered, and you'll manage things well when the time comes.

Needing approval is a very normal emotion. And some of my coworkers who insist that you have to get rid of it entirely irritate me a little. Most individuals find it very hard to entirely overcome, and those who never feel the need to seek anyone's approval tend to have traits that are close to narcissistic personality disorders.

Therefore, we don't necessarily need to let go of our need for acceptance; rather, we just need to make sure that we're directing it in the correct directions so that it may advance us rather than impede it. You see, the majority of individuals feel the need to win the approval of everyone and anybody. They are concerned about what total strangers may think of them. They pay attention when someone who doesn't understand what they're talking about advises them to do something differently because they feel awful when someone they care about disagrees with them, regardless of whether that person has any true expertise in the subject at hand. That presents a challenge.

Instead, we should be careful to only solicit this sort of criticism from the correct people—those in whose judgement we have faith that they are knowledgeable about the subject at hand and that their values are compatible with our own. For instance, I cherish my wife. She is perceptive, smart, and astoundingly capable of doing just much whatever she sets her mind to. She has built a life for herself that I appreciate. Regarding anything about which she is informed or in which our personal beliefs and philosophies coincide, I appreciate her views and pay attention to her comments. However, if my wife didn't like, say, how I set up my seminars, I wouldn't take it too personally. I consider myself very adept at planning and leading workshops.I have a tried-and-true method that I've been working on for well over a decade, and it has brought me a tonne of satisfied customers. It would be absurd for me to require my wife's approval on how I conduct my seminars when she has no prior experience. If I wind up altering how I do my seminars because of someone's unqualified comments, it may even turn out to be damaging. Don't misunderstand me. I will consider what my wife has to say if she has any recommendations or ideas for my workshop, since I appreciate her and her intelligence.

Now, if a colleague whose workshop planning abilities I valued offered me constructive criticism about my workshop, I would pay close attention. I'd probably put their recommendations to the test to make sure they align with my preferences, objectives, and moral principles. And if they do, the adjustments they recommend will be made permanently, and I will learn from the criticism and appreciate it rather than feel awful about it. What would I do, furthermore, if a total stranger approached me on the street and voiced some disapproval of my workshops? I wouldn't give it a second thought because I have no reason to pay attention to him. I am unaware of his expertise, background, morals, ideologies, or anything else relevant. So what I'm saying is that we should only accept constructive criticism and feedback seriously when it comes from a source that we respect for their knowledge, particularly within the subject they're providing us with input on. Even then, before accepting it as fact and taking action, we must carefully assess if it applies to ourselves.

Our harmful desire for acceptance can swiftly transform into a useful instrument that we can utilise for our own self-development if we practise doing this while also remembering not to compare ourselves to the ideal concept of others. And if we begin to see constructive criticism from others as an opportunity for us to learn and become better, we will begin to look forward to it. And even though she could have had an idea that I hadn't, that doesn't mean I'll feel awful about disagreeing with her or criticising her, or that I should follow her advice even if I don't agree with it. Due to my real experience with workshops, I would be inclined to believe that I would be correct if we disagreed.

Large picture, little steps Another option is to choose to concentrate on the things you can control. I know you've heard that advice a million times, so why don't we apply it more frequently? According to some estimates, up to 70% of our thoughts are focused on outside factors, which only fuels pessimism. To prevent getting dragged into irritating things beyond your control, create concern boundaries—lines you draw on what you will and won't worry about.Change is a factor in the decision's outcome.

How to maintain optimism while maintaining perspective?

Even those of us who are the most optimistic occasionally succumb to negativity. Maintaining perspective aids in maintaining a happy outlook. Utilise the three Cs of perspective to do this. Connecting with uplifting individuals is the first step. Decide who you want to be with, spend time with, and get perspective from, avoiding bad influences as much as possible. The most significant factor in leading a happy, good life is surrounding oneself with happy, positive people, according to a 71-year-long research at Boston University. That makes logical, no? That's how easy and difficult it is. I am aware that you cannot just cut certain individuals out of your life.But you must at the very least establish limits.

According to research, those who are negative frequently are unaware of the effect their negativity has on those around them. So let them know how it's affecting you and set a rule that you won't participate in the melancholy. Get insight from people who energise you rather than deplete you. You are the average of the five individuals "you spend the most time with," according to author Jim Rohn. Choose accordingly. Additionally, make minor offsets. It's vital to remember that you can always try to counteract negativity with doses of optimism, at least in your own tiny part of the globe.It doesn't have to be grand gestures like quitting your job to pursue one that serves others or giving away all of your assets. It may be as easy as concentrating on consistently following your ideals. For instance, being nice may be one of your basic values. Despite your struggles, you offer the coffee shop barista a kind greeting or compliment a coworker on their efforts. Living this way every day might help counteract the negative aspects of your life. It aids in making you feel less helpless. Furthermore, research demonstrates that our values are the most consoling, reorienting item we can repeatedly turn to when we feel lost.

Lastly, think about the past. Your prior unpleasant experiences are an excellent place to start to gain perspective. It's likely that you've experienced times of negativity that seemed especially intense at the time. Did you learn anything from those experiences that helped you become a little stronger or develop as a person, even just a little bit, when you reflect back on those times? It's critical to have faith in your resilience and know that you can overcome adversity because you have in the past. Getting through might indicate that you fully adapted to and conquered an event, or it can just mean that you discovered one little aspect of it that helped you become a little bit stronger. Thus, keep in mind the three Cs of perspective when creating.

"Concentrate all your thoughts on the work at hand. The sun's rays do not burn until brought to a focus."
-Alexander Graham Bell

You'll see a link between mindfulness practise and being able to attain your most critical professional goals with less effort. It is equally crucial to be physically active as it is to find calm. Surprisingly, we sometimes feel the most calm and still while we're moving around. When we exercise, our hearts pump more blood and send more oxygen to our brains. This oxygen boost helps us concentrate better. Many people make the mistake of saving their exercise and mobility for before and after work. While you may not want to break a sweat at work, think about your physical condition when you're preparing to settle down to work on a subject that requires concentrated concentration. If you want to enhance this talent for your present or future career, or simply for yourself, there are a few things you may do. The first, and, in my opinion, most essential, technique to enhance attention is to think hard and long about what you really desire.

"The only trouble is that they do it about a great many things and I do it about one. If they took the time in question and applied it in one direction, to one object, they would succeed." -Thomas Edison

Your body is constantly in the here and now, living in the moment. This habit of reflecting on a recent work interaction or reviewing plans while not feeling truly at ease and settled in your current life creates an undercurrent of unease and dissatisfaction. It also happens when you are in a form of virtual reality and lose touch with what is actually happening in the present. After learning about mindful awareness of the body, I recall taking a stroll through the woods. I could smell the sweet aroma of the apple trees and feel the soft wind on my skin, and my mind was at peace when I suddenly realised that my body and mind were in the same place at the same time. Even though everything seemed so straightforward, there was a deep sense of life. I was an active participant in the spring. Researchers have revealed that mindfulness meditation significantly reduces the area of the brain that detects the border between oneself and others. Meditators have reported experiencing a strong sense of connectedness. A profound sense of serenity and homeliness results from this.

Being mindful of your body's sensations may act as an anchor for being present with your experience, similar to how your breath can. Similar to the breath, you may calm a disorganised mind by maintaining concentration on physical sensations. Similar to the breath, you may calm a disorganised mind by maintaining concentration on physical sensations. You can contribute a sense of attention, ease, and well-being. I'll continue developing body mindfulness in this session by carefully and methodically scanning the entire body. Close your eyes and settle into a comfortable posture, whether you're laying down or sitting up. Take a few deep breaths, and with each exhale, let go of any stress. Start by focusing on the feelings at the top of your head while maintaining this open, relaxed awareness. Watch for pressure, pulsating, and tingling. Allow your focus to progressively descend as you feel the feelings in your ears, on each side of your head, and on the back of your skull. Take note of the feelings in your mouth, nose, cheeks, jaw, and the area around your eyes, forehead, and eyes. Give it some time. You are merely curious to experience the life of your body as it is, giving it gentle, receptive attention without trying to alter anything. As you carry out this scan, you could discover that there are areas of your body where you have numbness or no sensation at all.

Be advised that this is typical. Just allow your focus to drift in this direction for a short period of time. As your focus becomes more intense, you might discover that you start to notice softer feelings. Continue by focusing on your neck and throat region and observing any feelings there without passing judgement. Continually look down. From the inside, become conscious of your shoulders and take in their lives and feelings. Feel all the inside feelings as well as the volume and length of your arms. Turn your focus to your hands. Feel the fingers, palms, and back of the hands in a simple, uncomplicated manner. Take note of the pulsating, tingling, pressure, coolness or warmth, and liveliness of the body. Put your consciousness inside your chest at this point.

Allow yourself to gently experience the sensations around your heart and all over your chest. Slowly and with a soft, receptive focus, allow your awareness to descend into your stomach. Recognize the feelings in your abdomen. Pay close attention to your upper back at this point. Observe the feelings in the region between your shoulder blades. Slowly descend, paying attention to the middle and lower back first, then the entire spinal column.

Let your focus continue to progressively descend down your body. Let your awareness extend towards the pelvic area, keeping an open mind to the feelings in your buttocks, hips, and genitalia. Feel the size and volume of your legs as you descend. Bring your consciousness to them, experience them inside, and let your awareness permeate your toes and feet. And now, let your focus expand to fully include your entire body.

Consider the body as a fluctuating, floating field of sensations, a subtle energy field that animates and sustains each and every cell and organ in the body. Spend some time in present-moment awareness of your living body, seeing and sensing the presence of energy that makes you who you are. A good time to perform a body scan is when you first get out of bed in the morning or at night. And, as you go about your day, you can pause whenever you remember and perform a quick body scan whenever you feel yourself becoming tense or unsettled or when you need to regain a sense of well-being and stability. For instance, you can spend a few minutes scanning your entire body if you open an email and discover it includes unfavourable or distressing news.

What if you're only somewhat uncomfortable but realise that getting an aspirin right now isn't actually necessary? Everything takes on the taste of pain when our focus is fixed there. I am preoccupied with the issue's duration, causes, and potential solutions. I am concerned that it will make it difficult for us to complete a crucial project or interact positively with patients or clients. I am concerned that if we don't perform at our best, other people will judge us, and I will somehow be letting them down. While I can't always escape unpleasant circumstances, I can steer clear of the self-judgment and mental and emotional resistance that make pain the focus of our attention. When pain is resisted, misery results. And in the workplace, where I experience pressure to perform and worry about my ability to give my all, this is especially difficult.

Mindfulness is released here. Pain may still exist while I'm conscious, but it no longer has the same power over me.

A talented athlete learns how to move through discomfort rather than against it. When giving birth, a woman might accept the discomfort of her contractions rather than fighting them. In fact, studies have shown that people who practise mindfulness report less subjective discomfort. I create a spaciousness that can hold the pain more easily by maintaining a non-resisting conscious present. To compare, imagine adding a tablespoon of red food colouring to a glass of water. Glass as a whole turns crimson. What would happen, though, if you added a spoonful of red dye to a lake? The lake is large enough to easily accommodate the dye. In the same manner, practising mindfulness and paying compassionate attention creates a spacious consciousness large enough to more easily hold painful experiences. With this expansive awareness, I can perceive that what first appeared to be a solid, strong pain is actually a field of shifting feelings. You can gently bear this discomfort.

Make room as though you were cradling a sobbing baby. Take note of how the agony is always shifting, with waves of experience frequently arriving and departing around it. Pain gradually becomes manageable. It's crucial to remember that practising mindfulness isn't always the best or even an option when dealing with discomfort. Sometimes it's most shrewd and kind to change your focus or focus on something else that will make your body and mind feel better. But, as with all aspects of your mindfulness training, practise will help you find equilibrium and comfort in the midst of discomfort, which will help you stay stable during stressful workdays, when you're rushing to meet a deadline, and in all other situations in your life. Let's put this to use.

Allow yourself to find a relaxed seating posture. Take a few seconds to gather your focus with a breath as you become still. Sit back and enjoy the inflow and outflow. Maintain your calm, focused concentration on your breath. Also keep in mind to gently and steadily bring the puppy back if your focus wanders. Open your awareness to your body's feelings and look for any areas of discomfort. If you have any negative feelings, gently direct your focus there.

Practice focusing on any location that is causing the greatest or most noticeable feelings, if there isn't any discomfort there. Try to attract someone's thoughtful and interested attention. What do these feelings genuinely feel like instead of the term "pain"? You can gently describe them as tugging, searing, throbbing, twisting, stiffening, and firing if it is therapeutic. Take note of every detail of the encounter. What are their densities and textures? How large is the feeling zone? Where does the unpleasantness' edge lie? Is there a colour that goes with it? Hold everything in compassion. As you breathe slowly, try to feel the space beyond the pain.

Allow your feelings to float in your wider awareness. Even the space between the feelings may be felt. Right now, all you can do is watch while the sensations develop. Take note: do they become more solid and dense or less so? Do they move, alter, or transform into another type of sensation? Maintain your calm demeanour and let the feelings develop naturally as they will. It is important to gently direct your attention to the breath or, if that is more helpful, to a location in your body where there are pleasant or neutral feelings. This will help you regain resilience, equilibrium, and perspective if your mind ever becomes weary, fearful, or reactive, or if the experience feels overwhelming. For the time being, focus on practising extending a gentle presence to the intense feelings and returning as necessary to your resting place while keeping an open mind to any sensations that demand your attention. Keep in mind that this is not a race of endurance.

Instead, you're developing the skill of being a kind and compassionate observer, discovering a calm presence among the shifting currents of life, and developing your inner feeling of comfort, power, and freedom. Intense hunger, foot pain, headaches, allergic reactions, eye pain, exhaustion, itching, tight shoulders, and backaches are just a few of the frequent daily aches and symptoms people face while working. So, our bodies and brains may also experience stress, worry, and anxiety as pain. Being aware may be helpful. In the next few days, be aware of any aches you have and start to investigate the distinction between bodily feelings and mental resistance to them. Take note of the concerns and problem-solving that I bring to our physical experience, and then try, for a short while, softly acknowledging and kindly accepting the challenging bodily feelings.

Again, nothing needs to change. I'm just taking note of how the mind and ideas are functioning right now. Depending on your experience and amount of stress, you could have been generally at peace in your body, emotions, and mind, or you might have experienced some disruption. The first step in managing the tension that exists is awareness. Now that this exercise has come to an end, I ask you to make an intention for yourself, no matter how you are feeling physically, mentally, emotionally, or both. Who do you want to be for the remainder of the day? Do you want to be nice, approachable, and available, or are you more interested in being remote, closed, and unavailable? There is no right or incorrect answer; instead, respect the path you choose. I take three deep breaths to conclude this practice. The task at hand is to carry out that objective throughout the remainder of the day. Inhale deeply, then exhale slowly. Another quick one in, releasing all the air, and out. And then take one more deep breath, gently blink your eyes open as you exhale, and then resume your day with a better understanding of how stress affects you.

Being mindful might increase your productivity in today's hectic society. It eases tension, sharpens attention, and enhances your capacity to overcome obstacles at home and at work. With consistent practice, mindfulness may alter the path of your life. Practice while being coached by executive coach Henna Inam through activities that improve relationships, increase self-confidence, and broaden emotional intelligence. With these techniques, it's possible to overcome phobias, cope with challenging people, find inspiration when you least expect it, and manage change.

You may alter the structure of your brain to react to stressors by using the practises that go along with each lesson. Our world is quickly evolving. Develop a resilient mindset to face problems. Because it enables us to deal with each of these difficulties, mindfulness is a metaskill for the workplace. When we are in a state of mindfulness, we are able to observe what is happening in the here and now without passing judgement. Numerous studies have demonstrated that practising mindfulness truly alters the anatomy of the brain. Yes, it's true, my friends. Our reactive brain's activity is switched over to our thinking and reasoning brain.

According to some research, even three days of practise might make a difference. What are the main obstacles we face at work, and how might mindfulness help? We may use it to determine what is genuinely essential to us in order to have a better work-life balance. We may identify what energises and depletes us by observing our experience in the present. We may concentrate our attention on what is genuinely important to us once we have that self-awareness. We may utilise mindfulness to observe how we actually operate in order to better manage our workload. We identify efficient behaviours, situations where we might need to ask for assistance, and instances where we need to practise saying "no." We may recognise these tendencies in ourselves thanks to mindfulness. It also enables us to test out new, more beneficial habits.

"Lack of direction, not lack of time, is the problem. We all have twenty-four hour days."- Zig Ziglar

One of the most important abilities is time management, whether we're talking about business or life in general. Stress levels will increase if you let your day run haphazardly rather than consciously planning it. It also makes it too easy for other people to interrupt you. So let's consider a few practical suggestions that will enable you to master your time. First, think about getting to work early. Simply give it a shot. At least once a week, you should try to come 30 to 60 minutes earlier than usual. You might be surprised by your reaction. It works because there are so few triggers that increase our stress levels. People that make you anxious: ringing phones, doors opening and closing, etc.

The majority of individuals find that being quiet really reduces their stress. Thus, you become more productive and focused. Then, begin the day with your most difficult assignment. Don't be duped into starting with anything simple. We frequently believe that accomplishing an easy activity before beginning the difficult work would help us gain some momentum. Actually, no. Starting with a simple activity encourages you to do other simple activities, which ultimately serves as an escape from the work that you see as stressful. Of course, this entire procedure delays what really matters and, in fact, increases unnecessary tension. Start by doing the challenging task, and you'll feel much better once you're done. Then, intentionally take pauses for five to ten minutes each, at least three times every day. This is my 90/10 rule. You'll increase productivity and reduce stress if you work for around 90% of the time and take breaks for approximately 10% of the time.

"The key is in not spending time, but in investing it." – Stephen R. Covey

Most individuals believe that putting in long hours of work will result in greater productivity. Typically, that is not true. You know how sometimes turning off and then on your phone or computer will make it work better? In essence, your brain does the same action. When you take a little break from a hard activity and mentally disengage, you frequently return with less stress, more focus, and greater performance.So make a buddy connection, go for a stroll, or do a little personal project. Use the 90/10 rule to ensure that you don't deprive yourself of the brief rest your brain requires while being innovative and adhering to your company's regulations.

"My favorite things in life don't cost any money. It's really clear that the most precious resource we all have is time." – Steve Jobs

Finally, mindfulness may aid in improving our understanding of both ourselves and others, which can aid in dealing with coworkers. We frequently have to work with individuals whose styles are extremely unlike our own. Some of these individuals could annoy us or even be challenging to deal with. The mindfulness method helps us observe without bias. It makes it easier for us to understand others and their needs. We can influence and work with others more effectively when we can control our emotional response to them and accept them for who they are. These are just a few examples of how mindfulness practise may improve our ability to better lead ourselves, better lead others, and better lead through difficult situations. For this reason, I'm certain that if we can all learn to be more attentive, we can make work environments that are more inspiring, innovative, collaborative, and overall more enjoyable. We can have more influence, contentment, and wellbeing at work when we acquire these talents.

Everyone encounters stress in life in one form or another. Despite there being moments when it is advantageous, most of the time it makes our everyday life more difficult.

CHAPTER THREE

Transforming Yourself Through Mindful Resolutions

"Great acts are made up of small deeds." --Lao Tzu

The human mind is not designed to function in a chaotic environment. Your senses are easily distracted, and a small buzz in any part of your environment might cause our attention to shatter.

Do you understand why you lose concentration and become distracted? You probably have an idea, yet what you consider to be bothersome is frequently only a fraction of the whole. To enhance your attention, you must first identify the patterns that are causing you to lose it. Distraction patterns are unique to each individual. They're one-of-a-kind to you, and recognising them is crucial to improving your attention. You can recognise and adjust your distracting tendencies once you bring them to the surface.

You might have felt some degree of physical pain or discomfort while reading the final chapter of this book on bringing mindfulness to the various sensations in your body. I've been emphasising the importance of simply being present with feelings, no matter where they arise. However, you may wonder if it is wise to associate it with suffering. Why concentrate on the pain? Consider doing something to distract yourself from it or get it out of your head. Maybe you even remember George Carlin's words of wisdom: "My attitude is no suffering, no agony," he declared. But suffering is a necessary part of human life. Pain, from a survival standpoint, is a signal to pay attention. Of course, it's crucial to act in a way that looks proper to take care of ourselves. But what if you're experiencing agony right now and you simply can't seem to shake it? a backache, a migraine, a headache, or you recently underwent surgery. What if using painkillers or making other measures to lessen it don't work?

One of the most important things that most of you seem to understand is the importance of paying attention to the nuances of life. But, in truth, there's no way of knowing how much progress is being made when you focus on it every day. Unmasking the details reveals precisely what you desire, who you are, and what you want; the list is endless. It also assists you in becoming more present in the moment, and giving your life more clarity of purpose. When you remove everything in your environment that may cause disruptions, you will be more productive and have a higher chance of remaining focused. To reduce distractions, keep your phone in a different room or remain offline if possible. You will be more concentrated if you work alone or in a quiet atmosphere.

Can you imagine a sucessful outcome?

The notion of "visualising" could make you scoff. I did as well, up until I realised the underlying science. And I'll explain how you can use it to say no politely, easily, and more frequently. Starting off, let's define "visualisation." In general, it involves visualising a goal you want to achieve in your mind. not simply hoping and wishing, but picturing a specific result and what you'll do to get it. Leaders in business and top sportsmen use visualisation because it offers so many advantages, like boosting bravery, confidence, and resilience. It turns out that your mind is unable to tell the difference between fact and fantasy. Your brain is equally stimulated when you see yourself turning down a networking request, for example, whether you're actually doing it now or just visualising it happening in the future. The problem is this. Visualisation may either strengthen you or work against you. You've probably seen this in your own life. Maybe you previously felt hesitant to say no. You probably pictured yourself stumbling over your words or babbling. And I'll bet you that's precisely what tookay place. Why? Mostly because you trained your brain to behave that way. Now think about this. What if the situation was the same, but you prepared your brain mentally? You imagined yourself boldly entering the space. You were succinct and well-spoken. You may still feel anxious, but there is a far greater chance that you will present yourself forcefully. This is what psychologists refer to as the "finest possible self-visualisation."

First, revisit the situation where you'd like to say no that you specified at the beginning of this course. Next, inhale deeply and fully. Close your eyes while you exhale. Consider how you would behave in the situation if you were at your best. That indicates that you are at ease, confident, and in charge. That indicates that you are at ease, confident, and in charge. Give as much information as you can on how you felt at your best at that time. Are you calm, proud, or perhaps intrigued when you are being your best self and saying no? What are you thinking right now? Perhaps you're telling yourself again that you can handle it or that the way someone responds says much more about them than it does about you. How would you describe your body language? It's conceivable that your head is elevated and your shoulders are rounded. Before you say no, go over this visualisation two or three more times to ensure that it has actually taken root in your mind. You become what you think about and focus on the most, according to renowned athlete Jonathan Toews. Take that to heart and work to manifest your best self.

Do you wish to escape the cycle of negative thinking?

I must admit something. I used to try to please everyone. When I had to say no to someone in the past, I felt internally guilty. My nose was weak and unclear on the exterior. Perhaps you belong to the club of ex-people-pleasers, or perhaps you've gone the other way and unwittingly or wrongly delivered your no with hate and rage. In any event, it's imperative that you practise saying "no" in a calm, direct, and comfortable manner.

Alternatively, deliver it with confidence. Being aggressive does not have to imply being impolite. This means finding a balance between passive and forceful communication. being kind but stern. This shows that you appreciate the other person enough to be open and honest about your wants and preferences, as well as how much you value their time and your own.

To demonstrate an aggressive no, let's go through a few scenarios, starting with what it doesn't lookay like. When you say no in a passive manner, your message comes out as hazy and imprecise. You can just hope that the individual will forget to follow up after saying, "Uh, I'm not sure if I can commit; I'll have to see," or "I'm sorry, but..." Out of concern for upsetting the other person, you soften or obfuscate your message. It's okay to postpone a request, seek time to consider it, or check your calendar. Just be certain that this is not being said out of avoidance or fear. Delaying gives you the opportunity to take some time to think about the situation, weigh your options, and then make the best decision for you. On the other hand, there is a forceful no. When you do this, you become aggressive, confrontational, or contentious.

Every one of us has come across someone who became angry with us after we requested a favour. They may have assaulted you and said, "Are you for real?" I can't spend time doing that. Deliver an assertive no instead of a passive or hostile one, one in which you respect both yourself and the other person. You are succinct and lucid without being overly direct. You have a level emotional response, are considerate, and speak from your own point of view. This might be interpreted as: "I'd prefer not to participate." I'm forced to say no. I don't currently have the bandwidth. I'm not going to be able to do that. Or just say, "Thank you, but no." Note how succinct and straightforward these replies are. I'm composed, truthful, and up-front. I don't start out by saying, "I hope you won't be upset" or "I'm sorry to disappoint you but" in order to devalue myself. There is no room for doubt or ambiguity. I don't ask inquiries that lead the other person on and give them the impression that I'm interested or accessible, such as "When do you need this?"

When you say no, give some background information. It's been said that "no" is a full phrase. Most of the time, this is true. You have every right to set boundaries and guard your time. Providing a little light background along with your answer, though, can help a lot. Consider requesting a coworker's assistance with a task. This should be a reasonable request since you and I are on the same team. You send a kind, diplomatic email, and you receive the following response:

How would you be feeling right now? You can feel dismissed, taken aback, or even confused about what you did wrong to possibly upset them. If you get an email from a coworker saying, "Thanks for this request," Suppose you received an email from a coworker saying, "Thank you for asking." "My current family obligations prevent me from working extra." Significant difference, no? You got it. You are by default more sympathetic to their viewpoint. To avoid embarrassment, maintain our connection or your reputation, or when speaking with those in positions of authority above you, it is therefore helpful to provide a brief explanation for your no.

The other person will better comprehend your motive if you can provide them with just a small bit of information about your workload, priorities, or values. Additionally, it demonstrates that your rejection is unrelated to them and increases the likelihood that it will be accepted. Providing a justification can make the difference between being viewed as a team player and someone who doesn't contribute. You should just offer a brief context, no longer than one to three words. Let's imagine, for example, that a contact asks you out for coffee and you decline. Saying, "I have a lot of significant assignments at the moment, and I'm not available for coffee right now," is quite suitable in this situation, end of story.

Over-explaining or giving a protracted justification for your decision to refuse might come off as insecure. Additionally, it exposes you to resolving objections when someone tries to refute or convince you of your position. Likewise, refrain from being excessively sorry. I frequently see mistakes like these. I'm very sorry I can't go, or "Please forgive me," is a common response to a no. This is optional for you to do. You've done nothing wrong, especially if someone is using your valuable time while requesting a special favour. Change "apology" to "thanks." "Thank you for thinking of me," replaces "I'm so sorry I can't do that." Do not mistakenly believe that by declining someone's request, you are rejecting them.

When you say no, provide an alternative. Some of the best job advice I ever received was to always be solution-focused. Most likely, you've also heard this advice. For instance, your management doesn't want you to provide them with a list of grievances. Instead, they want you to outline the issue and suggest potential solutions. The same technique may be used to politely decline requests. By offering an alternate option, you can usually say no in a way that will help your counterpart meet their requirements and solve their problem. Several options are shown below.

You may start by expressing what you can do. Perhaps you were given a report to deliver with a tight deadline. Then you may respond by saying, "The whole report cannot be delivered by Friday afternoon." Does it sound okay? Alternately, you may propose to change the deadline by stating something like, I've heard this is significant. I can have everything ready for you by Monday afternoon, but Friday is not feasible. Keep in mind that you don't want to overburden yourself by helping the other person.

Let's say a buddy of yours gets in touch with you about an employment opportunity with your business. They ask you to speak well about HR. You might state that you don't feel comfortable doing that. I'm so happy you're interested in working here. It would be wonderful to have you at the business. I'm unable to reach HR. I can connect you with the individual who once had that role, though. She could know what makes a good applicant for that position. Another excellent method for preserving your time and fostering relationships is to make a referral. Offer to recommend the individual to a helpful coworker or a contractor they may employ.

Control your feelings. Some of your coworkers, friends, and family members may think it's a good thing that you've learned how to say "no," but others could become angry or irritated when they hear you say no, especially if they're used to hearing "yes" from you all the time. You can feel anxious and frazzled if, for instance, they raise their voice or become more combative. And the more tense you become, the more likely you are to give in and ultimately agree to do something you don't want to. This is the reason it's crucial to understand how to keep your cool when others aren't amenable to hearing no, namely by controlling your own emotions at the time.

Everything begins with your body. I like to claim that you can manage your physiology, notably your fight-or-flight reaction, and hence influence your psychology. This is a reference to the biological response that occurs when you experience stress. Your body starts to get ready to flee or fight back as your heart rate rises and your breathing gets shallower. Grounding exercises are a simple method to relax. Consider these to be intentional pauses. I now understand that you cannot take a break to journal or engage in prolonged meditation while things are tense. I prefer to advise my clients to do a few simple things, such as taking a deep breath. Now let's perform one together. Speaking out loud. Alternately, you may clench and unclench your hands or try to relax your hips into the chair's corner. Each of these relaxation techniques can help you unwind and change your brain's condition from one of dread to one of more serenity and control. Maintaining a glass of cold water nearby is another fast tip. Stress levels can be reduced by lowering the body's temperature.

Be mindful of controlling your thoughts as well. Don't personalise someone else's response. Verify your presumptions. If they're angry, it doesn't always mean you did something wrong. As a reminder not to absorb and internalise the wrath of the other person, many of my coaching clients find it useful to picture a glass pane standing between them and the other person. Your calmness is also aided by objectivity. Think about how someone you respect might respond to the circumstances. You may be better able to present your strongest self if you channel your inner hero. I'd like to leave you with a wise saying. If you respond emotionally to everything that is said to you, your suffering will not end. True power comes from taking a step back and analysing events logically. Restrained power is real power. If words have the power to manipulate you, then anyone can. Take a deep breath and let everything go. Accept that you have no control over how someone else will react if you say no in the end. Your own ideas and emotions are something you can control.

Feeling awful is, well, awful, right? It may be challenging to manage chronic stress and negative thinking patterns, so it's critical to learn how to quickly shift your viewpoint in order to be more optimistic and feel happy. Being happy will not only make your day better because you'll be in a better mood, but it may also have significant long-term impacts that increase contentment and wellness. People prefer to be around positive factors rather than negative ones; thus, it may affect others.

When communicating with another person, consider how their perspective differs from your own. For instance, if we had planned to meet someone for lunch at 12, but they arrived at 1:30 instead, depending on our perspective, we would feel a variety of ways. They may have insulted our time, which makes us upset, or we may be concerned that something horrible has occurred to them. From their perspective, though, they may have been in traffic or believed that noon was just a recommendation to strive for rather than a specific hour.

We are aware that we often see what we are looking for. Therefore, seek out favourable outcomes that will enhance or contribute to your life rather than those that would lessen it or reveal some defect or unpleasant consequence. You can create happiness by shifting your focus away from seeking it. According to Goldberg, when establishing a perspective on something, keep the big picture in mind and consider how this particular viewpoint or area of emphasis will fare in relation to the greater picture or the consequences in the real world. We may see things more clearly by opening our eyes to the bigger picture. It's as if we've suddenly gotten a bird's-eye view of the entire maze, rather than just individual walls.

According to research, practising thankfulness might help you feel happier with your life's circumstances, the people in it, and the environments you surround yourself with. If you're feeling down, consider anything for which you are thankful so that you may focus your attention on something positive that can help you forget your troubles and bad mood. Even if you're unhappy and smiling is probably the last thing on your mind, a quick grin and display of a few sparkling white teeth, as seen in the picture, may instantly improve your attitude. It can help you change your perspective on whatever challenge you are facing so that you feel better and are more optimistic about the future.

According to research, working up a sweat can increase happiness and mood levels. This is beneficial when you're feeling down and need to adopt a more optimistic outlook, gain some perspective, improve your mood, and begin to feel more at ease and less worried all around. Find a productive, fun hobby that you like doing. When you evaluate where you stand in comparison to others, people who may be suffering or are worse off than you are, it's simple to put things in appropriate perspective when you're feeling sad about yourself, as revealed in research.

Therefore, sharing a little money with others might make us feel happier. Spend a little money to make someone's day better. Numerous studies have demonstrated that sleeplessness causes substantially greater rates of anxiety and despair. You lose some of your capacity to regulate your mood when you lose sleep. Thinking holistically, getting enough sleep is essential for preserving a good outlook since it maintains the levels of hormones like dopamine and serotonin that are associated with a cheerful mood. Note the ones that make you feel depressed, hopeless, or trapped. Writing these ideas down can be helpful since it allows you to step back from them afterward.

Have you ever read a how-to book or attended a seminar and thought, "This is going to revolutionise my life," only to find that you didn't put what you learned into practice? Yes, I agree. It's something we do as people. It occurs in part because merely understanding something intellectually does not necessarily translate into action. Experience-based practise is necessary for new concepts to develop into skills. But it also occurs because it might be challenging to apply new ideas that we acquire in a socially engaged state while we're in a mobilised or immobilised state. For instance, even though you've learned important conversational strategies, you can still retreat or act aggressively when things become heated with a coworker. You know better than how you acted, but it was just a case of your nervous system taking over. The reason for this is that you truly don't have access to the portion of yourself that can respond consciously, whether you're in a mobilised or immobilised state.

You are only able to respond in a more basic way when your main priority is survival. Which gets me to the significance of practise and, more specifically, the significance of activities that will aid in nervous system regulation. This chapter offers a variety of techniques intended to calm your nerves or move you closer to a level of social participation. Additionally, the more consistently you engage in social interactions, the more likely you are to not only put what you've learned in this course to use but also to access all the knowledge and abilities you've previously mastered but may forget when circumstances are very stressful. I urge you to put the techniques in this chapter to the test and add the ones that are effective to your collection of resources for building resilience.

Have you ever been instructed as a youngster not to talk to strangers, not to take sweets from strangers, or not to go anywhere with strangers? If you were, it's probably for the best since it means you might have grown up in a neighbourhood where kidnappings could occur and that your parents wanted you to stick around for a while. However, as you got older, did anyone ever sit you down and explain that strangers in general aren't dangerous and that people are typically nice? Did they assist you in gaining confidence in your own capacity to discern between those you should perhaps avoid and those you don't need to be fearful of? In other words, did they give you the assurance to know which strangers to approach and which to avoid? If you answered "no" to any of these questions, you are in the same situation as the majority of people on earth. If someone did that for you, congratulations! You were lucky. This is only one of countless examples of norms we acquire as kids that continue to limit us as adults. They are the laws that gave rise to the superego, as it is called in psychology.

Your superego loves to warn you against doing anything that even remotely contradicts the rules you learned as a child, not because it's trying to protect you or even because the rules always make sense, but simply because the superego's only job is to get you to do the things you do in the way you do. The superego is described in psychology as the part of a person's mind that act as a self-critical conscience, reflecting social standards learned from parents and teachers. It accomplishes this by acting as the small voice in your mind that deceives you into thinking that you are listening to your own ideas, your own logic, and your own intellect. That is all it cares about and does.

I frequently remark that the superego's greatest ruse is making you believe something is you that it is not. You are not your superego. Your ego is not who you are. You are a human with a superego, and in the end, you are the one who decides whether to pay attention to what the superego is trying to tell you. It's crucial to understand that your superego has two ways of communicating with you. It may communicate with you through the voice in your brain that tells you you aren't clever, funny, or good enough to do what you want to accomplish. It may also warn you that others will reject, tease, or neglect you. It could even predict how you'll feel later on if you try something and fail.

How to control your identity and get rid of self-doubt?

Being able to recognise our superego is the first step in changing it. We need to be able to distinguish between the ideas and feelings that come from our own reason and logic and those that come from our superego. Fortunately, this is fairly easy. When you're at ease and comfortable, your opinions about anything are the result of your own logic. Your superego is the source of the varied ideas you have about the same item while you're under more stress. Your superego is triggered and fed by stress. You comply? Let's imagine that you have a huge meeting coming up and you want to present a novel proposal. The notion to tell everyone in your office about it comes from you when you're relaxed and at ease, perhaps when lounging at home and thinking about it.

However, if those ideas shift when you start to feel anxious or agitated, then your superego is feeding you new ideas. Therefore, if you suddenly change your mind about presenting your idea from being an excellent idea while you're relaxed and comfortable to a terribly horrible idea when the meeting begins and you start to feel a bit uneasy, that is your superego speaking to you. You must also exercise caution since your superego has a strong capacity for persuasion. It will frequently have a variety of justifications for why you shouldn't do it, all of which may sound sensible at the time.

However, the likelihood is that if you do, you'll come to regret it. Such how can we alter the superego so that it begins to assist us rather than hinder us? We only need to put everything you've previously learnt in this course to practise. You may begin to alter your superego by working on your development zone exercises since the superego only picks up new information through experience. We must demonstrate it since we can't argue with it. Your superego begins to adjust as you get more experience doing things you haven't done before or doing things you've done before in novel ways. Your inner confidence will emerge after your superego stops feeding you self-doubting ideas and becomes acclimated to this new way of operating. So here is your workout. Consider a task you can complete today or tomorrow that will undoubtedly cause you to experience some worry or anxiety when the time comes to complete it. After that, go perform that activity and observe how your thoughts alter from the moment you had the notion to the moment you were really doing it. Start with a simple, little project. This isn't about moving really far forward. It just involves becoming aware of the distinction between your thinking and your superego.

To put it another way, your superego is your self-doubt. It can also communicate with you through emotions, which is what typically happens when you don't have a good reason why you can't or won't do something, but the thought of doing it just makes you feel uneasy, uncomfortable, and perhaps even a little queasy. Any of it sound familiar to you? Isn't it a tremendous comfort to know that you aren't the one doing these things? They don't originate from your logic, thinking, or intelligence.

Additionally, they are not from the past or the future. They merely stem from an automatic mental process that was established by the teachings you learned as a youngster. I'm done now. Your superego relies on stale, habitual thinking that may be easily altered. Your superego is simply telling you not to talk to strangers because they might kidnap you, especially strangers who have something you want like status, authority, a job, or attractiveness.

However, your superego doesn't say kidnap because that doesn't work as well anymore in most situations. Instead, it might tell you to be wary of going to a job interview or feeling anxious about being in a room full of people you don't know. That would be an absurd concern for the majority of individuals to have during a job interview. That would be an absurd concern for the majority of individuals to have during a job interview. Since your superego will tell you whatever it can to keep you back, no matter how irrational, as long as it can merely make you believe it, it says "reject" rather than "kidnap," "mock," "despise," or "judge." Now that we are aware of the main causes of our self-doubt, let's go on to the following video and discuss some solutions.

How do you respond to reproach?

There is only one method to escape criticism, according to Aristotle: "Do nothing, say nothing, and be nothing." Not the criticism itself, but avoiding criticism is what weakens you. But it's not simple. If not handled appropriately, criticism feels like a fog of negativity. So let's examine how to respond to criticism appropriately utilising the who, how, and what framework. Choosing who has the right to criticise you is the first step. Not every reviewer is the same. Not every person is given a place at the table. Yes, your boss. either your spouse or your teammates. There is no need to absorb their words. I'm not advocating dismissing all critics. You miss out on some extremely useful criticism. Simply choose your critics carefully; you don't want to give people who shouldn't have influence the opportunity to influence you. Because we're four times more likely to recall criticism than praise, according to study. It's accurate for me. Then consider how to respond to criticism immediately. Only 15% of the criticism we get is justified and beneficial, according to research. However, we pay attention to more than 85% of every complaints. Regarding the 85% of unhelpful criticism you receive, keep in mind that you get to choose who gets to criticise you and how much weight you give their comments.

You must give someone permission before they may treat you unfairly. It may hurt, literally, when 15% of criticism is legitimate. In actuality, the same region of the brain that is activated by rejection is also activated when you suffer physical pain. Consider how Amazon's Jeff Bezos responds to criticism, which he frequently receives. Immediately, he thinks to himself, "Are they right?" Follow suit. If you are aware that the critic is telling the truth, and there probably is some truth in what they are saying, at the very least put aside pride and injured feelings, and gracefully embrace it as a gift that you will use. Instead of shrinking from criticism, acceptance and commitment in the moment help you develop from it. What should you do with criticism going forward? Keep it in perspective, then. Recognise that everything worthwhile will elicit both praise and criticism. Steve Jobs once said that if you want to make a difference or impact the cosmos, you will occasionally sustain dents in your armour. It is preferable to be judged than ignored. Simply take what you can from the critique, make the necessary changes, and keep going.

Popular stand-up comedians, for instance, rehearse their new act hundreds of times in comedy clubs before going on tour, receiving audience feedback each night and working on it to create a better finale and an even funnier show. The who, how, and what model puts criticism into context in order for optimism to follow.

How will you use adversity to create opportunity at work?

What do you do when a horrible incident occurs at work? Many have one of two responses. They either freeze up, unsure of what to do next, or they become too active in an effort to feel as though they are improving the situation. As a result, they do anything and everything, often the wrong thing. Overreacting or freezing up won't make a bad situation better. Instead, adhere to the 2P strategy and maintain your composure while keeping things straightforward and in focus. This is how it goes. Spend 50% of your energy, when anything goes wrong at work, on pragmatism, dealing calmly and logically with the unpleasant situation's repercussions. It feels fantastic to be making progress in the proper direction that will genuinely improve the situation. And what's this? Positivity results from feeling happy. Spend the remaining 50% exploring the options in that circumstance. What is the advantage? What chances arise as a result of the circumstances? You spend 0 percent of your time adding to the negative, since 50 + 50 = 100. I'm done now. Keep it straightforward, narrow your attention, and spend time being practical or considering alternatives to every challenging circumstance you encounter.

Let's discuss a few instances of this. Let's imagine you learn that a presentation you delivered didn't impress your supervisor. We've all experienced it, right? You may do nothing and worry about it all the time. You can overreact and send your boss an apology email while also putting your CV together quickly, right? Alternately, you can adhere to the 2P method by first pondering, "Okay, what are the implications here, and what should I do practically about it?" As a result, you may calmly arrange a meeting with your supervisor to discuss what you could have done better. Consider the alternatives in this circumstance as well. You may view the conversation with your supervisor as an opportunity to demonstrate your openness to criticism, your humility, and your desire to grow. The 2P method is especially effective for dealing with negative coworkers, who, to be honest, are a major contributor to the atmosphere of negativity at work. Imagine spending the entire day with negative people around you.

Keeping a cheerful attitude and being selective with your words. Did you know that the words you choose to express yourself aloud have an impact on how you think and see the world? Let's say a bad thing happens, right? You may declare how terrible this is. Or you may remark that this is difficult. Let's say you receive a list of brand-new assignments. You could remark that this will be tiresome. Or you may reply that this will be a chance to learn. You see what I mean. Using harsher language affects how you will really think about that incident in the future. It may have a negative impact on your outlook on other things. So, you say, hold on a second. My thoughts are beyond my control. What if I suddenly have a pessimistic thought? Am I destined to be trapped in a negative feedback loop? Easy, easy, easy. It all depends on the words you choose.

Research demonstrates that verbalising a negative notion as opposed to simply considering it is 10 times more detrimental to your positive outlook. Of course, it's preferable to make an effort to avoid having such negative ideas in the first place, but it may be much more difficult to manage. Whether or not you decide to express those ideas in words is something you can manage. That's where I can assist. Practice pausing just before you react to anything, considering what you're about to say aloud, and then telling yourself, "Words impact thoughts." After that, soften and neutralise the terminology you employ to define or describe the circumstance. This is not about being too optimistic or lying to yourself. Nevertheless, the reality was admitted. Just be cautious not to let the way you explain things bring you down. So be mindful of your wording if you want to promote positivity rather than the opposite.

Keeping a cheerful attitude through being in the present.

Not a happy mind is one that wanders. According to a Harvard research, our minds are off the task at hand 47% of the time, which artificially lowers our feelings of enjoyment and optimism. Contrarily, consider how a baby's presence may enliven a space. According to psychologists, it's not only because newborns are adorable; it also has a lot to do with how alert and involved they are in the present, their eyes wide open and focused on everything. Someone who gives their whole attention to what is in front of them is obviously magnetic. Much more good energy is generated when you are totally present than when you are disconnected or preoccupied. Practice the presence peak to achieve this. Three factors that when combined provide maximum present-moment awareness. Stop multitasking first, of course. The largest obstacle to being present is multitasking, which, by the way, doesn't get us anything near what we believe it will. According to research, multitaskers lose 40% of their productivity but have higher levels of emotional fulfilment, giving the impression that they are working more efficiently. No matter how excellent you believe you are at it, the mind just isn't capable of doing many tasks at once. Because of this, it has been said that texting and driving is the equivalent of having a blood alcohol level that is three times the legal limit. You can use neuroscience to your advantage.

What you can do is transfer your attention quickly from one item to another, which is what neurology refers to as task switching? But by doing this, you significantly increase the number of mistakes you make and the time it takes to do the jobs you're moving between. Stop trying to multitask and accept that the mind can only focus on one thing at a time. Continuing on, you get the idea. This means that you should make it a point to recognise when your focus is straying or wandering. If you must, excuse yourself and confess your mental state.

People will pick up on your attention-faking if you do it. To keep mindful, make short notes to yourself. Don't zone out, zone in is one of the ones I utilise. Keep your mind clear, don't allow it rule you, and practise mindfulness. Asking oneself this question when you see that you are wandering is one of my favourites. What now occupies my attention? Stopping your inner dialogue as it is happening is also beneficial. And taking a break to focus again. Psychotherapists advise slow, nasal breathing to aid with this since it induces a relaxation response, calms the mind, and makes it simpler to maintain focus.

Because of this, some martial arts teachers actually require their pupils to practise with their mouths full of water. You are compelled to breathe nasally as a result. Sending indications of absorption is the last step, which entails using bodily cues to show that you are totally present. People will notice them and immediately return more positive energy to you. It's a constructive cycle. Keeping eye contact, nodding at key moments, pausing to clarify, taking notes, and publicly indicating that you're paying attention are examples of signals right now. These signals let you properly receive messages and transmit the appropriate message. The key is to always be present, no matter where you are. Positivity results from presence.

Studies have shown that being optimistic at the beginning of the day increases your likelihood of being positive throughout the day by 80%. Every morning, you think about three things: your objectives, your affirmations, and your sparks. with goals first. Setting priorities for your day will prevent scheduling conflicts. I used to start my days by rushing headlong into whatever was in front of me without prioritising or making any sort of strategy. The day quickly came to an end, and to be quite honest, I felt like I had done nothing. It's not a good sensation. I discovered that the best way to start the day was by creating small, related macro and micro goals.

A traditional goal-setting method states that your macro objectives should be the one or two items that are most crucial for you to complete that day. Setting micro objectives, or the list of actions you must take to achieve your macro goals, is where the power lies. It shouldn't be on the list if it doesn't assist you in achieving your macro objectives. I'll use one as an illustration. Let's say that your daily macro aim is to complete drafting an essential report. One of your associated microobjectives may be to do the required research, and another would be to speak with someone who can provide you with crucial information. It is easier to stay focused on the right things when you have your macro and micro goals in front of you.

Moreover, a word of advice Setting global and micro objectives should not seem like a job, but rather inspirational. Now let's talk affirmations. You look at these encouraging sayings, ideas, or images each morning to help you think positively. Now, this may seem absurd, but a study demonstrates that it actually works. Every morning, I repeat a quotation from author Charles Swindoll that I like to think of as my attitude anthem: "Life is 10% what occurs to me, and 90% how I react to it." Make sure your affirmation goes beyond generalised optimism, such as "Anything's possible," and instead supports you in overcoming a particular obstacle to maintaining your optimism. I still have a tendency to react excessively when anything negative happens, so the attitude anthem serves as a good reminder for me. Lastly, a spark It takes a little more effort—both emotionally and physically—to create sparks of happiness to power your day.

Exercise in the morning, meditation, interesting reading, journaling, some me time, or even a nature walk are some ideas. These things have all been shown to promote joyful, upbeat attitudes for the day. For instance, studies suggest that taking a walk in nature may enhance pleasure levels and improve memory and concentration by over 20%. Choose what seems right to you, but make a commitment to lighting sparks. It plays a crucial role in a productive morning routine. In order to have a positive day, start each morning with your objectives, affirmations, and sparks.

How to be remained focus and take preparation for performance?

Let me ask you a few questions, and I'd like you to think about whether you've ever been in any of these scenarios. Have you ever laboured on a presentation or speech, going over every detail and nuance, only to have it fall flat in front of an audience? Even if you have useful knowledge to contribute, do you find it difficult to persuade others? When you're meant to be concentrating on the topic you're providing, do you find yourself sidetracked, thinking about what the audience might think? Almost everyone I've ever coached has expressed one of these fears, but I'll let you in on a little secret.

It's the key to a great performance. It's here. Speeches and presentations, like a live concert or a play, are performances. While content is king, how well it is delivered impacts whether or not the audience is persuaded, and how well it is delivered is determined by practise. I'd like you to think about it from the standpoint of performance. A talented musician recognises the distinction between practising and playing. Performers spend the majority of their time practising and polishing their talents, but all of the practise in the world won't help you if you can't deliver the skills you've acquired on stage, in real time, and under pressure.

There is a significant difference between the performance mindset and the practise mindset. You have the opportunity to play, test new things, review, and correct through practise. You're in go mode for the performance, though. You only have one shot to get it right, and you must keep going ahead. First impressions are crucial, and you must be prepared to deliver regardless of the circumstances. To stay focused on your presentation, keynote speech, major conference, or whatever your mission essential performance is, you'll need mental flexibility. The trick is to prepare for the performance in advance. Consider how you might prepare for your big occasion by practising.

Perhaps it's giving a presentation to a few trusted coworkers or practising your speech in front of friends or family at home. You want to get a sense of the tempo of what you'll be doing, as well as grow accustomed to being a little apprehensive. The observer effect is something to be mindful of. When you're being watched, a certain degree of self-consciousness comes into play. If this isn't something you're used to, being in the limelight may be rather nerve-wracking. However, once you start practising your presentations and key events, this will become nearly second nature to you.

So this is what I'd like you to do. Consider the next major public-facing event where you'll be presenting or speaking. I'd want to challenge you to think of some unique methods to prepare for this event in advance. Don't be concerned if your stuff isn't quite ready for prime time. It is not about the content in this case. It's all about the show. You improve your concentration game by continually detecting important behavioural changes and then reorienting your attention to needed locations. It comes with intentional practise, which is practising with awareness of all the components we want to develop and clarity on how to get there. It forces us to pay undivided attention to each activity we're performing at any given time, allowing you to track our progress and see if you're progressing or not.

How can you enhance your focus by regulating your attention?

Simply expressed, attention management is the act of determining what gets your full attention throughout the day. It's about regaining control over your attention and, hence, taking control of your life, explains Maura Thomas, author of Attention Management. While time management is frequently mentioned in relation to productivity, it does not necessarily work in the long run. Time does not change. It stays the same. Our focus, on the other hand, shifts, and it does so often at times.

Depending on what a person is doing at the time, the brain goes through several cycles throughout the day. Attention management is divided into four quadrants, according to Maura Thomas, and "depends on the degree of control you exercise over your attention." I was distracted and reactive. Your concentration is lost in this region, and you have no control over it. You're usually agitated because you're responding to what's going on around you or within your thoughts. You may be trying to complete your task, but even a little distraction might cause you to fall behind. Scheduling particular periods during the day can also assist in reducing "during work-hours consumption."

The simplest option is to turn off your phone's email notifications. Close any applications or online browsers that hold your email as well. I also manage my email with an app called SaneBox, which filters out messages that aren't important. At the very least, tidy your workstation once a week. On a Friday afternoon, for example, is ideal. This is a soft chore that can be completed quickly because you've probably already mentally checked out for the week.

When you multitask, you're more likely to make mistakes, think less creatively, and damage your brain. If someone initiates a conversation with you and you're busy, gently inform them that you don't have time to chat right now, but that you'll meet up with them after lunch. When you don't want to be disturbed, you may also send out signals without saying anything by wearing headphones, as previously suggested.

For entrepreneurs, relinquishing some control is never easy. However, you must delegate authority to your team. It doesn't imply you should completely check out if you aren't a micromanager. It entails keeping an eye on everyone and mentoring them throughout the day without interfering with their job.

Another approach is to designate one day each week for no meetings, such as the well-known "No Meeting Wednesday." Each week, having a day free of meetings helps everyone focus on their most critical responsibilities without interruption.

Reduce the number of decisions you make on a daily basis as a possible solution. This was accomplished by Barack Obama, Steve Jobs, and Mark Zuckerberg wearing the same attire every day. Others have found success by planning meals for the week, delegating onerous jobs, and automating certain activities, such as scripted email answers and appointment scheduling.

Select a task on which you want to concentrate, one that requires your undivided attention. Remove any visible distractions and settle down. Inform people in your immediate vicinity that they should not bother you until the building is on fire! Set a timer for 25 minutes, then focus entirely on the work at hand. If your mind wanders, bring it back to the present moment. Remind yourself that you only have a few minutes to maintain this level of focus. Take a 5-minute break when the 25 minutes are over. You can perform another "pomodoro," a 25-minute period of intense concentration, when you're ready. You'll be astonished at how well this boosts focus and how much you'll be able to do.

Anticipating at least some of the activities you like on a daily basis is the key to creating joy. Many individuals enjoy simply sitting quietly in peaceful thought for a few minutes. Others find a reason to grin or laugh on a daily basis. Throughout the day, deliberately seek moments of delight. Most people's capacity to focus at work will deteriorate if these mindfulness measures are not implemented. We're all dealing with information overload, more pressure to move quickly, and a work environment that's highly distracted. Our attention is always under attack, resulting in fewer outcomes. Have you observed a difference in your productivity, health, or happiness as a result of this? Now can be a good moment to sharpen your concentration. Harvard psychologists Matthew Killingsworth and Daniel Gilbert sampled over 2,000 individuals throughout their daily tasks and discovered that their brains were not engaged with what they were doing 47% of the time. Even more startling, participants reported feeling less joyful when their minds wandered. According to Killingsworth, "mind-wandering is a great predictor of people's pleasure." "In fact, how often and where our brains leave the present is a stronger predictor of our pleasure than the tasks in which we are engaged."

How will you cultivate habits to improve your attention to detail?

The human mind is not designed to function in a chaotic environment. Your senses are easily distracted, and a small buzz in any part of your environment might cause our attention to shatter. Someone plays a distant tune, and you become distracted; someone texts, and you become distracted; no one does anything, and you become distracted. That is how short your attention span is. Have you ever been watching a movie and noticed something hilariously out of place in a scene, such as a takeout coffee cup on a historical drama set? Perhaps it was a mistake in a book you were reading? In these cases, it indicates that someone was not paying close enough attention to notice these little mistakes. This should go without saying, but because this is a comprehensive list, you must mention it.

When it comes to focusing, the surroundings are the most important factor to consider. Remember to choose peaceful locations with few distractions, enough lighting, and a comfortable seat. Lay down however you choose and put any items you might need nearby, such as a water bottle or food. This will assist you in avoiding thoughts of hunger or thirst. Paying attention to detail entails taking your time and moving at a slower pace. To produce anything of great quality, you'll have to go over it numerous times, maybe over several days or even weeks. Taking the time to proofread your work might be the difference between presenting a document that is filled with errors and one that is completely free of them. Intrinsic motivation is the fuel that keeps you focused for the long haul. Habits of action and thought, high standards, high drive, intrinsic motivation, and passion all contribute to grit. It requires grit to pay attention to the minor things while keeping an eye on the broader picture. It requires practice, just like everything else.

Your first mindful resolution is to dream big.

Staying on target requires overcoming temporary, unpleasant, and unavoidable setbacks. That is why the ability to concentrate is so important. The first, and, in my opinion, most essential, technique to enhance attention is to think hard and long about what you really desire. Close your eyes and think of a goal you'd like to accomplish. Assume that you've already accomplished it. Feel the joy and confidence that comes with it now. Continue to consider the facts: where you are, who is in your immediate vicinity, and what you did to achieve this aim.

It may seem unusual, but thankfulness aids in the development of attention since it trains your mind to search for the positive in every scenario. You are focused on your current condition by being appreciative. You become more aware of the opportunities that are available to you right now. You become more aware of the people who can help you achieve your goal. You're also more aware of the measures you'll need to take to achieve your objective.

Make a commitment to yourself to focus on this objective and write it down. Then you must delve into the weeds. What are the little measures you need to take in order to reach these huge goals? Break down your larger ambitions into smaller, more achievable chunks. Now is the time to concentrate on finishing these stages. To reach them, what do you need to do on a daily, weekly, or monthly basis. Write them down in your grit notebook and keep track of your progress. Smaller objectives that are detailed and practical will help you endure, stick with it, and be tenacious. It all comes down to perseverance and long-term dedication.

Motivation is wonderful, but it is limited.

You all know that motivation fades quickly when you're weary or worn out, so you shouldn't rely on it alone to get things done. Instead, you may boost your drive by forming behaviours that will urge you forward. Here are three techniques to speed up the formation of beneficial habits. First, The capacity to focus is the most fundamental foundation habit that underpins all the others. Because that has been gravely harmed in the age of the internet, make sure you've switched off all alerts on both your phone and your computer. Second, start stacking habits. The anchor is a critical component in habit development.

Your second mindful resolution is always keeping a To-do-list.

Cut off the fluffy duties and focus on the most important elements to achieving your goals—delegate the rest. The easiest way to do this is to have a to-do list that you work on every day. I prefer to write my to-do list on a Post-it note because I enjoy the experience of writing it with a pen and scratching it off when each thing is completed. These low-effort tasks give you a sense of accomplishment and serve as a powerful visual reminder when you glance at your to-do list. You've completed something, which boosts your concentration! That's why having a to-do list is so important; if you have one, you can start accomplishing the low-effort items right away, which will help you gain confidence, drive, and a sense of achievement that you can use to tackle your more difficult activities.

It's crucial to reward yourself for keeping on track, since these emotions of achievement will help you focus on your broader goals. Another thing I've learned about how to increase attention is that if you become sidetracked, don't finish your to-do list, or don't keep a commitment you've made to yourself, there needs to be a consequence. Consequences for failing your concentration tasks are critical because when you don't do something you know you should, you experience a smidgeon of shame, which, if allowed to fester, can sap your drive and happiness. A guilty conscience is completely ineffective. Donating to a cause that you believe in is a terrific consequence you may have for yourself. This will help you retain your concentration since you will still feel good about yourself and will be able to redirect those positive sentiments back towards your objectives.

Your third mindful resolution to have healthy eating.

When you're eating, be aware of your surroundings, savour the flavours, chew carefully, and take pleasure in your meal. You will feel more satisfied with your meals if you chew your food slowly, sit down, and appreciate what you're eating. Being present and attentive to what you're eating will not only help you enjoy your meal better, but it will also help you lose weight. This is a tried-and-true strategy that my wife, a nutritionist, uses to help her clients feel more full and satisfied following a meal. The clever part is that by concentrating on mindful eating, you enhance your attention. Take a seat at a table and eat. There will be no television or cell phones.

Consume your meal and pay attention to how it tastes and feels. Enjoy your meal and pay attention to when you begin to feel full. Allow yourself to effortlessly stop eating when you feel full and satisfied by listening to your body. By being more conscious and focused on how you feel, you may develop the habit of going to bed on time and focusing on your body's fatigue cues. That way, you are providing your body with what it requires, which is adequate rest. When you should be going to bed, most of you disregard our weariness signs and linger online, queueing up the next Netflix film or playing games on your phones.

Your fourth mindful resolution to maintain cleaniness.

So pay attention to the structure of your nights so that you go to bed when your body tells you it's time to relax. Not only when you're tired. Make it a habit to tidy up your workplace desk at the end of each day. Make it a habit to empty your inbox on a regular basis. You don't want any unnecessary distractions to detract from your ability to concentrate. Working on these modest organised activities every day also helps to build that old attention muscle. There is no one-size-fits-all approach to focusing, but I find that clearing everything out and creating a little zone of calm attention works best for me.

Here are some pointers on how to go about it: Shut off your browser and email software. If you need to work in the browser, make sure there are no more tabs or windows open than the one you require. Turn off all notifications. It's hard to concentrate while anything is alerting you to an incoming email, tweet, or Facebook update. Turn off the computer. Turn off your computer, unplug your router, or better yet, go somewhere without the Internet. This is the most effective method for concentrating. Close all except the apps and windows you'll need for this one task. You have a critical responsibility to fulfill and build that amazing Android app, among other things. Make sure your desk is clear. There's no need to waste an entire day doing this; simply stuff everything into a drawer or a box to be sorted later. Don't mess with it right now. In fact, don't fuss with anything-don't stress about having the proper setting, notepad for writing, or anything else.

Your fifth mindful resolution is to detoxing mind-body at regular basis.

Do guided meditations at home to improve your attention-control abilities. Many applications, such as Buddhify, Simple Habits, and Headspace, provide these meditations. These meditations might assist you in being more aware of your thoughts and feelings. When you practise mindfulness, you are developing your capacity to regulate your attention and focus on what you choose rather than what others pick for you. Plug in the headphones. Wearing headphones and listening to decent, tranquil music is ideal if you have others around who could distract you. Use simple software.

Start working on your assignment once you've set up this environment which shouldn't take more than a few minutes. Don't do anything else but that one thing. Switching to another task is not a good idea. Our days have structure and a timetable thanks to schedules. However, not everyone works according to the same schedule. Our capacity to focus and produce is influenced by our natural cycles. The trick is to schedule your most important tasks during your most productive hours of the day. Keep an eye on your body clock.

The majority of us are most awake in the morning, and our attention begins to wane in the afternoon. Binaural beat technology is a sort of brainwave entrainment that uses auditory tones to change a person's main brainwave state into one that is more appropriate or relevant to the work at hand. In each ear, various frequencies of tones are played. Rather than hearing each tone independently, the brain will hear the difference between them.

You may calm and relax your mind by listening to the frequency difference between the tones, or boost your alertness and concentration by listening to the frequency difference between the tones. Binaural rhythms may be found in a variety of locations, including YouTube and Spotify. For obvious reasons, binaural beats must be listened to through headphones to operate correctly. Don't put these small activities off till later, and don't put them at the bottom of your to-do list. Simply do it in two minutes. You might be amazed at how much you can get done in a few minutes, such as writing an email or cleaning your desk. Caffeine, a natural stimulant, has been demonstrated in studies to accomplish precisely that. Coffee and other caffeinated beverages are cognitive enhancers that help you focus and concentrate better.

However, the more caffeinated beverages you consume, the more your body adapts to the stimulant and the less effect it has on you. Limit your intake to just one cup. Before you settle down to work, take a ten-minute stroll up and down a flight of stairs, or better yet, go outside and ride your bike or take a fast walk around the building or block. While it may appear that you are wasting time since you are not working, the opposite is true: you are preparing your brain and body to maximise your attention at work. While it may appear that you are wasting time since you are not working, the opposite is true: you are preparing your brain and body to maximise your attention at work.

Your sixth mindful resolution to Prioritise tasks in hand.

Don't worry if you can't concentrate on a single job for lengthy periods of time. That's quite typical. Technology and culture have conditioned your minds to switch jobs often. Switching to check email, blog updates, or Facebook/ Twitter is beneficial in one way: you are rewarded with a small morsel of satisfaction in the form of someone sending us a message social validation! or having something fresh and fascinating to read shiny and bright!. Switching tasks creates a positive feedback loop that is difficult to break. You only have so much time and energy, and you'll almost certainly never have enough of either to get everything done that you believe you need to do every day. A growing amount of evidence suggests that humans operate in natural 90-minute cycles. You're more equipped to engage and focus throughout these cycles. This is followed by around 20 minutes of lower frequency brain activity, during which you may experience brain fog and have difficulty concentrating.

Use this natural cycle to your advantage by working in 90-minute intervals and taking a break in between. What you really need to do is prioritise the tasks that are most essential to you. Not everything on your to-do list needs to be done right now. While deadlines can help with procrastination, research has shown that self-imposed deadlines don't work for serious procrastinators. Hard deadlines that are evenly spread out, on the other hand, are the most effective. Set strict deadlines with your supervisor or customer if you're having trouble finding your mojo for a project, and make sure they're realistic and spread out enough to complete the assignment.Giving yourself some "do not disturb" time isn't the only way to speed through your responsibilities. Inform your coworkers that you will be unavailable for meetings or appointments during this period. Cutting out concentrated time reduces interruptions and allows you to work more deeply. When you compartmentalise your time, your brain is able to isolate a task, allowing you to focus entirely on that activity without being distracted by something else.

Prioritising for the things that matter most to you.

People frequently tell me that they spend the least amount of time with the people who matter the most to them. What caused this to happen? The idea of a residual benefactor is central to the concept. A residual benefactor is the person, or chump, who gets the leftovers when a firm goes bankrupt. In most cases, the residual benefactor does not do well. And that idea has stayed with me because I remember thinking to myself, "Wow, I don't want to turn anyone I care about into a residual benefactor." That is to say, if individuals in your life are essential to you, they are entitled to a spot on your calendar. As a result, setting aside time for traction is critical.

I prefer to categorise how we spend our time into three categories. You have time in the middle sphere. It's difficult to care for and love people, much less do your best work, if you're not in good physical and mental health. Outside of yourself, there are significant people in your life, your community, your friends, and your family. Finally, there are your career and professional responsibilities to consider. As a result, we must arrange time in our day for each of these domains, beginning with ourselves.

Do you have enough time for sleep, mental sustenance, audiobooks, viewing things you like, enhancing our lives in various ways, and physical activity? All of it would fall under your area of influence. Then we have to schedule time for the key people in our lives so that they don't become residual benefactors. Finally, we must create time for these job duties, as well as all of the other things we must do in our daily lives to ensure that our careers are on track. The majority of folks do it backwards. They first fulfil all of their professional commitments, then leave the rest to the individuals who matter most to them.

Your seventh mindful resolution is practicing attitude of gratitude.

It may seem unusual, but thankfulness can help you focus since it trains your mind to search for the good things in life. Attention to detail is a necessary talent for many jobs. This is especially true in professions that require a high level of attention to detail. These can range from design to financing to construction and will require you to deal with people, language, figures, or a combination of all three.

"Constant interruptions are the destruction "of the imagination."

It's difficult to get back into the creative flow if you've been stopped when working on anything creative. Distractions obstruct not only the capacity to produce high-quality work on time, but also the deep and broad attention required to tap into great creativity. Finally, I'd like you to think about what measures you may take to reclaim control of your gadgets. Here are a few simple methods to start changing your habits and improving your attention.

- Use an internet blocker on your computer to manage your online surfing habits.
- Allow yourself to benefit from uninterrupted work periods. Rather than battling the difficulties of returning to your original task after a surfing session, eliminate the temptation.
- You may also wean yourself off of your smartphone. Unnecessarily, people look at their mobile devices hundreds of times every day
- Hougaard describes eight mental habits that everyone should develop in order to keep their minds clear and tranquil, as well as boost their overall productivity.
- Focus and mindfulness are built on a foundation of presence. It entails paying close attention to the people, objects, and ideas that surround you at all times.
- Patience is more concerned with long-term goals than with short-term fixes. Before reacting, practise stopping and taking a few deep breaths to calm yourself. Instead

of spontaneous reactions, give reasonable replies.

- Be considerate of others. Treat others with respect. as you would like to be treated. Practice by demonstrating attention, respect, understanding, and acceptance in all of your interactions with others.
- Practice by consciously rejecting any habitual perceptions and forcing yourself to be more curious about your daily activities. Approach every circumstance with the mindset of a beginner.
- Practice by deciding to go on without an inner conflict after all reasonable attempts have been exhausted.
- Avoid prolonged battles with problems you can't solve.
- Let go of a nagging problem or a constant source of distraction, such as a new email or text message. To concentrate your mind, practise relaxing and breathing at regular intervals. Let go of weighty thoughts and distractions consciously.
- Anticipating at least some of the activities you like on a daily basis is the key to creating joy. Many individuals enjoy simply sitting quietly in peaceful thought for a few minutes. Others find a reason to grin or laugh on a daily basis.
- Throughout the day, deliberately seek moments of delight. Most people's capacity to focus at work will deteriorate if these mindfulness measures are not implemented. We're all dealing with information overload, more pressure to move quickly, and a work environment that's highly distracted.
- Our attention is always under attack, resulting in fewer outcomes. Have you observed a difference in your productivity, health, or happiness as a result of this? Now can be a good moment to sharpen your concentration.

- When you go out, leave your phone at home or disable internet browsing and use it just as a phone.
- Break your day into time-bound, manageable pieces with particular activity items in mind to help you focus.
- In certain cases, time pressure is an excellent strategy to keep you focused.
- You can only stay concentrated for so long while producing high-quality work.
- Breaking your work into 20 to 30-minute pieces can provide you with a foundation for focusing intently in shorter sessions while also allowing you to stay on track without becoming bored.
- It's not about getting rid of your devices at the end of the day; it's about putting in place limits to better manage your concentration.
- Limiting internet access, locking your phone away, and setting time limitations as you plan your day will help you reclaim control of your concentration and be more productive.

You can choose what to refuse.

It's likely that you've come to this page because you need to refuse requests for your time or take on more tasks. While helping out or challenging yourself generally isn't improper, be sure you're saying yes for the correct reasons. Here are five considerations to bear in mind when you choose what is best for you. When your core work tasks may suffer, first think about declining. Assume you are a member of the product team but have been requested to assist with marketing due to a staffing shortage. Your main work tasks, such as user research or strategy, may soon start to suffer as a result of the amount of time you spend evaluating promotional items. While I would love to assist, there are some other responsibilities I need to attend to this week, so I'm sorry but I'm unable to. When it's someone else's responsibility, you should likewise decline.

Like the sales representative who suddenly finds themselves answering customer support calls, it's easy to get drawn into doing tasks that aren't your responsibility. Consider whether the task makes a significant contribution to your professional progress. If it doesn't, you may say, "It's outside of my scope, therefore I can't take it on." Offer an alternative that involves hiring a contractor or another team member to complete the task. And the third need is to refuse when there is no escape plan. When you are certain that you are aware of the entire extent of what is involved, only take on new duties. You don't want it to be an open-ended agreement because you want to avoid future misunderstandings.

Let's say your employer approaches you inexplicably for advice on a new project. Obtain details. How much time must you devote to the project? Which meetings are you required to go to? Once you've decided it's not a good fit, thank your supervisor for the chance. If you're feeling really brave, state that you don't feel like you'd be set up for success and that you couldn't pursue the project knowing you wouldn't be able to reach the objective since it doesn't line up with your professional goals. Saying no when a request is ridiculous is the fourth requirement.

Perhaps top management has asked for a brand-new business strategy within two business days. You provide a new deadline or describe which portion of the task you can finish in that time because you are aware that this is not achievable. The fifth and final criterion is to refuse when it conflicts with your ideals. For instance, if you know a coworker has a poor performance record, don't recommend them for a position at your organization. Most importantly, resist the urge to participate in any activity or assignment that you believe goes against your deepest convictions out of guilt. You may say, "I cannot, in good conscience, join in this initiative, but I send my best wishes your way." Even if you can't say no to everything, saying no when you have good reasons will make you feel more in control and secure.

How to deal with guilt while declining?

When we have disappointed others, fallen short of a standard, or committed a sin, we experience guilt. It's crucial to determine if you're feeling guilty because of good or bad behavior. Guilt that is healthy has a use. It alerts you to your improper behaviour and may inspire you to change your ways or at least make apologies. On the other side, unhealthy guilt is inappropriate. Even when we've done nothing wrong, we nevertheless feel it. Here are some strategies to deal with the toxic guilt that many of us feel when we say no. Start by assessing what is under your control and what is not. Pick up some paper and a pen. Draw a circle on it. If you'd rather use one, I've built one in the exercise files. Write down everything that is under your control inside the circle. This encompasses your ideas, deeds, responses, attitude, posture, tone, and even how well you eat and how much sleep you receive. Spend a moment doing this.

Next, list anything that is beyond your control on the outside of the circle. things like the opinions, sentiments, errors, or ineffective time management of others.

Furthermore, factors such as the state of your business or the economy play a role. I advise keeping this graphic handy or pinning it to your desk so you can refer to it the next time you need some more self-assurance. Self-talk modification is also essential. Saying no will only make you feel worse if you convince yourself that you are a nasty person for doing so. actively attempt to develop a more positive inner story. You may remind yourself that you have the same right to guard your time and energy as anybody else has. I personally find it beneficial to remind myself that it's possible to be both compassionate and firm at the same time. You haven't necessarily done something wrong just because you're feeling guilty. In reality, it shows that you are concerned. Reframe those negative emotions as a sign that you are establishing boundaries.

Finally, an idea that is extremely doable. Set a goal and a timer. According to research published in the journal "Motivation and Emotion," emotions of guilt normally persist between 30 and 90 minutes. Set a timer, and during that interval, give yourself permission to completely experience and process your emotions. After the timer rings, decide how you want to feel about going ahead and what steps will bring you there. Perhaps you want to feel calm. You may take a little meditation break or a break to take your dog for a stroll. Above all, be kind to yourself. You're a kind person, so work on putting your unhealthy guilt in perspective, and you'll see a shift in how you react over time. Be firm while denying something.

Active listening can help ease stress by: James was a customer of mine once. He spent a lot of his time telling people no while working as a product lead for a computer business. Naturally, in addition to leading the product vision and development, he frequently had to decline feature requests, give some tactics the highest priority, and let people down by selecting some team members for projects rather than others. James was adored by his direct reports, his employees, and the executive team despite frequently having to say no. Furthermore, it wasn't only due to his excellent product management abilities, which he possessed. It was partly due to the way he handled resistance. James didn't just ignore sales' demands for a new product dashboard, for example. Instead, he gave them the benefit of the doubt, and they ultimately came to a compromise. What then was James' technique for reducing tension? It was active listening, which is a term for strategies that support sympathetic interaction with others.

Let's go over some strategies for using active listening when dealing with the resistance that results from saying no. The first step is to validate the other person, or to let them know they are seen and heard. Validation might appear like this: "I am aware of how crucial having coverage is for this undertaking." "I would want to make sure we were ready if I were in your position. Another excellent expression is, "That is entirely logical." "I understand your perspective." Through your body language, such as nodding and saying, "mm-hmm," you may also validate someone. The next step is to paraphrase or restate the individual's objections. What I hear you saying is that you're disappointed that I can't make the meeting," and "It seems like the team's availability on Tuesday is what matters most to you."

How to overcome impostor syndrome?

According to psychologists, 70% of people will experience impostor syndrome at least once in their lives. Imposter syndrome is the belief or sense that we are faking everything right now and don't truly deserve what we have. It doesn't matter who you are, it just doesn't matter what you have. Even the famous individuals we watch on television and in movies, people who have all the success that most people only dream of, struggle with it. People who are multilingual and renowned, such as Natalie Portman, a Harvard psychology graduate. Ryan Reynolds, Meryl Streep, Emma Watson, and Daniel Radcliffe have all openly discussed having impostor syndrome in their professional lives.

No matter what we've accomplished, Tom Hanks claimed in an interview from 2016 that there comes a time when you question, "What brought me here? When will they realise that I am a phoney and seise what I have earned?" Imposter syndrome becomes important when it comes to boosting our self-assurance in circumstances when our mind tells us that we're just acting confident, that we're clueless, that people shouldn't respect or pay attention to us, and so on. These are all common sentiments for people who wish to be more confident but don't feel that way by nature.

As a result, when they stand up in front of a group and others pay attention, they begin to persuade themselves that those individuals are just being kind, feeling sorry for them, or other similar justifications. And thinking in this way simply helps to undermine our confidence. Along with working on the exercises I've previously given you in this course, it's crucial to keep in mind that you don't actually feel like an impostor. It's a notion you've conjured up in your head based on outdated assumptions or knowledge. No matter how you feel about it, if you can accomplish anything, you can do anything.Because, once more, those emotions aren't caused by what's going on outside of you or by others thinking you're a fraud. These fictitious ideas in your head are the only source of the impostor thoughts.

So, feeling like an impostor while performing an action is similar to thinking you don't know how to run while participating in a marathon. What you're doing and how you're doing it are genuine even though it doesn't seem like it, unless you're truly talking lies. And if you ever lose sight of that, even for a little moment, simply tell yourself that the impostor syndrome will pass if you just keep doing what's working.And if you ever lose sight of that, even for a little moment, simply tell yourself that the impostor syndrome will pass if you just keep doing what's working. Simply give your brain some time to catch up and acknowledge that you are now a different person.

How can negative self-talk be stopped?

An average individual has 60,000 thoughts each day, of which 45,000 are unhelpful, repeated ones. The objective is to silence the negative inner chatter, which is made more difficult by the fact that we create the majority of our negative ideas. We say things to ourselves like, "Ah, I'm such a loser." My supervisor doesn't seem to like me. I'm performing worse than my classmates. We continually criticise ourselves by engaging in restricting beliefs, actions, and attitudes. Why do we do it when we frequently aren't even aware that we're doing it, and even when we are, we still aren't able to stop?

How can you stop the self-talk and better embrace your differences?

By pausing to practise self-compassion there three steps are involved. Begin by just acknowledging your feelings without passing judgement. Don't punish yourself for punishing yourself. Then, at that same moment, speak to yourself as you would a buddy going through a difficult period.For instance, would you listen to a friend's tale and then tell them they are a total loser if they had just made a major error in a significant meeting and needed some encouragement? Of course not, so why would you speak to yourself in that manner? final stage Keep in mind the 90:10 ratio. A straightforward method to determine your worth is the ratio 90:10. Self-worth, your own self acceptance and admiration, and self-love should account for 90% of how you should feel about yourself, with 10% coming from assigned worth. how people, such as your boss or neighbour, perceive you. Those who believe that your self-worth should solely come from you and not from what other people think may not agree with the 10% allowance for external validation. But since I'm practical, I know that it's unreasonable to assume that individuals would always feel the need to receive affirmation from others. The issue develops when the 10% of external validation we occasionally require in that 90:10 ratio becomes to be a far larger portion of how we value ourselves. Keep your attention on the 90% and consider the 10% to be occasional affirmation. Seek sincerity rather than acceptance. Therefore, avoid engaging in negative self talk. Spring forward and let go.

How can you get over your fear of failing?

50% of individuals claim that their greatest obstacle to goal achievement is their fear of failing. Whoa, our paralysing fear of failing prevents us from taking the chances and doing the things required to go toward our objectives. Our huge ideas are snuffed out, our capacity to anticipate potential is diminished, and our optimistic attitude is crushed. Let's look at how the term "courageous," which stands for "be brave," might help us overcome our fear of failing and the associated negativity. B is for burn the boats; when sea-going ancient Greek forces arrived on hostile territory, they would do so before engaging in combat. There was no going back as a result. Simply taking the first step in your plan is one of the most effective strategies to overcome your fear of failing, according to research.

Fear of failure vanishes when you realise you can no longer run from failure and there is no turning back. Next, review your standards again. Perhaps you're holding back because you're worried that you won't live up to the unreasonable bar you've set for yourself. Say, for instance, that you have been dreaming of starting your own business but have yet to do so because your high definition of success is earning a million dollars in the first six months. Setting realistic goals aids in reducing fear.

Now, I'm not advocating lowering your standards unduly; I'm simply suggesting that you steer clear of establishing objectives that are so ambitious that you start to feel like you'll never achieve them. The first question is, "What exactly am I afraid of?"Most of the time, our fear of failure is unfounded. We're terrified of experiencing the shame that comes with failure, and shame is toxic because it makes you feel awful about who you are rather than guilty or remorseful about your deeds or attempts. Realise that failing is not anything to be embarrassed of. It indicates that you've changed how you present yourself to the outside world, which is excellent.

Also, consider if the things you are afraid of are actually likely to occur. Or do you just imagine the worst-case scenarios in your thoughts, which is normal? Validate your assumptions after that. Assumptions are used to replace uncertainty, which is, to put it bluntly, frequently useless and inaccurate. Determine the underlying presumptions that underlie your fear of failing and confront them. You could believe, for instance, that you are incapable of making an effective speech in front of a crowd because no one would be interested in what you have to say. Well, that is a presumption that has to be contested. The final step is to look at prior failures. You've failed before and managed to survive. Most certainly, it helped you grow. Consider times when you have felt defeated.Consider instances when, despite the anguish, failure helped you become a bit stronger.

Do not undervalue your capacity for recovery. Consider Oprah Winfrey, who was dismissed from a position as a television news anchor in the past, or prepare yourself for this one: Walt Disney, who was fired from a job as a newspaper reporter in the past for lacking creativity Don't let fear of failure dictate your actions; instead, be brave, take the initiative, and take a moment to appreciate the opportunity for good that will arise.

How do you keep your temper in check?

Have you ever gotten angry? Naturally, you have. Have you ever felt confident afterward? Most likely not. When you lose your temper, you either create or exacerbate a bad situation. So, how do you avoid it? Consider the balled-up fist as a representation of rage and losing your cool. Consider the image of palms up, or outstretched hands, as a sign of peace. When you notice that your anger is rising, recall the word "palms" and hold your hands palms-up, facing up.

Visualise writing it out with one of your hands. Each fingertip has a letter that stands for project, accept, laugh, measure, and separate. You may gently remove yourself from an agitated situation with the use of these phrases. Science has shown that maintaining your composure requires calm distance. Look at each one, Project.

Ask yourself what picture I'm about to convey if I lose my anger. It never turns out well. Frequently, angry words are regretted. "Think before you speak" is the Mayo Clinic's suggestion for preventing furious outbursts. Imagine how you're going to come across or the harm your words are going to do when you're thinking. Sincerity dictates that you move cautiously.

You may even visualise a camera in the room's far corner capturing and broadcasting your response to everyone. What will the world see that you will be proud of? Accept. Your fury may be erupting merely because you reject an opposing viewpoint, but there are more appropriate responses to have. In the heat of the moment, reminding yourself to acknowledge, rather than criticise, the opposing point of view demonstrates that you value the alternative perspective. I often quote the proverb, "If everyone thinks similarly, someone isn't thinking."

Acceptance is an important word for you if you occasionally have strong opinions or are closed-minded. Laugh. Finding humour in the situation helps calm anger. After all, laughing is the exact opposite of becoming upset. I used to crack jokes with my colleagues during tough situations. I used to crack jokes with my colleagues during tough situations. It made the atmosphere in the room more pleasant, prevented me from reacting furiously, and helped us stay on track. Sincerity be damned, my teammates informed me they admired what I was attempting to do.

The word measure is next. Measure the response you're about to deliver as soon as possible. Is it appropriate given the current offence? Probably not. If you're being honest with yourself, you know it's going to be over the top. And be aware that, according to the study, outbursts frequently result from a quick response to someone's tone. So pay attention to their purpose rather. For instance, consider what they are actually trying to convey before retaliating.

What point are they conveying by saying that their tone is obscure? Take a moment to think about this, refrain from overreacting, and replace it with curiosity. Finally, divide. Distinguish the individual from the point. Conflict frequently develops not from the issue at hand but from tension in an underlying connection. as an example. Focus on the arguments they're trying to make rather than what you think of the individual when you're engaging with someone who bothers you. You'll wrongly assess what they're trying to communicate if you don't. Yes, it might be challenging to keep your cool under pressure, but while you have no control over your feelings, you do have power over how you respond.

The body's direction is expressed through the actions it takes. A concept originates in the mind and is subsequently translated into certain physical acts. For instance, if the concept of anger is generated in the head, the body will undoubtedly feel it and express its wrath through certain acts. Therefore, we may certainly channel our life energy through these beliefs.

Everything on an intellectual level needs to be balanced, whether it's the quantity of thoughts produced or just a quality check. Only Prana can assist us in being intellectually sound and psychologically healthy. Prana gets boosted and strengthened as a result. Negative and pointless ideas produce negativity and drain energy. We only need to keep in mind how significant each notion is. We should occasionally take a little pause from our job to assess the type of thoughts we are generating.

Let them flow if they're good. We must swap out negative, damaging thoughts for constructive ones. We can't help but think. The brain's job is to generate ideas. Therefore, we must swap our negative thoughts for positive ones. This is true because our ideas, which are what shape our personalities, are what determine our fate. No personality programme has the power to alter us permanently. We are the ones who must put forth the effort, and awareness is the only way to achieve this. We should carefully build our thoughts since they shape our personalities and futures in every way.

Every idea we have is translated into an action, and that action then shapes our character and personality and ultimately our fate. As a result, it is believed that thought develops individuality and character. Unnecessary ideas and needless deeds merely waste and drain the body's vital energy, leaving it depleted and worn out. Only the absolutely necessary should be considered, and extreme caution should be avoided. Every idea we have should be constructive and beneficial. This improves the atmosphere around us. The outward circumstances of a person's existence will always be discovered to be harmoniously tied to his inner state because "thought and character are one, and thus character can only manifest and reveal itself via environment and situation." Allen James

We should carefully build our thoughts since they shape our personalities and futures in every way. Every idea we have is translated into an action, and that action then shapes our character and personality and ultimately our fate. As a result, it is believed that thought develops individuality and character.

Be mindful of your ideas since they influence the words you say. Be cautious about what you say because what you say affects what you do. Be mindful of your behaviour since it shapes your habits. Be mindful of your habits since they shape who you are. Be mindful of your character, since it determines your fate. Lao Tzu's Chinese proverb

There are wonderful sayings from the past that still apply to our day and merit repetition. We can learn that we were given instructions on how to control or steer our fate if we take our time and carefully consider what was said so many years ago. Most of the time, what we believe ends up in someone else's ears after we speak. Our words have an effect on how we feel about ourselves, as well as on how other people think and feel. Words serve as symbols via which we may express to ourselves and to others what is happening in our minds. With our words, we express our worries, grief, joy, love, and hopes.

Our words inspire movement. Our words may foster closeness or distance. We can use the power of our words to motivate people to assert their personal authority and achieve things they never thought they were capable of accomplishing on their own. In fact, words have the power to alter the course of a nation. So be mindful of your thoughts, the words that flow from them, and the actions that result from those words.

A habit is an action we frequently perform automatically. We just naturally do it. When we perform a certain activity and it feels good or produces the desired consequences, we frequently repeat it. Some behaviours might be helpful, while others can be harmful. It's often referred to as an addiction if it causes harm. It's said to be a good discipline if it's useful. Small, unconscious "habits" that we perform throughout the day fill our days.

Some of us have a tendency to be neat or dirty, early or late, impolite or polite, joyful or furious, or early or late. All of these are routine states of being. As a result, our habits shape who we are or our character. However, if I think positively and work toward my goals, my future may be one that is upbeat, joyful, and occasionally ecstatic. If my tendency is to get up one more time than I fall, my destiny will be one of success even if I stumble and acquire a few bruises in the process. Because of my optimistic outlook, people will want to be near me. They'll be curious to learn how I manage to produce so many lovely things in my life. I'll freely provide the happiness and love that permeate my heart because of my richness and my kind nature.

Thus, I develop a character intended for improvement by thinking positively and consistently acting positively. Our fate is determined by the ideas and deeds we repeat throughout time. Negative thoughts and judgments of others and myself will cause me to act in a negative manner, and I will attract what I concentrate on. Because they don't enjoy being judged, and they don't like hearing me evaluate others, most people won't want to be near me. My feelings of victimisation and loneliness will keep repeating, and eventually my future will seem grim. The core of your characters' identities are their ideas and convictions.

Every move they make, every line of conversation they use, and every gesture they make should be crafted with them in mind. But eventually, it's time to deal with the ideas themselves, not as the basis for other behaviours but as the essential aspects that they are. When that time comes, a lot of writers struggle to deal with such a crucial aspect of their characters and tale.

How will you become a detail-oriented person?

While it's a wonderful quality to have, what does it truly imply? Furthermore, should you be portraying yourself as detail-oriented when it's possible that's not the case? You frequently hear people characterise themselves as detail-oriented. Employers frequently state that they require the most detail-oriented individuals on their teams. It means the employees' ability to pay close attention and notice minute details is referred to as being detail-oriented. Employees that are detail-oriented are frequently good at recognising faults in procedures. An editor or writer, for example, can verify texts and materials for grammatical errors with great care. An accountant may be detail-oriented in the same way by guaranteeing numerical precision.

Employees that are detail-oriented work methodically to produce an efficient, high-quality output with few or no mistakes. Being detail-oriented entails cultivating habits that help you focus and become more aware of your surroundings. It entails establishing a mental pattern that might assist you in better planning your day and responsibilities. Being detail-oriented is an essential skill that enables you to advance in your career and become a reliable employee. A detail-oriented individual may devote their complete attention to a task and spot flaws, errors, or modifications before they become a greater issue.

- What does it mean to be detail-oriented?
- Are you a person who pays attention to the smallest details?
- How are you going to describe yourself in an interview about your detailed orientation?

Individuals who are detail-oriented do things that people who do not have the attribute do not. However, just because you do some of those things doesn't mean you're detail-oriented. At some point in your career, you've probably used the term "detail-oriented" to describe yourself on your résumé or in a job interview. Let's find out some characteristics of a detailed-oriented person.

- They are self-critical always seeking ways to improve themselves. Self-critical attention to detail is a trait that many people use against themselves.
- Intelligent in terms of emotions, Similarly, those who are detail-oriented are effective at picking up on other people's feelings. They pick up on clues that others miss, and they connect the dots to figure out what that person is really thinking and feeling.
- A strong accent, for example, may be detected by anyone, and faces can be remembered by anyone. People with above-average attention to detail have certain habits, I've discovered. If more than half of these apply to you, you're probably a detail-oriented person.
- A detail-oriented individual pays close attention to the smallest of details. They're meticulous, accurate, well-organised, and efficient.
- They are meticulous in their attention to detail.They recall people's names once they've been introduced to them, and they don't forget birthdays or deadlines no

matter how big or small.

- They try to figure out what is causing or what is causing a problem.
- They're a grammar geek or they could be an Oxford comma fanatic.
- They are aware of body language and social cues. This implies that they may pick up key clues about how to deal with someone by paying attention to their position, tone of voice, or emotions.
- Detail-oriented people pay extra close attention to the small details, but that sounds a little too high-level to be a trait that an employer can't live without, right?
- They are detail-oriented enjoy order and structure because it allows them to stay focused on the work at hand. Maintaining a procedure allows you to stay organised and on track.
- They value their time and are rarely late for meetings, deadlines, or activities. They have adequate time to take on new tasks and obtain new experience because they are skilled at managing time.
- They're obsessively organised thus they rely on their planners or Google calendars to keep track of their schedules.
- They have a high level of efficiency and effectiveness in their operations. They can contribute to the success of your team.
- Being a team player comes naturally to them. You know you can depend on them to bring something to the table, whether it's extensive reports, well-thought-out ideas, or exhaustive notes.
- It keeps this meticulous learner from learning new things every day.

- They arrive prepared for meetings, plan ahead for tasks, and set realistic deadlines. Detail-oriented people recognise that planning is essential to their own and their team's success.
- They provide a well-polished and high-quality work product. It's no surprise that people who are meticulous have high expectations.
- They Use attention to detail to understand the bigger picture entails seeing the ripple effects of each action.
- They may be relied upon by coworkers and friends to be the group's documentarian.
- Prudent people consider how their actions may affect the future. Thinking about "what if" scenarios necessitates a systems approach.
- They review it and double-check it for typos and grammatical problems, set it down, double-check it for context and completion, and do it all over again. They can repeat this process until they have a product that they are happy with.
- They ask probing questions to learn all there is to know about what they're attempting to achieve, why they're working toward that objective, and everything else in between.
- Detail-oriented people pay close attention to the structure and grammar of whatever they write. They want to put their best foot forward at all times. This is closely related to proofreading.
- They don't allow any details to fall between the gaps since they have an analytical mind.
- Detail-oriented individuals are incredibly perceptive, and they can read the moods of those around them by observing their body language, which becomes much more powerful once they speak.

- They're always ready to go. The name of the game is planning, and they play to win.
- They pay attention to the details pick up on signs like body language, tone, and emotions throughout encounters. By enhancing their emotional quotient and empathy, they become better coworkers and people.
- They are people who are usually quick to see problems and correct them. Their great attention to the smallest details aids them in avoiding mistakes even while the job is being done.
- They may keep notes of important dates, recurring tasks, and instructions related to their jobs. They can accomplish this by keeping track of time and tasks in a diary or by utilising a web or mobile application.
- They stay motivated to accomplish their deadlines throughout the day. They concentrate on one task at a time and avoid distractions in order to do the work quickly and accurately.

Some sort of direction is being given on what people have in terms of detail-oriented talents, so you can emphasise them the next time you're asked to be precise in a job interview.

- Inquisitiveness pays off when it leads to useful knowledge that they would not have discovered otherwise. Your inquisitive attitude helps you obtain knowledge and solve difficulties.
- Curiosity is the cornerstone of knowledge acquisition. The more you learn, the more informed you will be about the world.
- Time management is an important, detail-oriented ability. You're starting from a disadvantage if you don't

know how to effectively manage your time. This frequently entails planning and preparation so that you may attack a task head-on and completely equipped.

- Organising your workspace might help you be more productive and concentrate better. A tidy workstation reduces distractions and allows you to concentrate. It also alleviates the burden of looking for stationery, paperwork, or other necessities. Apart from keeping your desk tidy, it's also important to keep your computer data organised.
- Being detail-oriented necessitates paying attention to nonverbal clues, which may be useful in your profession. Active listening allows you to pay attention to the speaker and draw conclusions or important points from what they say. This might happen in everyday conversation or at business meetings. Listening intently to others encourages you to think and ask questions that may add a fresh viewpoint to the conversation.
- To boost effectiveness and avoid extended periods of distraction, take regular breaks and schedule them on your calendar.
- Meditation or yoga practise can also aid in focus and awareness. All of these exercises help your brain and body recharge and become more productive.
- You'll likely boost your effectiveness if you manage your time effectively by delegating tasks, eliminating needless procedures, creating goals, and saying "no" when it makes sense.
- Everything you do has a useful perspective as a result of this. So, in your daily life and beyond, don't be hesitant to ask questions and scrutinise the people and things you come across.

- Micromanagers want to be copied on every email, expect continuous updates, and may never appear satisfied with the final output. You may defend yourself against charges of being a micromanager by stating your "why" to your employees.
- What if you wish to recall the details yet are aware that you are forgetful? That's not an issue! Recognising that you're not great at remembering things is half the fight.
- To ensure you don't forget, use tricks like taking extensive notes in meetings, setting reminders on your phone, and adding crucial dates and information to your calendar.
- Proofreading your work before turning it in to your employer, or even an email before sending it to a friend, is standard procedure. Proofreading, on the other hand, isn't a one-and-done transaction for individuals who value accuracy. It's standard procedure for them to finish their task, set it aside, and return to it a few minutes to a few days later.
- Before you push send on that email, make sure you're portraying yourself at your best and that you've put your finest work forward before your big presentation. It can also help you avoid awkward situations in the future.
- By asking questions, you can guarantee that they completely comprehend what they're doing. They don't go into projects with any preconceived notions.
- Don't let your concern about coming out as a perfectionist prohibit you from producing high-quality work if you're detail-oriented.
- According to a study published in Harvard Business Review, emotional intelligence is responsible for over 90% of great performers' success. This talent is very

valuable at work. It is advantageous to know when and what to say at the appropriate moments, as well as when to be empathic.

- Organisation is a crucial, detail-oriented talent. To have a high-efficiency job and a personal life, you must establish a fool-proof strategy that works.
- Explain why the report's accuracy is so critical if you're requesting a tenth revision. Perhaps you'll be presenting to the CEO or the board of directors, and any errors will reflect negatively on you and your team.
- Strong organisational skills set a good example for your coworkers and demonstrate that you are serious about your work. Keeping things in order reduces stress, gives you more control, and helps you achieve personal achievement.
- Before diving into a job or project, identify potential roadblocks, conduct necessary research, and devise a strategy to help prevent complications on the back end and ensure a smoother overall process.
- Explaining your goal will help people see things through your eyes if you're making demands that might come off as micromanaging. Then it's up to you to believe that they're capable of doing the task.
- Effectiveness guarantees that you are contributing value to the work at hand while also completing it. While getting the task done correctly should be your top concern, detail-oriented people understand that time is money. To achieve your full potential, you must strike a good balance between efficiency and effectiveness.
- It's because they understand that the work they do reflects their brand. People learn that they can rely on you to get the job done, and more importantly, to get it done effectively, when you regularly create a fantastic

product. You're providing a product you can feel good about if you don't provide your seal of approval until everything is exactly as it should be.

- It also signifies that you're reducing distractions when working on a task. Yes, you're referring to your smartphone. Turning off alerts or putting your phone on aeroplane mode for a while can help you focus.

Here are the three most crucial things you should learn if you want to improve your attention to detail:

- Deadlines give all endeavours a sense of completion. One clever option is to work backwards from the set deadline to determine when your part of the project is due. You will never miss a deadline if you keep to the prescribed plan for finishing the mini-projects you have.
- Your team is working on projects alongside other teams who have their own tasks and deadlines. When you have a complete understanding of the work-flow plan, you may be able to contribute insight to the larger project or to a smaller element of it that others in the company would find useful.
- As the saying goes, "What may go wrong, will go wrong."Don't make unrealistic timeline promises. Something will almost certainly go wrong, but if you've budgeted time to correct it, no one will be alarmed. You probably already pay attention to a few minor aspects. Don't lose hope. You may improve your detail-orientedness by overcoming your lack of attention to detail. You've got this! You can overcome your deficit.

Do you find any flipside of your detail-orientation?

- It isn't always a terrible thing, but it is sometimes. When people place too much emphasis on the aspects of themselves that they dislike, it becomes a problem. Many people who are overly concerned with details must learn to appreciate the good in themselves.
- They're inquisitive curiosity may have killed the cat.
- It doesn't matter if you're meticulous, if you're not adding value. Their coworkers are probably envious of their attention to detail and steady work ethic.
- Neurotic as a personality attribute, attention to detail has both advantages and disadvantages. However, it has apparent job benefits, and it may help people deepen their relationships and avoid taking unnecessary risks if they can control their associated tendencies like neuroticism.
- High efficiency leads to maximum productivity, but high effectiveness indicates that the work is being done correctly.
- If you tend to become confused or overwhelmed by too many details, being detail-oriented might be a disadvantage. Recognise whether this is a problem for you, and make intentional attempts to raise your head from time to time so you don't become entirely engrossed in the details. Knowing how you work might help you avoid this setback and keep the overall vision in mind.
- They could be mistaken for micromanagers. Others may understand their obsessive attention to detail, but they may not like it when it is directed at them. If you're a

manager or team leader who points out minor mistakes in others' work, they can be caught aback by your *"pickiness"* and accuse you of being a micromanager.
- It doesn't imply that anything is grammatically accurate just because it sounds good.
- Some may misinterpret their many, thorough queries as a perfectionist attitude, which is sometimes true, but not always. Accuracy is sometimes misunderstood as perfection.
- Details can be found not only in tangible work products, but also in how you speak and carry yourselves.
- Their to-do list is probably color-coded, and their bookcase is probably organised alphabetically.

How can you improve your concentration and focus?

Our brain's capacity to concentrate on a particular goal has grown increasingly difficult in the ever-changing world of technology. You can train your mind to stay present with the appropriate mentality and practise. Understanding the advantages of keeping focused may be critical to our success and can help us determine where we can make improvements in our work lives. In this chapter, I have explained attention and offer strategies for implementing optimal concentration in the workplace with few distractions.

Someone's focus refers to how they pay attention to or concentrate on a certain person or item. When someone is concentrated, their attention is drawn to a single spot. An employee is focused in the workplace when their attention is directed toward achieving their primary aim or objective.

When you remove everything in your environment that may cause disruptions, you will be more productive and have a higher chance of remaining focused. To reduce distractions, keep your phone in a different room or remain offline if possible. You will be more concentrated if you work alone or in a quiet atmosphere. If you have a long list of activities to perform, it might be helpful to not only make a to-do list, but also to prioritise each item according to its priority. This will help you to move gradually through your chores rather than becoming overwhelmed and ineffective.

Participating in various brain training exercises is an excellent way to increase your cognitive abilities and, as a result, your capacity to maintain attention. By instructing your brain to become more disciplined, you may become more adept at paying attention to the work in front of you. You're more likely to get more work done when you're working alone or in a private environment. You won't be disturbed by coworkers or other noisy distractions from your workplace if you operate in a calm setting.

Taking the time to relax, breathe, and meditate can help you think more clearly. To improve your ability to concentrate at work, try doing yoga. Exercising on a regular basis stimulates and refreshes your brain. Physical activity can also help you remember things better and concentrate better. It will not only keep you energised, but it will also give you the boost you need to stay focused at work. Sleeping at least eight hours a night is an excellent strategy to ensure that you arrive at work in the best physical and mental condition possible. You slow down when you're drowsy. Getting a good night's sleep, on the other hand, helps you stay aware and awake throughout the day, especially in the morning.

When you focus your attention on a single activity, the chances of becoming distracted are reduced. Keep your brain actively engaged on one item at a time rather than multitasking. Concentrate on one job at a time to improve the quality of your work and your attention span before moving on to the next. When deciding what you need to do, consider the amount of time it will take you to finish each activity. Scheduling your day and practising time management skills can help you finish your job more quickly and keep on top of everything. For example, set aside 8–10 a.m. to do work one, 10–11 a.m. to finish task two, and so on.

However, we live in a world where you are continuously bombarded with distractions and notifications clamouring for your attention. The vast number of "shiny objects" that are always attempting to interrupt your attention is simply too much for your brain to handle.

According to Dr. John Ratey, who published a book about the influence exercise has on the brain, exercise enhances your attention for two to three hours after you finish your workout. Do you have a time of day when you just can't seem to get your thoughts to stop racing? Try exercising for 90 minutes ahead of time to ensure you have enough attention to compensate during your more difficult hours. Exercise boosts our confidence in our capacity to do difficult tasks. Entrepreneurs such as the late Steve Jobs and Facebook's Mark Zuckerberg are prime instances of self-assured executives who have benefited from exercise. Many entrepreneurs advise walking during the day on a regular basis.

Why multitasking doesn't work?

So I'm sure you've been taught a million times that you can't multitask. That isn't quite correct, and I'm here to tell you why. You can, in fact, multitask. Task switching is something you can't do properly. When we go from one activity to the next, we are said to be task-switching. As a result, our concentration suffers. And there are times when we aren't as effective as we would be if we just focused on one activity at a time.

Multitasking is a unique skill. You can, in fact, multitask. In reality, multitasking can help you get more done. This is referred to as "temptation bundling." And what we've discovered is that when we combine something we want to do, something that is a reward in one context, with something we don't want to do, we can actually boost our drive to engage in the activity we don't want to engage in. For example, I'm not a great admirer of exercise, but I listen to podcasts, novels, and audiobooks, which I enjoy, to help urge me to go to the gym. This provides me with the added drive to make that activity more pleasurable.

Multitasking is what I'm doing, but the main thing is that you may multitask as long as it's on different channels. For example, with the visual interface, you couldn't watch two television stations at the same time, right? At the same time, you can't have two streams of information on two different channels. Two audiobooks cannot be listened to at the same time. You can't work on two math problems at once. However, switching up those interfaces so that you're using the visual interface While watching a movie or listening to music through the auditory interface while performing some type of physical exercise may be effective multitasking, which is a terrific approach to getting more done in our day.

Multitasking does not assist, according to modern science. People who focused their attention, intelligence, and ingenuity to discover a solution to a human need created everything we see around us-your pen, mobile phone, watch, and the zip on your jeans. Focus may help us push the boundaries of our talents while also leaving a legacy for future generations.

Daydreaming In our technological age, these times are rare and far between. However, you are less likely to be distracted by outside forces in this sector and instead have a "silent moment" to merely ponder things. You're not completely focused on work or other activities, but you're also not distracted. focused and aware. This quadrant is all about being focused and knowing what you need to do to achieve your objectives. When your brain is in this state, you frequently take proactive steps to ensure that you remain focused. To reduce distractions, you could lock yourself off from people or wear earplugs or headphones.

"Concentrate all your thoughts upon the job at hand," Alexander Graham Bell said, citing how the sun's rays only burn paper when focused on one location. Yet, in most cases, our attention wanders, making us vulnerable to whatever distractions come our way – especially when our email inbox is flooded with urgent yet unimportant diversions. Then there's multitasking, which means moving from one narrow concentration to another since the mind can only keep one at a time in "working memory." As a result, switching from one job to another might take a long time to get back to your initial focus.

Single-tasking is the polar opposite of multitasking; it is the capacity to focus only on one job at a time. It comes naturally to us in such life-or-death situations when a deadline drives us to concentrate completely. But how can we maintain that level of focus for the remainder of our working lives – or our lives in general? One solution is to practise mindfulness. When we are attentive, we give our undivided attention to whatever is in front of us. It offers us the ability to shift our focus from one thing to another as we go about our day-writing a report, enjoying a meal, loving a child.

Do you multitask well, or do you aspire to be one of those people who can do five things at once? I've got some good news for you. Multitasking isn't all it's made up to be, and while you might believe it's a useful talent to have, it has its limitations, and it doesn't happen as often as you would think. While the continuous demands of computers and digital gadgets intensify our propensity to multitask, research has revealed that when it comes to more cognitively demanding activities, multitasking does not exist.

That's one thing if you're talking about walking and chewing gum at the same time. However, for more challenging jobs, you're actually task switching, which involves rapidly moving back and forth between tasks, and task switching has a cost. When you switch tasks, your attention declines in terms of length and quality. This indicates you're less able to stay concentrated and have a shallow focus. Your capacity to engage with ideas, initiatives, and other people really deteriorates. Distracted driving comes to mind as an example of how your capacity to cope with potentially risky circumstances deteriorates. Switching tasks can also make it difficult to acquire and retain knowledge.

When your mind jumps from one thing to the next, you're less able to monitor and control your emotions, leading to more impulsive or reactive behaviour. However, knowing all of this, however, does not change the reality that you may be besieged with requests for you to be able to accomplish several tasks in a short period of time. So, what are your options? Now that you're aware of the difficulties of task switching, you may practise mindfulness to enhance your task switching abilities and become more completely immersed in whatever you're doing. Multiple studies have demonstrated that practising mindfulness for even five minutes a day can help you enhance your task switching ability.

Find a relaxing spot, whether it's in your office or at home in a peaceful corner. You can sit in a comfortable chair or on a cushion on the floor if you prefer; it's not a big deal. So keep it straightforward. Set a timer for five minutes if you have a mobile device.

Please close your eyes and pay attention to the sound of your inhale and the rising and falling sensation in your chest as you exhale. Continue to focus on the sound and sensation of your breath. Allow each notion that runs through your mind to depart, to fade away. Return your attention to the sound and sensation of your breath. After a few weeks of doing this easy exercise consistently, you will notice a change in the quality and duration of your attention during task switching and in other areas of your life.

To obtain optimal outcomes, managing your attention entails keeping your mind focused and limiting distractions. It is critical to take a proactive rather than a passive approach. It's about taking control of your life and making decisions about your wants based on your goals. Specific components are required, according to Maura Thomas, an expert in the field of attention management, to properly control your attention in a way that is helpful to you overall. It is critical to develop a practise of attention, concentration, mindfulness, being present, and flow in order to achieve this. Many factors, both internal and external, might prevent us from focusing on the work at hand. However, if you focus on the things that matter most to you, you may dramatically enhance your productivity.

Keep in mind that one of the behaviours you may attempt to better is focus, which is an important part of regulating your attention. You'll notice a big boost in your capacity to focus on projects after you start practising the skill on a regular basis. Whether you work in a busy office with numerous interruptions, sounds, phone calls, and emails clamouring for your attention, or at home with the family, finding time to practise focus on a regular basis is the only way to develop the discipline. Focusing on a single activity might be difficult with all of the distractions that surround you on a daily basis. It's critical to develop methods for improving your attention and, as a result, your capacity to complete tasks.

"Successful people maintain a positive focus in life no matter what is going on around them. They stay focused on their past successes rather than their past failures, and on the next action steps they need to take to get them closer to the fulfillment of their goals rather than all the other distractions that life presents to them." - Jack Canfield

Concentration is a mental state that deals with being attentive. There may or may not be an element of interest involved. Concentration is defined as the capacity to focus on a single thought or subject while ignoring everything else in one's range of awareness. The capacity to control one's attention according to one's will is known as concentration. Concentration is the act of paying close attention to something. Concentration on any activity or task improves memory and other cognitive skills, including reading, writing, storing, memorising, and recalling. Better focus can help you improve your mental performance by improving your problem-solving, decision-making, provocative thoughts, and idea production abilities. Overcoming distraction refers to the brain's capacity to focus on the activity at hand or the task at hand. Both external and internal sources of distraction exist.

According to research and as I've found through many years of coaching, focus isn't one-size-fits-all. Depending on your position, the type of attention you require fluctuates. Depending on your demands, your emphasis might be broad or limited, internal or external, or many combinations. A broad focus offers you situational awareness, such as knowing what's going on on the field when playing soccer or being able to read the audience discreetly while giving a presentation. A tight concentration is intense, similar to a surgeon's razor-sharp attention while performing a dangerous procedure.

Internal focus is a possibility. Consider a violinist actively altering his finger position during a concert while watching his pitch. External concentration is another option. Let's take a look at some common focus situations. To successfully execute a job with a tight deadline, you must eliminate all distractions. To reach the finish line, you must persevere no matter what. To stay on track, you'll need a laser-like focus. Let's imagine you need to make an important presentation to a large group of people.

Being effective entails remaining on track while being present, interested, and invested in the information you're delivering. You must maintain a high level of enthusiasm and maintain eye contact with the audience. You'll need a broad exterior focus for this. Let's assume you need to tune in to your creative side and let ideas arise without being stifled by your internal critic. Distractions may stifle productivity, so maintain a broad internal focus. As you can see, each of them requires a distinct sort of concentration, and in some cases, a mix of two: wide and narrow, internal and exterior. Consider how you might tailor the emphasis to your own position and requirements.

Consider a period when you really needed to concentrate. What level of concentration was required in the situation? Now choose a current task that requires you to concentrate. Perhaps you're working on a project or preparing for a public speaking engagement, or perhaps you'd like to enhance your tennis game. Maybe it's just finding a way to get into the swing of things first thing in the morning. Take a moment to visualize yourself in the middle of whatever task you're working on. What does it resemble? What are the task's primary requirements?

"All I need you to do now is improve your attention. Your levels of attention are different at different times, and whatever the peak attention that you have had in your life at any time, that is still not all of it. You are capable of much more attention. don't try to pay attention to anything. Just become more attentive, and you won't miss a thing. If you pay much more attention to everything, if you heighten your ability to be attentive, that could be used in miraculous ways" -Sadguru

Focus is a mental skill that allows people to start working on a job without procrastination in the present and then sustain their attention and effort until the activity is completed. Video games can aid in the development of skills. When you're immersed in a pleasant and engrossing gaming experience, it's easy to lose track of time. Because focus is the entryway to all thinking: perception, memory, learning, reasoning, problem solving, and decision making, it is the most significant phenomenon. The core principles and operational principals that ensure the organisation's strategic orientation are known as "focus values." While the average time spent concentrating on a job is 45 minutes, some people may concentrate for hours on end.

Arjuna's Bird's Eye Test teaches us how to remain focused to our goals and achieve them. Arjuna is regarded as the most powerful of the Pandavas. Because of his superior warfare capabilities and astute intellect, he was a force to be reckoned with. Both the Kauravas and the Pandavas were taught the art of combat by Guru Dronacharya, who was a master of military techniques. Many people accused him of favouring Arjuna, especially Duryodhana. This account, on the other hand, explains why Dronacharya believed there was no warrior like Arjuna. Dronacharya once overheard Duryodhana accusing him of favouring Arjuna above the others. Dronacharya planned to prove him wrong by placing a wooden bird on a branch and putting everyone through a simple test. He collected all of his people and instructed them to hit the wooden bird's eye. He did, however, ask each of them a question before allowing them to fire their arrows. He initially called for Yudhisthir, the eldest of the group, and said, "What do you see there?" Yudhishthir responded, "I see a wooden bird, the branch and the tree, the leaves moving, and other birds." When Arjuna's time came, he firmly declared: "I can only see the bird's eye." Dronacharya grinned as he realized he had been proven correct. Everyone else had their gaze fixed on everything but Arjuna, who had his gaze fixed on his goal, the bird's eye. Arjuna's response demonstrates his ability to focus all of his attention on a single aim. This is where we learn about concentration.

While others struggled to distinguish their aim from the obstacles in their way, Arjuna was able to put everything else aside and focus solely on the prize. There are so many unimportant things that take up our efforts on a daily basis in life. We should always push the turmoil aside and focus on the important things.

Focus is a mental skill that allows people to start working on a job without procrastination in the present and then sustain their attention and effort until the activity is completed. Video games can aid in the development of skills. When you're immersed in a pleasant and engrossing gaming experience, it's easy to lose track of time. Because focus is the entryway to all thinking: perception, memory, learning, reasoning, problem solving, and decision making, it is the most significant phenomenon. If you have the ability to focus, you don't have to pay attention to anything. There's nothing else like it. They have told you that you can focus on this or that, which is a contemporary psychology fallacy. Nothing piques my interest. Simply said, I'm paying attention. Everything in my immediate proximity instantly catches my eye. When you wake up in the morning, do you look to see if the sun has risen or not? Not at all.The sun has invaded your body as you have awoken. Because you are awake, everything around you penetrates you.

Practice builds habit when it comes to meditation; practise does not make perfect. The difference between doing something correctly and incorrectly requires less perfection. I'm interested in developing the practise of mindfulness and being present in this situation. You can only respond fully to what is in front of you at this moment, whether it is something that stresses you out or something that calms you down. One of the most common misconceptions about mindful meditation is that you're trying to get there, that you have a certain place in mind to go, or that there are right and incorrect ways to do it. Today, I'd want to ask you to embrace the concepts of practise and exercise rather than the idea and notion of performance. To be able to relate to anything, whether it be an extreme feeling, a struggle in your thinking, or a challenge in your life, practise making this a habit and incorporating it into your everyday life. The gift I gain from this exercise today is to practise and to be present rather than flawless.

When I wash my teeth, it is the cumulative effect of everyday brushing that provides us with fantastic or superior dental hygiene. This is one of the analogies I like to employ. It is not necessary to wash your teeth correctly the first time. It's not about reaching a specific location or achieving a certain level of oral hygiene. It is all about doing it frequently and making it a habit. And you gain from that habit. Therefore, the practise for today will consist of basic mindfulness, which involves paying attention to the breath, concentrating on the feeling of inhaling and exhaling, and then opening to what is known as open awareness. This cannot be done properly. There isn't a wrong way to accomplish this. I'm only asking you to come along. There isn't a wrong way to accomplish this. I'm merely asking you to join me in this moment's exercise.

Let's start now. Breathe in deeply through your nose. As you exhale, close your eyes, relax your shoulders, open your jaw if it's clinched, and soften your belly if it's being held in. releasing and relaxing the knees if they are squeezing, as well as the hips and gluteal muscles. On your own, perform a light scan, slowly going up and down the body with each breath, to check for any remaining muscular tension, holding, or squeezing. breathing in, observing, exhaling, and investigating. observing the sensations the body has with each breath. Ask and answer this question to yourself while you take a good, deep breath in through your chest and belly, releasing your attention from the physical body as you exhale, and take some time to settle into a meditative zone.

Why are you here now? What attracted you to this method? Do you currently have a personal objective or goal while you meditate? There is not a requirement. When you breathe, you usually get a tiny bit of reflection. Another deep breath in, fully expanding it, and as you exhale, releasing the mind from any thought-processing and allowing the attention to be the anchor of your practice, This essential aspect of your daily life occurs constantly. The breath is constantly in action, whether it is coming in or going out. In response, you are invited to carry out that move. Observing the singular experience and feelings of the breath coming in and noticing the singular experience and sensations of the breath going out. Whatever breathing rate you choose is okay. Test your ability to independently count five breath cycles. One breath is one inhalation and one exhalation. When the counting has already left the mind, start afresh or take up where you left off, counting all the way to five. Let's take one more deliberate breath together right now, starting by exhaling as much air as you can. And pay close attention to how your breath feels as you inhale and exhale.

Allow yourself to return to your usual breathing pattern. There's no need to change it in any way. And in the last stages of this practise, shift your attention from being focused to being open when there isn't anything specific you need to pay attention to. Instead, it's more like an open, floating state in which you are conscious of everything in your experience and allow it to exist as it is as you watch, observe, and feel. I take a deep breath in and exhale as I softly, slowly, and comfortably blink open my eyelids to let some light in. With that, I've completed my practise for the day, which was focused on developing the habit of mindful meditation. I wish you continued growth in your relationship with stress management.

Anxiety is common. We all go through it on a daily basis, day in and day out. And if stress is common, then I can get better at managing it and dealing with it. This is not intended to prevent stress from occurring. It's about enhancing our capacity to react to it. I need to practise if I want to increase my capacity for expanding my stress management skills. Practice being aware and understanding how it affects our life, as well as our bodily, emotional, and mental bodies. Then, sit in a mindful meditation practise where I can step back from the edge of its intensity, even if only for a moment. This consistent, regular exercise improves our ability to deal with pressures that will always exist. The task at hand is for you to continue doing this steadily for the next one, two, or three minutes, all the way up to 90 minutes. The regularity of doing it every day is more crucial than how much time is spent doing it. I'm going to issue you a challenge: Try it for a week; try it for two weeks. Experience what it's like to continue living your life as usual while also adding the daily practise of mindful meditation. Your capacity to handle stress and become more robust in your daily life will grow as a result of this constant exercise. a set of meditation techniques that help you stay present, rooted, and focused at work. Learn how to make the most of your commute so you arrive at work prepared, whether it's a two-hour trip or a quick stroll. Learn how to foster a positive work atmosphere and improve your relationship with your supervisor. Learn how to make the most of your downtime, stop counting down the minutes so you can live in the now, and make meetings productive and collaborative.

Finally, develop the ability to leave work with awareness and return home in the present. There are many opportunities for us to bring our best selves to work and to be mindful about how I show up in the work environment every day. I have seen in my work with organisations all over the world on how to create the best environments to bring out the best is one of the things I have seen in my work with organisations all over the world on Methods for incorporating mindfulness into every situation so that you arrive at work, spend your time there, and leave work feeling like your best self—connected, rooted, and attentive.

Create habits and abilities that promote positivity.

Our viewpoint, presence, and performance are all impacted by negativity. When constant negativity surrounds us at work and in life, even the most upbeat among us can become depressed. In this course, you'll discover how to maintain positivity over the long term by putting the principles of positivity into practise and by deriving optimism from greater mental power. I'll help you develop a concrete strategy for cultivating a lasting optimistic outlook, even in the face of repetitive pessimism and doom. This effort will be worthwhile because a wealth of data demonstrates that positivity is strongly associated with better health, happiness, and success. I'll work with you to develop daily optimism habits as well as specific positivity abilities, such as how to deal with criticism and negative individuals. We'll look at real-world examples and teach you how to be optimistic even when it appears that everyone is trying to bring you down. So come along as I will show you how to maintain your optimism in the face of adversity.

How does thought affect behaviour?

One idea can result in a significant shift. Every thought influences our future and shapes our personality. We must alter who we are on the inside if we want to make a lasting difference. Every idea we have has an impact on how we feel physically and spreads to others around us. Words are less powerful than thoughts. Every idea we have immediately produces an emotion.

A strong, positive idea will make us feel good, whereas weak, negative, wasteful thinking will make us miserable. Our bodily components experience favourable effects whenever we feel well. Every time we have a bad thought, it has an adverse effect on several regions of our body. This is the reason why humans continue to experience a wide range of ailments despite all of the contemporary scientific study, development, and production of countless medications and cutting-edge surgical treatment techniques. This is due to the fact that the majority of the ailments we currently face are brought on by our psychosomatic illnesses. Therefore, the majority of them are brought on by prolonged periods of stress and strain. As a result, everyone nowadays advises letting things go in order to avoid worry and strain.

The more we can remove ourselves from stressful situations, the healthier we can remain. But we can't simply go to another location if we want to be stress-free. People take a short leisure trip and feel rejuvenated when they return. People take a short leisure trip and feel rejuvenated when they return. But how frequently and for how long can they do it? Not everyone has the same budget. People who cannot afford it do not necessarily have to live in constant tension.

The entire transformation is only a thought away. Everything changes when the mindset changes. We don't have to wait for other people or the environment to change. Simply changing our ideas is all that is required. We must alter our thoughts if we are to change. Even in a hectic setting, we are the ones who form thoughts, even on a leisurely vacation.

Therefore, we are unable to place blame on or hold people accountable for our feelings. When we are on vacation, we feel wonderful, but it isn't because there is some magic that protects us from stress; the real reason is because we cultivate the positive emotions that make us feel good. We frequently place the blame for our poor behaviour on other people and hold them accountable. This is untrue, though. We are powerless to influence either our surroundings or other people. Only we can alter ourselves. When faced with a catastrophe, we should think positively and maintain our composure.

No matter how tough things may appear to be on the outside, everything is peaceful within. A soul that is at peace is able to deal with whatever challenging situations come his way quite well, but a soul that is inwardly very unstable readily gives up. As a result, self-control is necessary. Every thought elicits an emotion. Every emotion must be examined. Whenever we get a bad emotion, we should pause and look within to see what is causing it.

A notion will be the root reason. We need to immediately swap that particular way of thinking out for an empowering and positive one. Because of our belief systems, we tend to think such negative things. Therefore, we need to alter these belief structures and replace them with new ones that will foster positive thinking and a happy internal experience.

Feelings are really powerful things. The same type of sensation arises from repeated ideas. If, for example, we think negatively about a certain individual, we may begin to feel resentment toward him that may even be critical or judgmental. If we don't pause to catch ourselves, we will continue to think of him in the same manner. As a result, we will gradually develop similar feelings toward him over time, and our character will undoubtedly be negative.

Negative emotions always result in the development of bad character. We acquire diverse personalities or attitudes toward various people, places, and things as a result of this. Not everyone experiences things the same way. We don't all react to someone with the same level of harshness. We do not all share our compassion in the same manner. Because we think in various ways about different individuals, locations, or things, our character changes for each of them.

People are frequently counselled to alter their behaviour or attitude. It cannot be altered, though. One needs to alter their thinking in order to alter it. When children rebel and treat adults disrespectfully, their attitude is challenged to change. They work on it and make an effort to be respectful, but as soon as a circumstance comes that is unfavourable to them, they act in the same manner. This is as a result of their attempts to alter it merely on the surface. They didn't test it out at the very beginning, which was by altering their way of thinking. You cannot hide your attitude. It manifests itself through action. Positive actions include remaining at peace, obeying others, speaking the truth, placing a high value on loyalty, becoming detached from expectations, attempting to become completely detached, etc. Negative actions include losing our temper, disobeying, speaking a lie, attempting to be disloyal, creating expectations, interfering in other people's karmic accounts, etc. When these attitudes are used often, they become habits. It gets ingrained in us.

People claim that it is hard to break a habit. This is due to the fact that it did not grow over time. It evolved through time and now has a powerful shape. We must now focus on our thinking processes in order to modify any of our poor behaviours, and in order to change our thought processes, we must swap out our outdated belief systems with new ones. Each personality is nothing more than a collection of behaviours. They could include some nice ones and some negative ones. The personality that impacts others is the one made up of only positive behaviours. When a person develops good habits like serenity, love, contentment, wisdom, and bliss, for example, this enhances his personality.

Everyone wants world peace. This is true because every soul's fundamental essence is serenity. As a result, everyone experiences comfort when they are at peace and depression when it is disturbed. Our fate is shaped by our individuality. We are in control of our future. We either make or break it. Everything that happens in life is a result of our thinking. We have a million ideas in a minute without even thinking about how they will affect our relationships with others and with ourselves. To develop a decent personality and build a happy, fulfilling future for ourselves, we must direct our thoughts in the appropriate directions.

The mind's function is to think. It continues to generate ideas. We believe that since we are not in charge of the mind, neither the quantity nor the calibre of our ideas are up to our control.We're simply living in a kind of illusion right now. We must realise that we must control our thoughts rather than letting them dominate us. As a result, since we are the ones producing the ideas, we have the ability to assess their quality. If necessary, we may edit them or modify the quantity of thoughts we have produced. The most essential force in our bodies, Prana, can be guided by our thoughts if we learn about it and become conscious of it.

Are you calm, proud, or perhaps intrigued when you are being your best self and saying no? What are you thinking right now? Perhaps you're telling yourself again that you can handle it or that the way someone responds says much more about them than it does about you. How would you describe your body language? It's conceivable that your head is elevated and your shoulders are rounded.

Say no with confidence, "I have a confession to make." I used to try to please everyone. When I had to say no to someone in the past, I felt internally guilty. My nose was weak and unclear on the exterior. Perhaps you belong to the club of ex-people-pleasers, or perhaps you've gone the other way and unwittingly or wrongly delivered your no with hate and rage. In any event, it's imperative that you practise saying "no" in a calm, direct, and comfortable manner. Alternatively, deliver it with confidence.

How to move forward?

- Focus your attention on one subject at a time. The basic idea is to concentrate on one thing at a time, but the deeper significance comes when you've realised that awareness and thought are two different things. There may be 10 things in your head, but you only need to focus your consciousness on one of them.
- Set up task timers.This aids your productivity by providing you with a certain amount of time to complete a task. Of course, if you need more time, you can devote additional time to the activity, but time boxing allows you to concentrate intensely without being distracted.
- Take part in this online game. The game asks you to recall both letters and square placements on a tic-tac-toe grid. It's one of the more well-known games for gaining attention.
- Concentrate on a dot or a location on the wall in front of you for as long as you can until you can't hear anything anymore. Make a list of potential distractions and keep it close to your workspace.
- Do not carry out any of the tasks on the list. Take anything in your hand and stare at it for a minute without saying anything.
- Gather more information. Take in your surroundings and notice the small details. Start with something as simple as gazing at your own hand as it lies on your office keyboard.
- Take note of the minute lines, veins, and where they lead, the colour shifts in various regions, and how your hand moves as you write. The more you can see in life, the better off you will be! Everything becomes more intriguing the more you pay attention.
- Identify the duties that come naturally to you, such as email and texting, and contrast them with the tasks that

are more difficult for you, such as dealing with customer complaints or confronting coworkers.

- When you practise balancing awareness, you'll notice a difference in your amount of immediate distraction and long-term avoidance.
- Maintain a healthy balance of quick rewards and uncomfortable effort.
- Consider the mind's eye to be a flashlight. This lamp is capable of finding something positive or negative at any time.
- The key is to be able to regulate that spotlight and search for the good in everything. You're playing to win when you do that. You're able to retain your optimistic attitude by focusing on the right things.
- Also bear in mind that a leader must not only focus her mind's eye, but also assist others in doing so.
- The more you concentrates on the job at hand, the better you learn. If you have a tendency to push through, you will undoubtedly sabotage your learning. When the entire effort should be concentrated on the goal, you can't be sidetracked by the means to the goal.
- Taking care of yourself might help you avoid burnout. While it is critical to complete duties consistently, allowing your mind to recharge and rest may be extremely helpful to your mental health.
- If you're stuck on a task, taking a break for a few minutes might give you a new perspective. Allowing your brain to shut down and take a rest might also give you the boost you need when you return to work.
- Place your most important project on your desk in front of you. Now, sweep away any additional distracting things with your hands so they are out-of-sight and out-of-mind.

- To achieve tunnel vision, place a hand on either side of your face. As a result, your primary priority is in-sight, in-mind, and top-of-mind, both literally and metaphorically. When you utilise your hand blinkers every time you need to telephoto focus, that physical action becomes your Pavlovian trigger for switching from dispersed to focussed.
- Meditate A method of training the mind or inducing a state of awareness, either for the purpose of achieving a goal or as an end in itself, is meditation. With practice, meditation can undoubtedly assist you in focusing and improving your attention.
- Maintain a healthy lifestyle by exercising often. Exercise often to help enhance the flow of oxygen to your brain. Go for a stroll in the fresh air. Staying healthy will give you the capacity to focus, among other things. Vacations are important. Your brain is not a machine that runs 24 hours a day, seven days a week.
- It requires relaxation and entertainment. Take a trip and make the most of it. Concentration may be improved by rejuvenating oneself.
- Sleeping at least eight hours a night is an excellent strategy to ensure that you arrive at work in the best physical and mental condition possible. You slow down when you're drowsy. Getting a good night's sleep, on the other hand, helps you stay aware and awake throughout the day, especially in the morning.
- Make a healthy snack station at your office. Dry fruits, for example, are constantly available. You just eat a handful of almonds or walnuts whenever you're hungry. You may provide staff with a flex schedule, allowing them to arrive at work later in the morning to escape the rush. If you're an employee, you may inquire with your

manager about whether any of these options are viable alternatives to your busy commute.

Finally, advice learning to say no is sometimes all that's necessary for effective time management. You don't always have to stop what you're doing to chat to or assist someone just because they are your coworker or supervisor. It's okay to respectfully decline an invitation and ask if you may follow up with them later while working on significant tasks or when there are tight deadlines. Managing your restricted time isn't difficult if you keep in mind the most effective strategies. Use the strategies we just discussed to effectively recapture the time you need to concentrate and be productive. Put at least three scheduled breaks of five to ten minutes on your calendar straight away. Use them to take a break from your job, and you'll really finish more of it. It's true.

Mindfulness practise will assist you in being more efficient and juggling several chores. You'll pay more attention to each activity and grow more adept at switching between new ones. So commit to a basic mindfulness practise for 90 minutes each day.

About The Author

Dr. Amit Das, is a renowned executive advisor, consultant, educationist, author, speaker, counsellor, and coach whose 25+ years of business experience provides high-impact, practical solutions that support his clients' leadership development and organisational transformations. He worked for fortune 500 companies and left rich leagacy of organising transformational learning workshops. He has transformed more than 5000+ working executives through his path breaking capability building learning workshops. Dr. Amit Das is recognised as an innovative, principled thought leader who combines intellectual rigor and discipline with an ability to translate theory into practice. His operational skills are coupled with a strategic ability to analyse, develop, and implement successful strategies for profitability, growth, and sustainability.

Dr. Amit Das has a successful track record in aligning learning and training solutions to key business strategy with a strong focus on flawless execution excellence to facilitate individual, business divisional, and organisational performance. He keeps relentless focus on measuring training impact and ROI, people capability building graphs, training process governance, performance coaching, and strategic thinking. These have been some of his key individual success traits. His core capabilities include performance coaching, designing training and development frameworks, psychometric assessment and analysis, competency framework development and assessments, content design and facilitation of soft skills and leadership programmes, Learning Management Systems, Learning Impact Measurement, Talent Analysis, and Performance Coaching and Counselling.

Dr. Amit Das has authored multiple management and self-development books, like Change Your Perspective Change Your Life, The Alchemy Of Resilient Leadership, Redefining Organisational Excellence, High Impact Leadership, Redefining Corporate Spectrum, Create Your Leadership Edge, Love-Laugh- Live With Happiness, SMART Parenting @ Zero Cost, Redefining HRM, Building Organisational Capability, Ethical Road Map, Attomic Attention, BYPB, Redefining The Power Of Mentoring, Making The Most Future Fit Organisation, Redefining Talent Management, Defining Your Success Factors, Lead or Plead, Make The Most Of Your Life, Better Half or Bitter Half, Psychology Of Learning And Development, The Transformative Mind & Soul are few of them.

He has a Ph.D. and a Fellowship in strategic learning, along with his first class degrees in Human Resource Management, Marketing Management, International Business, and Corporate Laws from the top business schools in India. He is a certified Psychometric analyst, HR Analyst, OD Interventionist, Human Psychologist, Lifecoach, Leadership Developer, Black Belt (LSS), Strategic Thinker, Talent Analyst, certified professional trainer from the U.K. and certified behavioral coach from the U.S.A.

Dr. Amit Das likes googling, reading books, writing articles & books, cooking, listening to old melodies, and counselling people to unleash their true potential to build a strong nation. He is married and blessed with a son. He would love to hear about your experience after reading his books. You can email him and share your thoughts, or you can use his services for life coaching, positive behavioural counseling, educational support, and mentoring for young, promising students pursuing their B.B.A. and M.B.A. degrees.

References

- *Yoga Essential Yoga Poses For Taking Control Over Your Mind by Jen Solis, 2016*
- *Focus, A Simplicity Manifesto In The Age Of Distraction by Leo Babauta, 2010*
- *Limitless Upgrade Your Brain, Learn Anything Faster, and Unlock Your Exceptional Life by Jin Kwik, 2020*
- *Radical Focus by Christina R Wodtke, 2021*
- *The First 20 Hours by Josh Kaufman, 2013*
- *Focus, Elevating The Essentials To Radically Improve Student Learning by Mike Schmoker, 2018*
- *Focus Bringing Time, Energy, and Money into Flow by Pedram Shojai, 2020*
- *Total Focus by Bradon Webb, John David Mann, 2017*
- *Daily Habit Makeover by Zoe Mckey, 2018*
- *Deep Work: Rules for Focused Success in a Distracted World by Cal Newport, 2016*
- *The 80/20 Principle: The Secret to Achieving More with Less by Richard Koch, 2009*
- *Eat That Frog!: 21 Great Ways to Stop Procrastinating and Get More Done in Less Time by Brian Tracy, 2007*
- *The Checklist Manifesto: How to Get Things Right by Atul Gawande, 2010*
- *Getting Things Done, The art of stress-free productivity by David Allen, 2015*
- *The one thing by Gary Keller, 2012*
- *The compound Effect by Darren Hardy, 2015*
- *First Things First by Stephen R. Covey, 2007*
- *Vision top Reality by Honoree Corder, 2011*
- *Make Smart Choices by Som Bathla, 2017*

- *The Effective Executive by Peter F. Drucker, 2006*
- *The Life-Changing Magic Of Tidying Up by Marie Kondo, 2014*
- *The power of Less, The Fine Art Of Limiting Yourself To The Essential Business and in Life, 2009*
- *Finding Focus In A Busy World by Joshua Seth, 2015*
- *How To Stop Procastination by Charlie west, 2019*
- *18 Minutes Find Focus, Master Distraction, and Get The Right Things Done by Peter Bregman, 2012*
- *The Leadership Challenge by James M. Kouzes, Barry Z Posner, 2017*
- *Unsubscribe How To Kill Email Anxiety, Avoid Distractions, and Get Real Work Done by Jocelyn K Glei, 2016*
- *Time Management strategy by Debra Conn, 2020*
- *The Distraction- Proof Advisor by Paul Kingsman, 2015*
- *The Pomodoro Technique by Francesco Cirillo, 2018*
- *Self Discipline by Jimmie Powell, 2019*
- *Great At Work by Morten T. Hansmen, 2018*
- *Do The Work: Overcome Resistance and Get Out Of Your Own Way by Steven Pressfield, 2015*
- *The Seven Habits Of Highly Effective People by Stephen R. Covey, 2013*
- *The power of Habit: What We Do In Life Nad Business By Charles Duhigg, 2014*
- *Getting Results the agile way by J. D. Meier, 2010*
- *The Power Of Full Engagement by Jim Loehr and Tony Schwartz, 2003*
- *The Willpower Instinct: How self Control Works by Kelly McGonigal, 2013*
- *The Power Of Story: Change Your Story, Change Your Destiny by Jim Loehr, 2014*
- *Ready For Anything by David Allen, 2004*

- *Now Habit by Neil Fiore, 2007*
- *Thinking Fast and Slow by Daniel Kahneman, 2013*
- *The Great Mental Model by Farnam Street, Shane Parrish, 2020*
- *Shine Rediscovering Your Energy, Happiness and Purpose by Andy Cope, Gavin Oattes, 2018*
- *Procastination Cure by Faith P. Blake, 2019*
- *20 Principles Of Productivity by Alex Genadinik, 2017*
- *Aware The Science and Practice Of Presence by Dr. Daniel Siegel, 2018*
- *The Leading Brain by Friederike Fabritius, Hans W. Hagemann, 2017*
- *The Time Cleanse by Steven Griffith, 2019*
- *Attention Pays by Neen James, 2018*
- *Atomic Habits by James Clear, 2018*
- *Noise Living and Leading When Nobody Can Focus by Joseph McCormack, 2019*
- *Concentration Maintain Laser Sharp Focus and Attention For Stretches of 5 Hours or More by Kam Knight, 2019*
- *Mind Hacking by Dr. Xavior Trafford, 2019*
- *Productivity Habits and Procastination*

www.ingramcontent.com/pod-product-compliance
Ingram Content Group UK Ltd.
Pitfield, Milton Keynes, MK11 3LW, UK
UKHW040005200726
13854UKWH00001B/39

9 798888 837443